The Moral Work of Teaching and Teacher Education

Preparing and Supporting Practitioners

The Moral Work of Teaching and Teacher Education

Preparing and Supporting Practitioners

EDITED BY

Matthew N. Sanger
Richard D. Osguthorpe

Foreword by David T. Hansen

Teachers College, Columbia University
New York and London

Published by Teachers College Press, 1234 Amsterdam Avenue, New York, NY 10027

Library of Congress Cataloging-in-Publication Data can be obtained at www.loc.gov.

The moral work of teaching and teachers education : preparing and supporting practitio-
    ners / edited by Matthew N. Sanger, Richard D. Osguthorpe ; foreword by David Hansen.
      pages cm
    Includes bibliographical references and index.
    ISBN 978-0-8077-5430-6 (pbk. : alk. paper)
      1. Teachers—Professional ethics. 2. Teaching—Moral and ethical aspects. 3. Teach-
    ers—Training of. I. Sanger, Matthew N.
    LB1779.M68 2013
    371.12—dc23   2013002551

ISBN 978-0-8077-5430-6 (paper)

Printed on acid-free paper
Manufactured in the United States of America

20   19   18   17   16   15   14   13   8   7   6   5   4   3   2   1

Contents

Foreword

Any teacher educator who takes this book in hand may be in for a bit of a shock. It won't be the sort of verbal sting that Socrates was known to inflict on people who presumed to know more than they did. Rather, it will be a pleasant surprise, even amazement, at seeing an entire book devoted to the moral dimensions and aims of teacher education. Such a focus on deep purpose is rare in today's policy ethos. Teacher educators, like their comrades who teach in elementary and secondary schools, face a labyrinth of externally mandated prescriptions and standards that all but obliterates discussion of fundamental aims in education. Readers will find a breath of fresh air in the fine set of studies edited adroitly here by Matthew Sanger and Richard Osguthorpe.

The editors and contributors agree, as I read them, that a fundamental purpose of education is the cultivation of moral beings: that is, of persons with a humane, reflective, and responsible approach toward other people and the shared features of public life. They also agree that teaching is saturated with moral meaning and consequence, even if that meaning or consequence may be microscopic in the passing moment. Teachers literally cannot move in educational space without expressing moral values, without expressing a judgment (which may or may not be their own) that "this is beneficial for human beings" while many other things are less beneficial or not beneficial at all. And, the authors agree that teacher education should attend much more formally than it does at present to what Sanger and Osguthorpe call "the moral work of teaching." The editors describe, and the chapters in the book illustrate, how this moral work encompasses both "teaching morally"—in a spirit of fairness, truth telling, and the like—and "teaching morality"—focusing explicitly with students on virtues such as justice and courage. According to the arguments in this book, teacher educators need to include in their programs a form of moral education in its own right: namely, experiences and activities that help candidates both understand and know how to enact the moral work of teaching.

The contributors differ on how to characterize this work. Some lean toward direct modes of moral instruction, which have traditionally been associated with what is called character education. They suggest teachers need to inculcate morals such as fairness, respect, and honesty, and that teacher education needs to prepare them how to do this sort of teaching. Other contributors accent preparing teachers to engage their students in meaningful dialogue that embodies moral values and aims. Here the goal is less the inculcation of particular morals, as such, and more the education of civic- and social-minded individuals who can think and act well in the larger world. These different emphases echo John Dewey's play with the distinction between ideas *about* morality and *moral* ideas (in his classic *Moral Principles in Education*, published in 1909). For Dewey, an idea about morality (i.e., about goodness, or justice, or truth) does not in itself translate into mind and action. But a moral idea, he argues, is any idea—mathematical, historical, philosophical, scientific, religious—that takes effect in and influences a person's actual conduct in society for the good. Dewey believes indirect instruction about morals, in which they may not even be mentioned by name, can generate moral ideas more naturally and fluidly than can ideas about morality.

Dewey's provocative, contested distinction highlights another debate about the moral education of teacher candidates that readers will find in this book. Should teacher education programs feature specific courses on the moral dimensions of teaching and education? Or is it better to infuse attention to the moral throughout all of a candidate's experiences? Moreover, should programs engage candidates explicitly with the moral work of teaching before they begin any sort of fieldwork, or in conjunction with it, or after it? These questions are variants on the age-old, unavoidable issue of the relation between theory and practice in education. A core aim of teacher education, as I see it, is to equip candidates to appreciate both the necessity of the question about theory and practice and its unanswerability in any final sense. Part of a teacher's professional growth is to grasp why a deepening capability at the work will generate new theoretical and philosophical questions, just as such questions will become lenses to perceive new possibilities in the classroom.

A chief reason this book will be valuable to the teacher education community is not only that it articulates the terms of the debates touched on above, but also includes telling evidence in support of the various sides. It is possible that without an explicit course or set of courses on the moral work of teaching, the topic may dissipate and become invisible, especially given the great pressure teacher education programs are under to include a host of externally mandated standards. But it is also possible that without infusing a focus on the moral throughout a candidate's experience, it may not have an enduring effect. This ambiguity is how things must be until we have sufficient systematic, longitudinal studies that shed light on the matter. Moreover, as the editors note, much depends on the actual, unique circumstances and resources enjoyed by each teacher education program.

The book will also be valuable because it brings together scholars with disparate disciplinary backgrounds who nonetheless share an abiding commitment to helping candidates understand and enact the moral work of teaching. In these pages philosophers of education and teacher educators write side by side with educational psychologists. These communities have not always gotten along. No

doubt every teacher educator has heard caricatures of the "dip-stick" approach—
"Aha, this candidate is at stage 3.42 of moral development!"—as well as of the
"hortatory" approach—"Candidates *must* believe in social justice! No, it's democratic education! No, it's (fill in the blank)!" The collaborative tone of this book,
as expressed in Sanger's and Osguthorpe's irenic editing, is much welcome and
may lead to fresh collaborations across disciplinary boundaries in the future. That
consequence would be splendid for foregrounding the moral work of teaching in
teacher education.

As someone who has worked for years in teacher education, as well as studied the moral aspects of teaching for just as long, I found it fascinating to see
how differently—and meaningfully—teacher educators and their programs can
incorporate explicit attention to the moral aspects of teaching. I was encouraged
to find repeated evidence that teacher candidates often respond well, if given the
opportunity and the support, to the challenge of grasping fully why their work is
at heart a moral as well as intellectual endeavor. Some candidates, like many veteran teachers I have known, find this truth sobering but also deeply moving. It is
as if they have been waiting for someone, as one of the contributors in this volume
puts it, to give them "permission" to talk in serious, morally reflective ways about
the important work they do with children and youth. The editors and contributors
help us appreciate that many candidates come to the work precisely because of
abiding moral commitments—to help others, to make a difference in the lives of
the young, to give something back to society. But they also help us see how crucial
it is to give candidates systematic support in coming to grips with the meaning of
these commitments, and how to translate them into pedagogical action for the
well-being of students and society alike.

—David T. Hansen,
Teachers College, Columbia University

Acknowledgments

We equally shared the responsibilities associated with editing this volume, and we are grateful for the excellent support that we received from Teachers College Press with that process. We also thank the Center for School Improvement and Policy Studies at Boise State University and the Office of Research at Idaho State University for their generous contributions that made this volume possible.

The ideas that led to this project grew out of our work as doctoral students with Gary Fenstermacher and Virginia Richardson at the University of Michigan. That experience, and their ongoing intellectual and moral support, continue to be invaluable to our work. We are ever grateful for their examples of scholarly and human excellence. Likewise, we thank David Hansen for providing meaningful feedback on our work over the years and for serving as a critical friend during the early stages of this project.

We are also indebted to the authors who have contributed this volume. They exceeded our perhaps impossible expectations (given the nascent state of the field), and their impassioned attention to the moral work of teaching continues to invigorate our research and practice.

Finally, we thank our students, colleagues, and families as ongoing sources of learning and inspiration. They sustain us in, and bring meaning to, all our pursuits.

Part I

INTRODUCTION

Part I provides a framework for understanding and probing the moral work of teaching from the perspective of teacher education research and practice, and sets the context for the chapters that follow in Parts II and III.

In Chapter 1 Matthew Sanger, Richard Osguthorpe, and Gary Fenstermacher lay out the purpose and rationale for this book, in part by claiming that all teachers are engaged in *teaching morally* and *teaching morality*. They then probe the distinction upon which that claim is based to illustrate the value it has in considering, conducting, and studying the *moral work of teaching* (MWT) within teacher education, and how this distinction frames the remaining chapters.

In Chapter 2 Richard Osguthorpe and Matthew Sanger present and analyze candidates' reported beliefs about the MWT. The authors summarize the themes within those data related to both teaching morally and teaching morality. They discuss how teacher educators might address the beliefs candidates bring with them to their teacher education programs and highlight examples and opportunities pointed up by the work of contributors through the rest of the book.

CHAPTER 1

The Moral Work of Teaching in Teacher Education

Matthew N. Sanger, Richard D. Osguthorpe, and Gary D Fenstermacher

Anyone teaching in a classroom, to varying degrees and with different levels of success, engages in teaching morally and teaching morality. This educational truism frames our introduction to this book, which begins by unpacking what it means to teach morally and to teach morality as two facets of what we have come to call the *moral work of teaching* (henceforth MWT) (Sanger & Osguthorpe, 2005). Our intention is to draw out the implications of the moral nature of teaching for teacher education research and practice, making an extended case for why teacher educators would do well to attend to it in meaningful ways within their programs. That case will in turn set the stage for the chapters in this book and the critical insights they provide into just how we might pursue the MWT in teacher education as a domain of inquiry and practice.

THE MORAL WORK OF TEACHING

Inquiries at the nexus of teaching and morality are founded on the very broad (and exceedingly rare) consensus in education that teaching, by its very nature, is moral work. As indicated by Marvin Berkowitz's (2002) quip, "If you work with or around children, you cannot *not* be a character educator" (p. 59), the assumption that teaching is unavoidably moral in nature is a common and well-supported one. There appears to be no active camp denying some essential connection between teaching and morality (however, see Barrow, 1992).

Teaching Morally and Teaching Morality

Broadening Berkowitz's notion somewhat, the connection between teaching and morality is itself twofold. As Campbell (2003) explains it, teaching involves both being a moral person as well as being a moral educator. These two sides of the MWT coin can be understood as *teaching morally* and *teaching morality*:

> To teach morally is to teach in a manner that accords with notions of what is good or right. That is, to conduct oneself in a way that has moral value. To teach morality is to convey to another that which is good or right. In the first instance, the teacher is being a good or righteous person; in the second instance, the teacher is providing to another person the means for becoming a good or righteous person. (Fenstermacher, Osguthorpe, & Sanger, 2009, p. 8)

While this framing has a number of virtues, there are also difficulties in keeping these two categories entirely distinct. To take a clear and significant example, if one is concerned with teaching morally, one cannot avoid the possibility of also being taken as a model of moral conduct or character, which is a powerful means of teaching morality. This does not mean that teaching morally can simply be reduced to teaching morality (or vice versa), but rather that these categories do overlap in this and other ways (see Fenstermacher et al., 2009). However, we are not trying to make hard and fast cleavages in the MWT here, nor do we need to. Rather we use this framing because of how it helps us make sense of this complex domain—for its utility as a conceptual lens. In particular, these categories help us identify and understand two importantly different ways of thinking about the components of the MWT that are both helpful in the context of teacher education research and practice and also reflected in the chapters of this book.

Further, these components do not merely sit at the periphery of teaching and learning in classrooms. When teachers understand the MWT and are able to enact it in practice, it infuses *everything* they do in their work, such that morality acts as modifier to content knowledge and methodological skill. Teachers who teach morally teach in light of considerations of honesty, fairness, respect, compassion, and so on (Osguthorpe, 2008), no matter the activity in which they are engaged, be it grading a test, communicating with students, or designing a lesson plan. Similarly, these same everyday activities are laden with moral content that might contribute to the moral development and functioning of students—with teaching morality—including the construction of classroom community, showcasing students and their conduct, and the design of academic task structures, among others (see Fenstermacher, 2001).

The Significance of the MWT

But even if we accept that teaching is unavoidably moral in these ways, teacher educators might still question the significance of that moral nature, asking whether the MWT has that much value relative to the rest of the content of teacher education, and/or the extent to which they can address it in meaningful ways in their work. Addressing the first question in this section, we argue that there are at least two sources of support for the claim that the MWT has value: philosophical claims regarding the nature and purpose of teaching and schooling, and empirical evidence that people support those philosophical positions (see Sanger & Osguthorpe, 2011).

The first of these two sources of support is backed by an extensive, wide-ranging literature, which is far beyond the scope of this chapter to review, or even summarize (see e.g., Biesta, 2010; Goodlad, 1997; Rothstein, Jacobsen, & Wilder, 2008). We therefore simply highlight a few salient claims that effectively provide this link in our case. Key among those claims is that education—and teaching and schooling as constituents of our educational system—have a broad and complex range of purposes, extending far beyond what is measured by standardized tests of students' content learning in core academic areas. These purposes include promoting students' physical well-being and development; their social, emotional, moral, and cognitive growth; and their acquisition of skills and capacities that will prepare them for productive work in our economy and productive participation among our citizenry. But even if one were to buy into the increasingly narrow and instrumental view of education that dominates contemporary educational reform, one might also note the evidence relating positive academic performance with environments rich in caring relationships; an atmosphere of trust, respect, and shared purpose; and opportunities for the exercise of one's body and emotions, as well as one's cognitive faculties (see e.g., Battistich, Solomon, Watson, & Schaps, 1997; Centers for Disease Control and Prevention, 2010). And we can take this link a step further, considering the extent to which

> teaching and schooling are not simply enriched by the presence of personal, moral, aesthetic, and democratic elements, and thus impoverished by their absence, but that these elements are essential to the basic function of teaching and schooling as educational enterprises. (Sanger, 2012, p. 297)

As Fenstermacher and Richardson (2010) suggest in their commentary on contemporary reforms,

> The all-consuming attention to high stakes accountability . . . make[s] it so very difficult to treat the classroom as a setting where moral virtue, aesthetic sensibility, and democratic character are intentionally nurtured by teachers, and where the school administrators are rewarded for an organizational climate that encourages these prized educational ends. The pursuit of these ends requires classrooms that have the characteristics of a coherent community, where teacher–student and student–student relationships are fostered in ways that promote mutual regard, reciprocity of interests, and a shared pursuit of goals believed to be for the common good. It is in such settings that we can make significant contributions to moral, aesthetic, and democratic enlightenment. (p. 8)

The suggestion here is that teaching, in both a practical and a conceptual sense, *requires* substantive moral engagement on the part of teachers.

Lending credence to the many forms of philosophical support for a broad view of the nature and purpose of teaching and schooling is the empirical evidence that people at all levels of involvement in education subscribe to some form of it (see Rothstein et al., 2008). There is common support for teaching and schooling that addresses a broad range of purposes, including moral matters (and we might note that originally schools in the United States were primarily driven by a concern for moral matters; see McClellan, 1999).

But more salient to teacher education practice are the views of prospective and practicing teachers. As a number of studies have shown, teachers and teacher candidates commonly report choosing to become teachers because of altruistic reasons: wanting to help others, to give back to society, and to make a difference in the lives of children. These moral reasons just begin to illustrate how the individuals who populate our teacher education programs believe that teaching is moral work, and that they seek to work in schools because of this fact. This point has significant curricular and pedagogical implications for teacher education, as we will explore further in Chapter 2, and adds to our case that the moral work of teaching is not simply a flight of fancy of educational philosophers or psychologists with highly specialized interests. It is a central and unavoidable part of teaching and schooling, and the value that educators and the public place on it reflect that fact. Teacher education should do so as well.

The Role of Teacher Education in Supporting the MWT

But how can teacher education programs make a substantive contribution to practitioners' capacity to teach morally and to teach morality? This piece of our case begins with the observation that we have an extensive amount of knowledge that can serve as a basis for such development. We know a great deal about the nature of morality, its manifestations in the context of schools, and how practitioners might productively make sense of and respond to those manifestations (Goodlad, Soder, & Sirotnik, 1990; Hansen 2001). We also have a substantial and growing knowledge of the moral development and functioning of children and youth and how it can be supported in schools (e.g., Killen & Smetana, 2006; Nucci & Narvaez, 2008). In our view, these bodies of knowledge could inform a professional knowledge base for the MWT, if supported by research and practice that demonstrates what elements of each are necessary or helpful for practitioners and how to deploy them in the context of teacher education (Sanger & Osguthorpe, 2011).

Given the substantive beliefs of teachers and teacher candidates related to the MWT, addressing those beliefs in support of professional knowledge, skills, and language of the MWT seems apt. Just as children have been shown to be anything but removed from or uninterested in the moral world that they are immersed in, educators are quite naturally and understandably engaged and driven by the moral aspects of teaching and schooling. Using Damon's (1988) words, "Morality is a fundamental, natural, and important part of children's lives [and we suggest teachers' lives as well]. . . . It is not a foreign substance introduced to them by an outside world of people who know all the answers" (p. 1).

And this is precisely where the teaching morally/teaching morality distinction helps provide some insight into how to think about the task of preparing teachers for the MWT in teacher education. More specifically, conceptualizing the MWT as teaching morally and teaching morality distinguishes two questions that need to be addressed in preparing for and engaging in both aspects:

- What does it mean to engage in each?
- What does it mean to do so well?

Answering each of these questions requires different resources, and also different criteria for evaluation, all of which bear directly on how teacher education prepares and supports practitioners in their moral work as teachers. To highlight these differences, consider what a practitioner would need to know, and be capable of and motivated to do, in order to teach morally and to teach morality:

> [To teach morally] practitioners would need to know what is good, right, caring, and virtuous and be able to enact those things in their practice (roughly: to know the good and to practice it). [To teach morality] teachers would need to know what contributes most effectively to their students' moral development, and be able to incorporate those things into their teaching practice (to know what contributes to the development of good people, and to provide it). The first sense raises practical and philosophical issues in normative ethics. The second sense raises psychological and pedagogical issues that have practical implications that extend beyond teachers being good. (Sanger, 2008, p. 176)

Clearly, these two lines of inquiry have implications for the content of teacher education research and practice in that they identify components of the MWT that every practitioner is necessarily engaged in. As an analogy, we use our knowledge of the nature of language and language learning to help teachers use language well and foster the literacy of the students in their classrooms. Similarly, in teacher education we can draw upon our understanding of morality and moral development to help teachers to teach morally and to teach morality in their classrooms.

One reason why we are optimistic about prospects for advancing teacher education practice in this way is the years of experience we have had working with teachers and candidates who share the common understanding that teaching is moral work, but who often lack the professional language, knowledge, and skills to pursue that moral work with the same level of intentionality and expertise as other areas of their practice. In Chapter 2 we formally share our research on teacher candidates' beliefs related to the MWT to illustrate how teacher education programs can address this aspect of practice. More anecdotally, our experiences have repeatedly shown that engaging candidates and teachers in inquiries into the moral dimensions of their practices often provides what one veteran teacher suggested was a rather cathartic grant of "permission" to acknowledge and pursue those moral dimensions in meaningful, explicit, and well-guided ways, rather than leaving them as part of the hidden curriculum of teacher practice (Fenstermacher, 2001; Sanger, 2001).

In sum, it is abundantly clear to us that in a variety of ways, the MWT is not just an unavoidable but an essential part of professional teaching practice. Further, there are ample resources that could serve to inform the MWT as a professional practice, a project that teacher education can meaningfully contribute to. Doing so would go a long way toward making the professional practice of teaching consistent with a broad view of the purposes of teaching and schooling so commonly supported by the public, and also responsive to the kinds of beliefs and motivations of teachers who commit their lives to the fulfillment of those purposes. However, the literature on the MWT in teacher education is also clear that these potential contributions of teacher education to the MWT have yet to be fully realized, and it is that piece of our case to which we now turn.

THE GAP IN TEACHER EDUCATION RESEARCH AND PRACTICE

Empirical research from a number of countries consistently documents a substantial gap between the fact that teaching is significant moral work, and the lack of attention to the MWT within programs of teacher education (for a review, see Sanger & Osguthorpe, in press; see also Jones, Ryan, & Bohlin, 2003). That is, while practitioners, teacher candidates, teacher educators, and program administrators commonly acknowledge the presence and the value of the MWT, teacher education programs and practices just as commonly lack explicit, substantive, and intentional treatment of it.

We find Bergem's (1992) analysis of this phenomenon in Norway to be not only consistent with much of the research in the United States, the United Kingdom, Canada, Sweden, the Netherlands, and elsewhere, but also provocative in the context of current educational discourse and practice:

> Prospective teachers do not acquire a moral vocabulary during formal teacher education. On the contrary . . . there is a marked shift from the use of normative concepts to technical concepts pertaining to teaching and teacher's responsibilities. . . . [Participants] speak fluently and with great enthusiasm about how teaching can be improved by the use of good planning and efficient teaching methods and techniques. In contrast, few are able to explain what it really means to be sensitive to the needs of the individual child, to be committed to all students in the classroom, and to behave as a figure of identification for the students. (p. 359)

On our reading, Bergem's findings suggest that teacher education programs may not simply fail to address the MWT, but actually play an active role in obscuring the MWT through the use of technical language that frames teaching in terms of effectively producing academic learning outcomes (Sanger, 2012). In this light, the notion that there is a gap or lacuna in teacher education may not accurately reflect the current situation. This finding begs the question of whether teacher educators are culpable for either ignoring or actively (if unintentionally) suppressing moral language and thought in their programs. While this question is as fascinating as it is troubling, we must leave that analysis for another time, underscoring how consistent the evidence is that teacher education typically fails to support teachers in developing an explicit, professional understanding of this basic component of all teaching practice.

FILLING THE GAP

The gap described above can be particularly frustrating, given that teaching is inherently moral, that the MWT is valued in multiple ways, and that we have ample resources to draw upon to make the MWT a substantive part of professional preparation. Contributing to that frustration, and the sense of urgency for putting together this collection of essays, there are a number of knowledgeable and skilled scholars who do fill that gap in their own programs, adding to our understanding of how to do so in meaningful and successful ways. Because of this, we thought it was important to put together this collection of essays, bringing together not only the scholarly knowledge of experts doing research related to the MWT, but their collective wisdom of practice accrued across many years, even decades, of work in this domain. The chapters of this book do not entirely fill the larger gap described above, nor do they simply occupy a part of that space. Rather, they provide a wide-ranging view of the path toward increasingly robust programs of research and practice to prepare teachers for and support them in the MWT. While there are contributions to theory that might guide both research and practice to be found in these chapters, you will not find theory disconnected from actual teacher education practice. Similarly, contributors reporting data link them to critical elements and issues of practice at the classroom and/or program level.

This collection of contributors is an intentional mix of well-established experts and up-and-coming scholars, all of whom have substantial experience in preparing and supporting practitioners, working in or with programs of teacher education. Further, we have intentionally invited scholars who have a disciplinary background in educational philosophy and/or teacher education, as well as those whose training and expertise is grounded in educational psychology, removing this common but counterproductive barrier to comprehensive treatments of the MWT. We have arranged the chapters to follow our framing of this introduction. Chapters 3–7 in Part II primarily focus on supporting teachers in teaching morally. In addressing this aspect of the MWT, this group of chapters considers elements of candidates as moral beings: from critical reflection skills and dispositions to their moral character, being, and identity, along with their capacity to think, speak, and respond morally as a teacher. In Part III Chapters 8–11 primarily focus on preparing teachers to effectively teach morality, drawing upon our understanding of how students function and develop in the moral domain to help teachers effectively support those processes in classrooms (much like we use educational psychology to inform other aspects of teaching and teacher education). Finally, in order to leverage as many meaningful, practical implications for teacher education as can be drawn from this collection, teacher education scholar Virginia Richardson provides an insightful analysis and commentary in the closing chapter of the book.

We can imagine that there might be some resistance to our categorizing of the book's chapters, such as the following:

Of course I support the development of both aspects of the MWT in teacher education, and in teaching practice—we all want teachers to be good people and do what is morally right for its own sake, and also to be effective moral educators throughout their teaching—but you can't really separate the two!

To that we would note that we are once again not making radical cleavages in the MWT with our distinction, acknowledging that the categories overlap, and pointing out that we are ascribing a *focus* to these two groups of chapters. Further, we believe that this framing holds up quite well throughout the book and points to the robustness of the distinction it is based upon. That distinction reveals not only important differences in how we might think about the MWT in the context of teacher education, but the differing resources and strategies used to support teacher learning and development on both sides of the MWT coin, which the chapters in Parts II and III elaborate so well.

THEMES TO CONSIDER WHILE READING FURTHER

In addition to the distinction between teaching morally and teaching morality, we believe readers of the chapters in Parts II and III would benefit by having in mind certain additional themes (see also Chapter 12). The first of these is the curriculum model that is being used (and often explicitly advocated for) in each chapter. A number of authors make a strong case for infusing the MWT throughout the teacher education curriculum, including fieldwork, while others focus on specialized courses. We suggest that a key issue in the development of this domain will involve not just what is pedagogically optimal, but politically and programmatically feasible.

Next, as we have suggested, this collection was motivated in part by an interest in what can be said about how to prepare teachers for the MWT, given all that we can draw from extant scholarship and teacher education practice. This interest raises the question of the state of teacher preparation for the MWT as a domain of inquiry and the state of our knowledge about this practice and how it might be advanced. We see this domain of inquiry as very much in its early stages of development. On the one hand, we see little dispute over the range of components that can be successfully drawn upon in teacher education for the MWT, and the value of comprehensive approaches that reflect the complexity of morality and moral development. But on the other hand, the lack of comparative studies that might suggest what actually is most effective in which contexts, or longitudinal studies that track the effects of teacher education programs on subsequent practice, reveal how far this field still has yet to travel, as well as the nature of the work needed to advance it (e.g., addressing the relative merits of infusion versus specialized integration of the MWT into the teacher education curriculum, and how to do either well).

But despite the claim that this collection of essays represent a nascent domain of formal inquiry, they provide a tremendous set of practical resources for teacher educators who share a broad vision of teaching and schooling, one that includes the MWT as something worthy of explicit and intentional effort in the preparation of teachers. Again, our contributors bring with them not only many decades of scholarly expertise, but also practical wisdom that warrants due consideration of their examples and recommendations by teacher educators.

To summarize and close this introductory chapter, we entered this book project with a keen appreciation of the need to inquire into preparing teachers for the MWT, partly based on the research we report in Chapter 2. That appreciation has been accompanied by a sense of urgency as we continue to watch the discourse around teacher education follow the trend of focusing more and more narrowly and instrumentally on the production of evidence-based increases in student academic learning outcomes. In the process, schools are moving further and further away from the broad project of educating fellow human beings for meaningful lives in a democratic society (and from the call for both teaching morally and teaching morality by professionals well prepared for those tasks). After spending time with the chapters in this book, our appreciation and sense of urgency is now joined by a much greater sense of the possibilities for teacher education research and practice to advance the preparation of teachers for the MWT. We hope you find similar rewards and join us.

REFERENCES

Barrow, R. (1992). Is teaching an essentially moral enterprise? *Teaching and Teacher Education, 8*(1), 105–108.

Battistich, V., Solomon, D., Watson, M., & Schaps, E. (1997). Caring school communities. *Educational Psychologist, 32*(3), 137–151.

Bergem, T. (1992). Teaching the art of living: Lessons learned from a study of teacher education. In F. K. Oser, A. Dick, & J.-L. Patry (Eds.), *Effective and responsible teaching: The new synthesis* (pp. 349–364). San Francisco: Jossey-Bass.

Berkowitz, M. (2002). The science of character education. In W. Damon (Ed.), *Bringing in a new era in character education* (pp. 43–64). Stanford, CA: Hoover Institution.

Biesta, G. (2010). *Good education in an age of measurement: Ethics, politics, democracy.* Boulder, CO: Paradigm.

Campbell, E. (2003). *The ethical teacher.* Philadelphia: Open University Press.

Centers for Disease Control and Prevention. (2010). *The association between school-based physical activity, including physical education, and academic performance.* Atlanta, GA: U.S. Department of Health and Human Services.

Damon, W. (1988). *The moral child: Nurturing children's natural moral growth.* New York: Collier Macmillan.

Fenstermacher, G. (2001). On the concept of manner and its visibility in teaching practice. *Journal of Curriculum Studies, 33*(6), 639–653.

Fenstermacher, G. D., Osguthorpe, R. D., & Sanger, M. N. (2009). Teaching morally and teaching morality. *Teacher Education Quarterly, 36*(3), 7–29.

Fenstermacher, G., & Richardson, V. (2010). What's wrong with accountability? *Teachers College Record.* Retrieved from http://www.tcrecord.org/Content.asp?ContentID=15996

Goodlad, J. (1997). *In praise of education.* New York: Teachers College Press.

Goodlad, J., Soder, R., & Sirotnik, K. (Eds.). (1990). *The moral dimensions of teaching.* San Francisco: Jossey-Bass.

Hansen, D. (2001). Teaching as a moral activity. In V. Richardson (Ed.), *Handbook of research on teaching* (pp. 826–857). Washington, DC: American Educational Research Association.

Jones, E., Ryan, K., & Bohlin, K. (2003). *Teachers as educators of character: Are the nation's schools of education coming up short?* Washington, DC: Character Education Partnership.

Killen, M., & Smetana, J. (2006). *Handbook of moral development.* Mahwah, NJ: Lawrence Erlbaum Associates.

McClellan, B. E. (1999). *Moral education in America: Schools and the shaping of character from colonial times to the present.* New York: Teachers College Press.

Nucci, L. P., & Narvaez, D. (Eds.). (2008). *Handbook of moral and character education.* New York: Routledge.

Osguthorpe, R. D. (2008). On the reasons we want teachers of good disposition and moral character. *Journal of Teacher Education, 59*(4), 288–299.

Rothstein, R., Jacobsen, R., & Wilder, T. (2008). *Grading education: Getting accountability right.* New York: Teachers College Press.

Sanger, M. N. (2001). Talking to teachers and looking at practice in understanding the moral dimensions of teaching. *Journal of Curriculum Studies, 33*(6), 683–704.

Sanger, M. N. (2008). What we need to prepare teachers for the moral nature of their work. *Journal of Curriculum Studies, 40*(2), 169–185.

Sanger, M. N. (2012). The schizophrenia of contemporary education and the moral work of teaching. *Curriculum Inquiry, 42*(2), 285–307.

Sanger, M. N., & Osguthorpe, R. D. (2005). Making sense of approaches to moral education. *Journal of Moral Education, 34*(1), 57–72.

Sanger, M. N., & Osguthorpe, R. D. (2011). Teacher education, preservice teacher beliefs, and the moral work of teaching. *Teaching and Teacher Education, 27*(3), 569–578.

Sanger, M. N., & Osguthorpe, R. D. (in press). The moral vacuum in teacher education. *National Society for the Study of Education Yearbook.*

CHAPTER 2

Teacher Candidate Beliefs About the Moral Work of Teaching

Richard D. Osguthorpe and Matthew N. Sanger

Despite the fact that so many teacher educators have been engaged in preparing candidates for the de facto moral work of teaching (MWT) for many years, there are few research reports that explicitly consider not only where teacher candidates need to be, but also what teacher candidates bring with them to the process of teacher preparation. In our recent research, we have begun to provide that data and analysis, suggesting a learner-centered approach to preparing teachers for teaching morally and teaching morality that meaningfully addresses their most basic beliefs about that very work (Sanger & Osguthorpe, 2011). Specifically, we have examined teacher candidates' beliefs regarding:

- The nature and purpose of teaching
- Their reasons for wanting to be teachers
- Their understandings of the moral aspects of their future work

Analysis of the data reveals that teacher candidates hold a range of philosophical and psychological conceptions of, and strong personal commitments to, the MWT. This chapter summarizes some of the emergent themes among these teacher candidate beliefs and analyzes the implications of these beliefs for teacher education practice. In that analysis, we also point readers to chapters in Parts II and III that describe teacher education programs and courses in which these teacher candidate beliefs are addressed in meaningful ways. But first we present the theoretical framework for our study.

THEORETICAL FRAMEWORK

This chapter is grounded in a number of basic theoretical assumptions. Clearly, a central assumption guiding this inquiry is that teaching is an inherently moral endeavor, as we explained in Chapter 1.

Second, the inquiry is guided by the assumption that effective education must be informed by the central beliefs of the students being taught (Donovan & Bransford, 2005). This basically constructivist assumption has been productively applied to teacher education in the teacher change literature (Raths & McAninch, 2003; Richardson, 1996; Richardson & Placier, 2001), which has in turn built upon the work of Pajares (1992) and Fenstermacher (1979). They suggest that candidate beliefs have the potential to be the most significant element that teacher educators address in their research. Thus if we are to prepare teachers to effectively and responsibly carry out the MWT, we assume that the process should be informed by an understanding of the beliefs our candidates hold about that moral work.

Third, we assume that the nature of the beliefs in question—those related to the MWT—are particularly important to elicit and process due to the centrality of these beliefs to our candidates' understanding of themselves and their world (Richardson, 1996, 2003). That is, we suggest that it would be difficult to identify beliefs related to teaching that are more deeply held by candidates than those that reflect their personal views of morality, moral development, and education.

DESCRIPTION OF DATA GATHERING AND ANALYSIS

The data referred to in this chapter come from an ongoing study of teacher candidates at Boise State University that examines their beliefs about the MWT. The data include two sets of writings. The first set comes from 267 essays that teacher candidates submitted for application/continuance in the teacher education program during the 2008–2009 academic year. The essay is a requirement of all teacher candidates who desire a placement in schools, and it is a response to the following prompts:

- Why have I decided to become a teacher?
- What professional goals do I expect to achieve as a result of my decision to become a teacher?

The second set comes from responses of 92 teacher candidates to an open-ended questionnaire that they completed as part of an assignment in an undergraduate educational foundations course during the 2008–2009 academic year. This course is typically taken in a student's sophomore or junior year and is required for admission to the teacher education program. The questionnaire was distributed via an electronic survey software system midway through the semester as part of an upcoming class activity regarding the MWT. The survey questions had not been attended to in the foundations course, nor is it likely that these teacher candidates had encountered them (or related questions) in other courses (as these candidates had not yet been admitted to the teacher education program). The questionnaire asked students four questions:

1. Can we teach children to be morally good? Please explain.
2. How does moral development occur?
3. What is your definition of morality?
4. What is the purpose of schooling?

Students submitted their responses anonymously and then participated in an online and in-class discussion related to their responses.

The questions for the survey were derived from the Moral Work of Teaching Framework (Sanger & Osguthorpe, 2005, 2009), and they bear directly on the ways in which teachers teach morally and teach morality. This framework consists of four categories designed to assist examination of the moral domain as it relates to the practice of teaching:

1. Psychological beliefs related to the nature of moral development
2. Philosophical beliefs related to the nature of morality
3. Educational beliefs related to the point and purpose of schooling
4. Contingent factors that help explain the content of the other three categories

Each of the questions in the survey elicits beliefs related to one or more of the categories of the framework:

- To examine teacher candidates' psychological beliefs, we asked them how moral development occurs and whether or not we can teach children to be good.
- To identify philosophical beliefs, we asked them to provide their definition of morality.
- To explore educational beliefs, we asked them to describe the purposes of schooling.
- To elicit contingent factors, we examined their reasons for choosing a career in teaching.

Content analysis was the primary method used to examine teacher candidates' writings (essays and survey questionnaires alike). *Content analysis* here refers to a "qualitative data reduction and sense-making effort that takes a volume of qualitative material and attempts to identify core consistencies and meanings"

(Patton, 2001, p. 453). Following this basic mode of qualitative inquiry (Huberman & Miles, 2002; Marshall & Rossman, 2006), the teacher candidates' writings were read and reread in the first stage of analysis, and an initial list of codes was created that reflected the categories of the Moral Work of Teaching Framework. Within these categories, inductive coding techniques were used to generate and refine themes, and we held data-analysis meetings to triangulate those themes and build code books. In what follows, quotations represent general themes that emerged from the data; students quoted are identified by numbers to protect their identity.

DISCUSSION OF EMERGENT THEMES

Five themes in candidate beliefs have emerged from the data that we find particularly relevant to the work of teacher educators:

1. Moral development occurs primarily via modeling.
2. Moral values are transmitted via direct instruction.
3. Moral development is a joint responsibility between home and school, but parents are the most influential.
4. Morality is primarily a function of behavior.
5. The purposes of schooling are primarily academic.

In the discussion that follows we examine the implications of each of these themes for teacher education research and practice, and then we identify relevant chapters in this book that address these themes programmatically and in specific coursework—connecting what is known about morality and moral development to teacher education practice. In doing so, we also encourage more explicit and intentional links between actual teacher candidate beliefs about the MWT and the experiences of teacher candidates in teacher education programs.

Modeling

One of the most conspicuous and consistent themes that emerged from candidates' writings is the psychological belief that they can successfully teach children to be good by simply being a moral exemplar (Sanger & Osguthorpe, 2013). While this belief is intuitively appealing (and seemingly obvious in the eyes of our candidates), it understandably does not reflect the complexity of creating the conditions necessary to be effective as a model—such as creating a caring classroom community (see Battistich, 2008) and integrating the necessary steps related to intentional moral character development (Narvaez, 2006, 2008). Moreover, our candidates' responses suggest an overreliance on modeling as the mechanism for moral development in schools—despite the lack of empirical or conceptual evidence that such a relationship obtains between teacher and student in schools (Osguthorpe, 2009). That is, many of our candidates describe various ways that moral development occurs (for example, via direct instruction, life experiences, and observing consequences of actions), but they suggest that modeling is the primary vehicle: "Moral development has many different forms but in my opinion it predominantly occurs through modeling" (#122). In short, our candidates profess a strong belief in an intuitively appealing mechanism for influencing moral development, but it is not clear whether or not they understand how modeling actually works nor the extent to which it might have an impact on moral development in schools.

Thus candidates' expressed beliefs on modeling appear to be ripe for processing and development in light of the knowledge represented in the literature, both in terms of the process of modeling itself and the extent to which it might have an impact on moral development. The extant literature that teacher educators might bring to bear on these candidate beliefs includes conceptions of how modeling works in the context of observational learning theory (Bandura, 1986) and in care theory (Noddings, 1984), as well as the role of imitation in moral education (Warnick, 2008) and the foundational work of Aristotle on the cultivation of virtue (Aristotle, trans. 1985; Burnyeat, 1980). In using these resources, teacher educators can assist candidates in processing the common beliefs that they hold—for example, identifying the conditions that are necessary for modeling to have any effect (particularly on moral development) and understanding how moral education in the socially complex environment of schools goes beyond a linear process of the teacher simply modeling good behavior for students. The moral development and moral education literature connected to modeling is extensive, providing teacher educators with multiple entrees to assisting their candidates in developing more robust conceptions of this belief that they so strongly hold.

Authors of the chapters in this volume highlight some of these entrees. For example, in Chapter 8 Lapsley, Holter, and Narvaez describe how they address and emphasize the importance of modeling in Integrative Ethical Education. And in Chapter 6 Fallona and Canniff describe how they help their teacher candidates understand the role of modeling in developing a moral stance to teaching. These examples (and the others referenced in this chapter) are not explicitly and intentionally connected to the prior beliefs that teacher candidates hold about the MWT (modeling, in this instance), but they provide meaningful ways to address such beliefs in teacher education practice.

Direct Instruction

Another prominent belief that has important application in teacher education is our candidates' view that moral values are transmitted to students via direct instruction. In candidates' statements there is an explicit and prominent belief that teachers influence the moral development of students through explanation of values, encouragement of norms, enforcement of rules, definition of exemplary traits, and so on. For many candidates these methods of direct instruction map directly onto their conceptions of the direct instructional methods for typical school subjects such as math and reading: "I believe we can teach children to be good the same as we can teach them to read or write. Many teachers do this as much as they teach other subjects" (#63).

This conception of method has important ramifications for teacher educators. For example, to the extent that the belief that morals can be taught through direct instruction is true, it suggests that teachers need to know the content of what they are teaching. Thus they would need some philosophical understanding of the moral domain and concomitant capacity to explain and support the examination of philosophical issues regarding what is good/right/virtuous within that domain. In this sense, knowledge of morality is to the moral educator what mathematical knowledge is to the mathematics educator. However, similar to the findings of Sockett and LePage (2002), our candidates' conceptions of morality do not generally reveal a robust understanding of morality, nor do our candidates appear to have the moral language necessary to discuss the inherent philosophical issues within them. This apparent lack of moral language related to the content of morality suggests an important educational opportunity for enrichment of teacher candidates (see Campbell, Chapter 3, for an in-depth exploration of helping teacher candidates develop a language of ethics).

The importance of developing moral language goes beyond increasing teacher candidates' understanding of different conceptions of morality. Teachers need more than just content knowledge; they also must know how to effectively convey that content or facilitate experiences that allow students to acquire that content in some sense (Shulman, 1986). On this score, many of our candidates' responses are cause for worry, as they seem to suggest that teaching is synonymous with telling, which we know is insufficient for teaching academic subject matter, let alone for something as complex and multidimensional as morality.

The chapters in this book, however, have much to offer teacher educators on how to address this commonly held belief related to direct instruction (as one element in a more complex view of the moral work of teaching). For example, in Chapter 9 Watson, Benson, Daly, and Pelton suggest how teacher educators might help teacher candidates understand the role of direct instruction in developing a caring classroom community, while Shields, Althof, Berkowitz, and Navarro in Chapter 11 detail multiple direct instructional strategies for character education that their teacher candidates encounter in program courses.

Preeminence of the Parental Role

Most of our candidates suggest that moral development is a shared responsibility between home and school, but they posit that "moral development starts in the home" and that parents are the most influential. Additionally, some candidates perceive this shared responsibility as problematic because they believe it takes away the right of parents to instill their own beliefs in their children (especially in cases where the moral code of the school is different from the moral code of the home). Still other candidates perceive this shared responsibility to be problematic because they believe it is difficult for schools to compensate for homes that are bereft of morality (in cases where students come from homes in which "morality is not taught and parents don't care"). Thus many candidates seem to believe that schools should either (a) not interfere with parents' rights to instill moral values in their children or (b) act in *loco parentis* for the moral development of children who come from homes devoid of morality.

These beliefs are worthy of addressing in teacher education programs because they suggest a misconception about the moral nature of schooling, an ill-conceived teacher role, and/or a deficit model of students and their development. That is, some of our candidates seem to assume that it is possible to avoid moral value and moral education in schools; or, alternatively, some candidates appear to conceive their role as replacing supposed delinquent parents of children who lack any moral foundation. These beliefs portend problems for moral development in schools because they deny the very moral nature of schooling, position teachers as missionaries, or distort the process of moral development as simply identifying supposed moral failings and remediating them.

There are multiple examples in this volume that shed light on how teacher educators might attend to these candidate beliefs. First, many chapter authors highlight ways to emphasize the moral nature of schooling in teacher education, such as Campbell (Chapter 3), Nucci (Chapter 10), and Shields et al. (Chapter 11). Second, and similarly, Stengel (Chapter 4) shows how democratic education serves as a guiding value in her course and assists candidates in developing a genuinely shared responsibility for moral and civic development.

Third, regarding beliefs that suggest there are students who come to school devoid of morality (because of delinquent parents), it seems that teacher candidates might benefit from addressing those beliefs in connection with the problems and complexities of teaching according to a deficit view (see the model of Johnson, Vare, and Evers for helping teacher candidates develop an asset view of students in Chapter 7). Moreover, because deficit views commonly are based upon a lack of understanding of the actual values and life circumstances of others, there is a need for candidates to actually come to know families in the communities where supposed deficits exist, laying the groundwork for developing teacher understanding, as well as open and supportive relationships with students and families (see Watson et al.'s approach to developing such relationships and understanding in Chapter 9).

Finally, these beliefs related to the respective roles of parents and schools in moral development also highlight the relativism that seems to pervade our candidates' conceptions of morality, and we believe it is valuable to address these beliefs in order to limit the potential paralysis or avoidance of thinking in explicitly moral terms (because the answers are not clear and can involve conflict) that often arises from such beliefs (Ternasky, 1993). This avoidance of explicit moral thought is apparent in candidates who hold that the moral code of parents is most influential and should not be interfered with by the school, except in cases of delinquent parents. In other words, these candidates appear to believe that morality is relative except when it is not. To meaningfully address these beliefs would require candidates to either stake their claim of relativism upon the moral code of parents or examine what constitutes an acceptable moral code in the home, thereby designating an appropriate moral code and level of intervention for the school. In this volume Campbell (Chapter 3) and Blumenfeld-Jones, Senneville, and Crawford (Chapter 5) provide rich examples of how teacher educators might attend to the relativism of teacher candidates and examine the ethical self.

Morality as a Function of Behavior

Most of our teacher candidates describe moral development and define morality in behaviorist terms. The prominence of this belief alone points up a need to help candidates understand the degree to which the belief is true, its limitations, and its needed complements in terms of understanding and practice. These needed complements include relational and affective elements of moral development. Very few of our candidates seem to understand what it means to view morality (or other domains of learning) in behavioral terms, or the importance of morality's cognitive, emotional, social, and relational dimensions. In particular, we noted that in describing the process of moral development or providing a definition of morality, an explicit or implicit reference to an ethic of care (Noddings, 1984) is conspicuously missing—the word *caring* (or its derivatives), for example, occurs only four times in the 92 candidates' responses to the survey questions.

The apparent behaviorism among candidates is apt for addressing in teacher education programs for at least two reasons. First, many of our candidates profess to want to be teachers because they "love children," and it seems appropriate to attend to this belief because there is ample research that details the importance of love and caring in the MWT. Second, many of our candidates also want to be teachers because they "want to make a difference and be a role model." Thus responding to the relative absence of caring and relationships in their beliefs about moral development might also be beneficial because they rely so heavily on relational and altruistic reasons for choosing a career in teaching. Put another way, from a constructivist perspective, understanding and responding to teacher candidates' own reasons for choosing a career in teaching necessitates the study of caring in teacher preparation, signaling the opportunity to provide a deeper understanding of ethics and moral development that fit candidates' reasons for becoming teachers (in this volume, see Nucci, Chapter 10; Johnson et al., Chapter 7; and Fallona and Canniff, Chapter 6, for examples of providing this deeper understanding and connection).

The implications for teacher education here include not only explicitly attending to care ethics and relational approaches to moral education in teacher education programs, but also processing candidates' behaviorism in light of their approach to teaching and moral commitments to the profession. For example, our teacher candidates might benefit extraordinarily from examining how their often deeply behaviorist approach to classroom management might be enhanced/reconstructed by attending to an ethic and a psychology of caring relationships and Developmental Discipline (see Watson et al., Chapter 9). Or, similarly, they might benefit by processing their behaviorist beliefs via coursework aligned with the relational focus undergirding components of programs described by Lapsley et al. (Chapter 8) and Nucci (Chapter 10). Regardless of the specific approach to teaching, addressing these beliefs from a relational perspective promises to both enhance teacher candidates' understanding of moral education and meaningfully connect them to the affective moral commitments that led them to choose a career in teaching in the first place.

Purposes of Schooling

There appears to be a possible tension between the purposes of schooling that our candidates espouse, their reasons for choosing a career in teaching, and the prevailing ideology of schooling that focuses on high-stakes standardized testing and accountability (Sanger, 2012). Again, many of the reasons that our candidates put forward for choosing a career in teaching are connected to the moral work of teaching, such as "being a role model" and "making a positive difference in the lives of others." Likewise, when asked about the purposes of schooling, some of our teacher candidates suggest a broad view of the purposes of schooling, including sociomoral purposes. However, most of them also emphasize purposes of schooling that are primarily academic and related to preparation for employment and the "real world," and there is no indication that they recognize the possible tensions in the interplay of their moral motivations to teach, their beliefs about the primary purposes of schooling, and the prevailing educational ideology that emphasizes academic outcomes. We believe this possible tension to be a rich one for exploration within the context of teacher education, one that reflects a gap between the dominant form of discourse on schooling within programs of teacher education, and the basic reasons that motivate teacher candidates within those programs. In this volume, Stengel (Chapter 4) provides a in-depth example of how teacher educators might assist teacher candidates in bridging this gap by attending to the purposes of schooling as a foundational element of a course, grounded in moral considerations.

CONCLUSION

The candidate beliefs discussed here both reinforce and significantly extend the point made by Sanger (2001), that educators have beliefs that are relevant to the

MWT, and relevant to consider in teacher education. Our data extend his narrative account of how two teachers view the moral nature of their work, by documenting a number of common beliefs about the MWT held by teacher candidates.

The summary of data and analysis in this chapter also gives teacher educators a clear empirical foundation for teacher education practice that connects the beliefs teacher candidates bring with them to their program to what we know about the MWT. We believe this connection to be sorely lacking in teacher preparation, and we submit that making this connection is necessary to both effectively and responsibly prepare teacher candidates for their future work in classrooms.

To this end, the connections to chapters in this volume (presented above) might serve to inform teacher educators about ways in which these potentially deep-seated beliefs can begin to be effectively and responsibly addressed in teacher education practice in a way that draws on what we know about the MWT, as well as what we know about teaching subject matter that is prone to misconceptions and naive understanding. The chapter authors in this volume provide rich descriptions of practice that address all of the emergent themes in our data, including modeling, direct instruction, the role of the school in moral development, behaviorism, and the purposes of schooling. We recommend a careful examination of these approaches to addressing the MWT in teacher education in relation to the beliefs that teacher candidates hold, and we also encourage further research that explores these and similar programmatic efforts related to the MWT.

The upshot of appropriately addressing these beliefs is teacher candidates who know how to intentionally pursue and fulfill their most basic motivations to teach and who are able to assist in the moral education and development of the students in their classrooms. And we are certainly encouraged by the possibilities that each of the chapters in this volume hold for addressing these beliefs and accomplishing this charge in teacher education research and practice. To this end, we urge more explicit and intentional links between actual teacher candidate beliefs about the MWT and the experiences of teacher candidates in teacher education programs.

REFERENCES

Aristotle. (1985). *Nicomachean ethics* (T. Irwin, Trans.). Indianapolis, IN: Hackett.

Bandura, A. (1986). *Social foundations of thought and action: A social cognitive theory.* Englewood Cliffs, NJ: Prentice-Hall.

Battistich, V. (2008). The Child Development Project: Creating caring school communities. In D. Narvaez & L. Nucci (Eds.), *Handbook of moral and character education* (pp. 328–351). New York: Routledge.

Burnyeat, M. F. (1980). Aristotle on learning to be good. In A. O. Rorty (Ed.), *Essays on Aristotle's ethics* (pp. 69–92). Los Angeles: University of California Press.

Donovan, M., & Bransford, J. (Eds.). (2005). *How students learn: History, mathematics, and science in the classroom.* Washington, DC: National Academies Press.

Fenstermacher, G. D. (1979). A philosophical consideration of recent research on teacher effectiveness. In L. S. Shulman (Ed.), *Review of research in education, 6,* 157–185. Itasca, IL: Peacock.

Huberman, M., & Miles, M. (Eds.). (2002). *The qualitative researcher's companion.* Thousand Oaks, CA: Sage.

Marshall, C., & Rossman, G. B. (2006). *Designing qualitative research* (4th ed.). Thousand Oaks, CA: Sage.

Narvaez, D. (2006). Integrative ethical education. In M. Killen & J. Smetana (Eds.), *Handbook of moral development* (pp. 703–733). Mahwah, NJ: Lawrence Erlbaum Associates.

Narvaez, D. (2008). Human flourishing and moral development: Cognitive and neurobiological perspectives of virtue development. In D. Narvaez & L. Nucci (Eds.), *Handbook of moral and character education* (pp. 310–327). New York: Routledge.

Noddings, N. (1984). *Caring: A feminine approach to ethics and moral education.* Berkeley: University of California Press.

Osguthorpe, R. D. (2009). On the possible forms a relationship might take between the moral character of a teacher and the moral development of a student. *Teachers College Record, 111*(1), 1–26.

Pajares, M. (1992). Teachers' beliefs and educational research: Cleaning up a messy construct. *Review of Educational Research, 62,* 307–332.

Patton, M. Q. (2001). *Qualitative research and evaluation methods* (3rd ed.). Thousand Oaks, CA: Sage.

Raths, J., & McAninch, A. (Eds.). (2003). *Teacher beliefs and classroom performance: The impact of teacher education.* Charlotte, NC: Information Age.

Richardson, V. (1996). The role of attitudes and beliefs in learning to teach. In J. Sikula (Ed.), *Handbook of research on teacher education* (2nd ed., pp. 102–119). New York: Macmillan.

Richardson, V. (2003). Preservice teachers' beliefs. In J. Raths & A. McAninch (Eds.), *Teacher beliefs and classroom performance: The impact of teacher education* (pp. 1–22). Charlotte, NC: Information Age.

Richardson, V., & Placier, P. (2001). Teacher change. In V. Richardson (Ed.), *Handbook of research on teaching* (4th ed., pp. 905–947). Washington, DC: American Educational Research Association.

Sanger, M. N. (2001). Talking to teachers and looking at practice in understanding the moral dimensions of teaching. *Journal of Curriculum Studies, 33*(6), 683–704.

Sanger, M. N. (2012). The schizophrenia of contemporary education and the moral work of teaching. *Curriculum Inquiry, 42*(2), 285–307.

Sanger, M. N., & Osguthorpe, R. D. (2005). Making sense of approaches to moral education. *Journal of Moral Education, 34*(1), 57–71.

Sanger, M. N., & Osguthorpe, R. D. (2009). A theoretically descriptive analysis of the Child Development Project. *Journal of Moral Education, 38*(1), 17–34.

Sanger, M. N., & Osguthorpe, R. D. (2011). Teacher education, preservice teacher beliefs, and the moral work of teaching. *Teaching and Teacher Education, 27*(3), 569–578.

Sanger, M. N., & Osguthorpe, R. D. (2013). Modeling as moral education: Documenting, analyzing, and addressing a central belief of preservice teachers. *Teaching and Teacher Education, 29*(1), 167–176.

Shulman, L. S. (1986). Those who understand: Knowledge growth in teaching. *Educational Researcher, 15*(2), 4–14.

Sockett, H., & LePage, P. (2002). The missing language of the classroom. *Teaching and Teacher Education, 18*(2), 159–171.

Ternasky, P. L. (1993). Coping with relativism and absolutism. In K. A. Strike & P. L. Ternasky (Eds.), *Ethics for professionals in education: Perspectives for preparation and practice* (pp. 117–131). New York: Teachers College Press.

Warnick, B. (2008). *Imitation and education: A philosophical inquiry into learning by example.* Albany: State University of New York Press.

Part II

TEACHING MORALLY

In a variety of ways, the chapters in Part II speak to preparing and supporting teachers in *teaching morally*—drawing primarily upon views of the moral conduct, character, identity, and thought of teachers, and their development in teacher education.

In Chapter 3 Elizabeth Campbell describes the professional and pedagogical responsibilities of the ethical teacher and how to attend to these responsibilities in teacher education practice. To provide analytical context, she describes her recent research that examines how other professions attend to these ethics of practice in the preparation of practitioners and then draws on her own practice to make recommendations for teacher education. She examines many of the difficulties of attending to these responsibilities across the teacher education curriculum, and her recommendations focus on the curriculum and pedagogy of a specialized teacher education course addressing the MWT.

In Chapter 4 Barbara Stengel presents a conceptually and practically dynamic account of her work with candidates to see, experience, and probe teaching through the lenses of pedagogical *responsibility* and its relational cognates: *response*, and *responsiveness*. She illustrates how these concepts and associated practices play constructive and critical roles in the developing practical judgment and action in the work of aspiring teachers, linking the work of preparing teachers for the MWT with the purposes and constituents of liberal education.

Maintaining a focus not just on supporting teachers in what we have termed *teaching morally*, but on developing our *moral being*, Donald Blumenfeld-Jones and his colleagues Don Senneville and Mary Crawford in Chapter 5 illustrate how we all (teachers, teacher educators, and teaching candidates included) live amid unacknowledged forms of ethical conflict and confusion. They present how they, and the teachers and teaching candidates in their summer institutes and courses, go about constructing an aware ethical self. This process, informed by an ethics of humility, provides a basis for teachers recognizing and responding to the ethical conflicts and confusions of teaching practice.

A more programmatic examination of preparing teachers for teaching morally is provided by Cathie Fallona and Julie Canniff in Chapter 6. These authors describe a nearly decade long practice of developing a moral stance in their teacher education program at the University of Southern Maine. Their

Aristotelian conception of a *moral stance* is embodied in their department's equity framework of wisdom and justice. The authors discuss how they support the development of teaching wisdom and justice in practice, reporting findings from a case study of recent graduates, elaborating the ways in which these graduates exemplify the program's moral stance.

Another programmatically oriented view comes in the work of Lisa Johnson, Jonatha Vare, and Rebecca Evers in Chapter 7, as they describe the recent redesign of their teacher education program at Winthrop University. Combining the psychological perspectives of Lawrence Kohlberg and Carol Gilligan with the philosophical work of John Dewey and Nel Noddings, their program supports the development and assessment of teacher candidate dispositions, focusing in particular on the disposition of fairness. They describe their assessment framework, based in theories of justice and care, that assists teacher educators in longitudinally tracking, linking, and supporting teacher candidate coursework and clinical fieldwork related to dispositions. Their conclusions emphasize the need for integration and theoretical grounding in order to infuse the MWT across teacher education programs, and their attention to both teaching morally and teaching morality provides a nice transitional chapter to Part III.

CHAPTER 3

Cultivating Moral and Ethical Professional Practice

Interdisciplinary Lessons and Teacher Education

Elizabeth Campbell

I didn't feel we were specifically taught ethics; I didn't feel that we were taught how to handle ethical situations. One of the instructors did talk about being fair, about being equitable, but did she really talk to us about what that looks like, sounds like, and feels like? I don't think she did, and that's what we need to see. What does it look like when you treat someone with respect? She never said the words, "Would you feel okay if someone went and did this to you?" I think that's really important, to say, "Now I'm going to do this to you, I'm going to call you up here to the front of the class and I'm going to do this to you—how does that make you feel? How do you think it would make a child feel if you were to do this?" I don't think this was really ever done, but I wished it had been. (Student teacher, unpublished data from the "Cultivation of Ethical Knowledge in Teaching Project," Campbell, 2005–2008)

In a review of articles published over the past 20 years in the journal *Teaching and Teacher Education* that have addressed the moral and ethical dimensions of teaching, Robert V. Bullough Jr. (2011) summarizes that the articles collectively advance the claim that "ethics are at the heart of the teacher's disciplinary knowledge . . . [and] to teach is to be embedded in a world of uncertainty and of hard choices, where what a teacher does and how he or she thinks is morally laden" (p. 27). This observation reflects more broadly the expanding body of literature during this same time that conceptualizes in rigorous philosophical analyses and illustrates in vivid empirical accounts the moral work of teachers as ethical professionals (Hansen, 2001; Jackson, Boostrom, & Hansen, 1993; Richardson & Fenstermacher, 2001; Sockett, 1993, 2012; Strike & Ternasky, 1993). While theoretically varied, this scholarship reveals attentiveness to how ethical and moral principles such as fairness, empathy, honesty, patience, diligence, kindness, trustworthiness, consistency, constancy, courage, conscientiousness, and integrity, as fairly uncontestable "goods," underpin the teacher's often routine yet complex practices. Teachers' ethical knowledge (Campbell, 2003) as a foundation of their professional practice is grounded by their awareness of the moral nuances of their work and by their capacity to reflect on how their behavior within classrooms and schools can both honor and jeopardize the realization of ethical virtues such as those identified above.

Teachers need to acquire ethical knowledge about all aspects of their curricular, pedagogical, and evaluative choices as well as in their relational and interpersonal connections with students, parents, colleagues, administrators, and others. Professional programs in teacher education would seem to provide an obvious and reasonable starting point for preservice teachers' initiation as ethical professionals. While student teachers obviously bring to such programs intuitive moral sensibilities rooted in their personal character, background, and experience, they need some kind of formalized education in ethics that transcends intuitive wisdom to show the relevance of moral virtues in their application to the practicalities of teaching.

In a way, ethics instruction is about making the familiar more obvious; it illuminates how generalized interpretations of moral values translate into the professional appreciation of one's work through a lens of ethical clarity. It should enable prospective teachers to know, among other things, when they are being—or not being—fair to students, honest in their evaluation of them, respectful in their instruction of them, and patient and kind in their treatment of them. Further, it should embolden them with a sense of ethical confidence as they anticipate and navigate the morally layered complexities of the situations they both create and encounter. As Strike (1993) noted about his student teachers, while they "rarely provide arguments that identify moral principles or seek to appraise ends, they do recognize the importance of such considerations once they are pointed out" (p. 103). While they may lack the "moral language" (Sockett & LePage, 2002) to articulate ethical values and principles as virtues of practice, they often can recognize them as relevant concepts with which to grapple in an effort to make defensible choices and principled decisions about how best to conduct their professional lives. Thus it is the task of ethics education, whether in teaching or other disciplines, to stimulate enlightened ethical consideration of practice and draw it to the forefront of how professionals define their responsibilities and engage in their work.

THE INVISIBILITY OF AN ETHICS CURRICULUM
IN TEACHER EDUCATION

More than 15 years ago I first addressed the teaching of professional ethics in an article in the *Journal of Teacher Education* (Campbell, 1997). In it I described my pedagogical and curricular goals and practices as a teacher educator, many of which

I continue to use, as I discuss later in this chapter. I concluded that, ideally, ethics instruction should be infused and embedded across the teacher education curriculum rather than siphoned off as an individual course or unit separate from the study of curriculum, pedagogy, classroom management, assessment, and other foundational components of most teacher education programs of study. By weaving ethical considerations into the discussion of teaching materials, styles, approaches, and other technical aspects, teacher educators are well placed to make the ethical real, concrete, and readily applicable to all components of teaching practice, instead of an abstract philosophical concept remote from the daily work of teachers.

In the subsequent years since the publication of that article, experience and empirical research have combined to compel me to revise my opinion. While infusion may still seem to be a preferred approach to integrating ethics into the teacher education curriculum, it also threatens to render the topic invisible. It is too easy to overlook or lose the focus on the moral and ethical nature of teaching if it is made implicit within the context of other curricular content. Ethics becomes, in essence, "the missing foundation" (Campbell, 2011) of teacher education unless it is highlighted in its own right, not hidden within what is usually a highly content-intensive program. Explicit and nonelective courses or units of study that consciously identify their objective as being the cultivation of ethical practice in teaching may be more successful in making the moral dimensions of teachers' work visible, authentic, and significant.

Such success does not seem to be evident, as literature in this field, which has always been critical of a lack of ethics instruction, continues to identify neglect on the part of teacher education programs to sensitize their students to the moral and ethical aspects of their chosen profession (Sockett, 2009; Willemse, Lunenberg, & Korthagen, 2008). My own study of whether and how some programs in Canadian faculties or schools of education contribute to an understanding of applied ethics and the moral work of teaching on the part of student teachers echoes what the literature uniformly claims—that minimal, if any, instruction in ethics exists in teacher education curricula. Although the findings of this qualitative study[1] are reported elsewhere (Campbell, 2008, 2011), I think it is useful to give a brief synopsis here of what the investigation revealed.

First, if ethics were mentioned in their programs at all, it occurred within a broader context of legal requirements and restrictions or as an excessively narrow and superficial nod to official local professional standards and codes without an accompanying application of such standards to the actual realities of teaching. The following compilation of responses from participants is fairly typical:

> The Ethical Standards document? I guess I could say it means nothing to me because I don't really remember anything specific from them. . . .
> We got a big pamphlet thing about the ethics of teaching, and I remember a lot of my course teachers were surprised to see them and read them. They talked with us but it was just kind of an informal meeting that was held once for an

hour during the school year. . . . The Ethical Standards? Do I know what they are? I couldn't name them. No, nope, I only had to do them for the one time; I know one of them was honesty, integrity, I remember words like that but, no, I can't tell you what they were. It was at the first part of the year, and ethics were never, ever, ever, ever touched on again.[2]

Second, while student teachers were not conversant with the ethics of teaching or moral principles that pervade its practices, they were introduced to elements of social justice education. While most identified this as somewhat different from ethics, some did collapse the sociopolitical language of social justice (e.g., equity, oppression, diversity, power, and antidiscrimination) with the language of moral and ethical principles (e.g., fairness, equality, care, and empathy). I have elaborated elsewhere (Campbell, 2008) on my arguments that social justice and the moral/ethical dimensions of teaching are distinct and separate fields of study, and that social justice education is not an adequate substitute for the focused instruction in the ethics of teaching.

Third, most of the student teacher participants in my study recalled alarming episodes of "negative role modeling" during their clinical practice in schools. They claimed that they witnessed teachers act in cruel, dishonest, careless, unfair, negligent, gossipy, spiteful, and subversive ways; such experiences brought their own moral sensibilities into focus as they recognized such conduct as unethical. However, efforts to address these experiences upon returning to their teacher education programs were silenced or ignored. One student (whose supervising teacher humiliated and yelled at her Kindergarten students daily, played games of favoritism, neglected those who could not keep up with class activities, threatened to "wring the neck" of one child, and referred openly to another who had autism as a "burden on society") recalled:

> I went to my course coordinator [teacher educator] and I said that I couldn't stay at this school, and she told me exactly these words, "suck it up. If we got rid of all the bad associate teachers, we'd lose 50%. I can't do anything for you . . . kids adapt, they'll be okay."

The student and novice teachers interviewed for my study all said they would have wanted clear and focused instruction in the ethics of teaching. They sensed the moral nature of the teacher's role, but were mostly unable to identify specific aspects of practice in moral and ethical terms beyond vague and generalized references to treating students with respect. As several stated:

> I think every instructor could have looked at his or her course and could have been a bit more thoughtful about putting it [ethics] in. . . . I didn't feel we were specifically taught ethics. I didn't feel that we were taught how to handle these situations [moral and ethical dilemmas]. . . . Teachers need a starting point, and, as a new teacher, I

would have liked to have that starting point because it's difficult to figure out [ethics of practice] on my own. (Campbell, 2008, p. 13)

The rest of this chapter explores ways to make visible and prominent in teacher education curricula the study of ethics in teaching and the moral work of teachers. Using qualitative empirical data from interviews with educators in professional preparation programs in disciplines other than teaching, this discussion considers by comparison what they do to teach the ethics of practice and moral complexities of their respective professions. Using this evidence as a catalyst for envisioning approaches teacher educators could adopt, along with examples from my own practice in teaching ethics to preservice teachers, the discussion proposes some practical recommendations of a curricular and pedagogical nature to enable the education of new teachers to be more attuned to their future ethical responsibilities.

WHAT OTHERS DO

A supplementary component of my study of ethics instruction in teacher education, referenced in the previous section, involved the interviewing of university faculty members from a range of professional programs in other disciplines. It is important to note that this component was not intended to provide comparative data from which to draw conclusions about the relative effectiveness of various programs. Students in these programs, unlike in the dominant teacher education part of the project, were not interviewed, so I have no empirical evidence to support any speculation on the impact of the programs. It may be that they too are minimally influential in the preparation of ethical professionals. Nonetheless, what became apparent is that descriptions of other professional programs revealed at least a serious curricular *intention* to familiarize students with the professional ethical standards and complexities of their respective fields. The purpose, therefore, of this brief overview is to highlight several perspectives on and approaches to teaching ethics that could offer some formative suggestions for those of us involved in teacher education. These include a belief that ethics must be a focused and required component of professional preparation that transcends personal opinion or intuition and reflects foundational knowledge in the discipline. Such perspectives also affirm explicit goals for teaching ethics that move philosophical theory and formalized codes or standards toward their concrete application. Instructional approaches involve the extensive use of case study pedagogy and attention to debriefing the details of students' clinical practice in ethical terms. My study interviewed 11 faculty members teaching in eight different professional disciplines. However, I have limited my discussion here to those teaching in nursing, social work, and physical therapy, since the nature of these disciplines as caring professions is more relevant to teaching than other fields, and the comments of these educators are more obviously transferable to teacher education.

A Focused and Mandatory Component Called Ethics

First of all, the three faculty members each acknowledged that issues of ethical significance "come up" continually throughout their programs and that they are addressed across the curriculum—both in the theoretical courses and units and, importantly, in relation to the clinical or practical components. However, while this highlights the importance of grappling programmatically with professional ethics in an integrated way, it is not the only way the topic is addressed. They all spoke of at least one course or unit specifically dedicated to the issue of professional ethics that is focused, mandatory, and evaluated as a core aspect of the program. In social work, it is part of a "foundations course" on the "theory, knowledge, and values" of social work practice, and one-third of it is devoted explicitly to the subject of ethics. Similarly, in nursing, ethics is a core part of an introductory foundations course on "the discipline and profession of nursing," which includes units on legal and professional issues as well. And in physical therapy, the third educator explained:

> Ethics and professionalism is one of the themes that cuts across all the units; . . . however, we try to build a foundation of ethics right at the beginning of the program and then intersperse it throughout their other content. . . . Later, in second year, they write an assignment where they identify an ethical issue in physical therapy and write about what the ethical issue is and what they see as a way forward or a conclusion.

Furthermore, the ethics components are clearly identified as such and involve direct reference to core ethical principles of autonomy, beneficence, justice, nonmalfeasance, and confidentiality; and students are pushed to develop their knowledge of these principles in a systematic way. Again, the physical therapist educator explained:

> I teach them that there's a better answer. There may not be one particular answer but there's usually a better answer. . . . Students get stuck on any answer is acceptable, right, so every answer's just as good. And I try and push them into, "no, there's a better answer and you need explicit reasons. You need to defend it." So even learning how to make an argument I think is a huge issue and a skill that they don't necessarily have.

By comparison, the social work educator stated:

> We tell them there's no right answer . . . but they need to pull in other materials, sources, and supports to help them make a decision. The thing we don't want them to do is act in isolation, keep secrets, not identify things, not refer to any codes and just be out there on their own, thinking, "I'm going to

do this because I think it's a good idea." We want them to have some sort of systematic way of working it through using, first of all, their own professional code of conduct and also other resources.

Despite different perspectives on teaching "right answers" what seems clear is that in each of the three disciplines, students are told, first of all, that their professions involve extensive ethical complexities and that, as professionals, they will need to base their decision making on much more than personal feelings and moral intuition. In this respect, such a message is just as relevant for teacher education.

Explicit Goals and Pedagogies

The faculty I interviewed described their ethics components in terms of not having implicit, naturally occurring, or embedded characteristics, but rather having clear and explicit goals, aims, and pedagogies. In some cases, they start by introducing the philosophical underpinnings of professional ethics and then move to focus mostly on their concrete application. Others initiate the topic with reference to the professional codes of ethics, as relevant. In all cases, the programs make extensive use of case studies of real practice. The nursing educator notes that "without a case, their [the students'] eyes will glaze over immediately and it means nothing to them." She, like the physical therapy educator, writes her own cases based on years of clinical experience, and "in case discussions we would look at different ways of using a theory to articulate the ethical dimensions." What is significant about their stated intentions for their programs is that ethics is a planned curricular component rather than just a haphazard point of reference that surfaces in the context of other lessons or discussions on other topics. It is consciously built into the programs, not left up to chance to be "touched on" in embedded ways.

The ethics lessons are based on theoretical evidence and resources, codes of ethics and standards, and "real-life" case studies that vividly depict the actual nuances of everyday ethical practice. In fact, they seem centered more on dilemmas of practice than on abstract theorizing about practice. One educator stated, "I hope that they come out being able to recognize ethical issues when they see them, to, at least, at first be able to label it as an ethical issue." Another concurred, "I used to present it more in a theoretical way . . . but thinking about what do these students need when they go out and practice? They need to have a sense of how to work through ethical problems themselves and to identify what's going on."

One could criticize the idea of focusing on ethical dilemmas of practice to define teaching's moral and ethical essence, especially given that teachers have a distinctive role among professionals to be responsible not only for their own ethical conduct, but also for the moral instruction of their students. However, while it is true that the moral complexities and nuances of teaching (and, I suspect, of the other professions mentioned above) transcend dilemma resolution, it does seem that one way to appreciate such aspects is to conceptualize them within the context of potential dilemmas or even normative situations compelling the application of moral judgment on the part of the professional. The case study pedagogy described by those above provides a solid practical basis through which to apply ethical decision-making skills, and I believe it could contribute to the kind of ethical knowledge development that may be lacking in many teacher education programs.

All three participants discussed at length their professions' codes of ethics. Unlike in the teacher education programs of the students in my study where the ethical standards seemed all but ignored, the codes were positioned prominently in these programs. As one explained,

> The code of ethics is part of their readings in first year, first term. They have to dedicate it to memory basically. We're not going to let them practice in the field, even in the practicum, without knowing it. So they take this course before they go into practicum, and they need to know it down cold.

Despite the obvious priority placed on formal ethical standards in a way that may be foreign to teacher education, all three participants stressed that such codes are only a small piece of professional ethics. As one said, "Your ethics don't come from your regulatory body even though they have a code of ethics." As in teaching, the ethics of these professions are seen as messy, complex, fraught with dilemmas, and reflected in the details of seemingly routine practice. They all recognize this reality and seek to impart it to their students.

A similar perspective on the legal aspects of their professions is taken. The nursing educator regards law as "a minimalist ethic. They need to consider the law, but being ethical usually requires a bit more than the bare minimum." The physical therapy educator echoes this belief: "I'm hoping students see ethics and law as different. Again, that's one of the things we do in first year, address this relationship. So we talk about how laws come from ethical principles but that doesn't mean that every law is ethical." The teacher education students in my study also seemed to acknowledge that law and ethics are not one and the same thing; however, their examples of ethical lessons they remembered, albeit dimly, seemed focused more on legal considerations about professional misconduct than on other ethical aspects of teaching practice.

Another pedagogical approach to consider relates to how these three professional programs debrief the practical and clinical experiences of their students. They all acknowledge that ethical issues abound in the clinical setting, not only relating to "their observing of bad practice, as sometimes what's happening in the real world isn't best practice," but also of ethically infused decisions that they face. They spoke of the "ambiguities" that present themselves in "real-life" practice where right and wrong answers are not always evident. In all cases, there is a structure in place for students to discuss and share their experiences using ethics as their term of reference. Some write ethical case studies based on their experiences.

In another program the students are debriefed:

> One of the things we do is every time the students go out on placement, the week that they come back we do a debrief with them. The clinical coordinator does the debrief, but I always go to those [as the ethics instructor]. Often I don't have to ask if there have been any ethical or professional issues that have come up. The students have stories and they have problems, and they've had trouble dealing with it and they want to talk about it. To me, it's a great teaching moment. "This is what's really happened to you. How did you deal with it? How do you wish you'd dealt with it? How could you have dealt with it?"

From my own experience, teacher education often seems reluctant to take this approach for fear of encouraging gossiping about and criticizing colleagues' practices in schools. However, I believe this fear is little more than a blind commitment to collegial loyalty in the guise of professional relations. There are professional ways to enable student teachers to discuss openly, yet confidentially and respectfully, their experiences, ethical dilemmas, and concerns in order to cultivate an educative opportunity that could enhance students' appreciation of the moral and ethical challenges in teaching. This is, from my perspective, infinitely more preferable than leaving student teachers with the message that they should shut their eyes and close their ears to unethical practices they may witness in schools.

As stated previously, I have no way of knowing whether or not students in the three professional programs referenced in this section came away from their formal education with a keener sense of professional ethics than the teacher education students who participated in my study. However, what does seem likely is that they experienced more focused programs that highlighted the centrality of the professional's moral responsibilities in explicit principle-based language. Ethics instruction, as a mandatory part of the programs, was grounded theoretically in order to enable students to hone their ethical judgment as something more than personal intuition. Pedagogically, the aim was to close the conceptual gap between philosophical theory, as well as formal codes or standards, and their concrete application to the ambiguities of real practice. To this end, case study pedagogy—based on both instructor- and student-generated scenarios from their unique field and clinical experiences—was extensively employed. Ultimately, professional ethics was not simply something students had to divine from the curriculum for themselves, but rather was an intentional aspect of their preservice preparation.

In this respect, I believe there are lessons to be learned for teacher education, despite differences among the disciplines. There may well be many teacher educators who already do address ethics and the moral nature of teaching in their courses and programs. However, for the most part, their work remains localized and hidden from the collective view of researchers in this field who maintain, as my study concurred, that the moral and ethical nature of teaching is a neglected area of preservice teacher education. Consequently, the next section, in which I provide an overview of my own teaching of ethics to preservice students, is certainly not meant as a necessarily unique or distinctive description of pedagogy that I alone use. Rather, I present it for illustrative purposes to offer some curricular suggestions.

WHAT I DO

I am fortunate to be currently teaching about the ethical and moral dimensions of teaching to preservice students in a small (150 students), 2-year master's program. My course is a required component of the program that prepares both elementary and secondary school teachers. In the past I taught versions of this course in a much larger undergraduate preservice program, in which it was an elective option available to approximately 35 of the 1,000 students registered in the 8-month program. The difference between teaching ethics as a focused and core element of professional preparation and teaching it as an add-on interest course for those who might find it of some relevance to their future career is palpable. By focusing squarely on the ethics of teaching as an essential component, student teachers have both the time and extended exposure to the language and concepts of ethics to become accustomed to the idea that familiar aspects of their daily practice are, in fact, morally laden, and that their attention to the ethics of what they do as teachers, not just the technicalities of what they do, is at the core of their identity as professional practitioners.

In his discussion of his own experience teaching ethics courses to preservice teachers, Strike (1993) observes that "students find moral ideas familiar even though they are not the kinds of considerations that come to their minds first and they often need help in finding the words to express them" (p. 104). As classroom conversations evolve, Strike notes a "transformation" in his students marked by a shift in their language from that associated with strategic or instrumental problem solving to realize specific ends, to that which requires the appraisal in moral terms of right and wrong of the means and ends. They conceptualize problems in new ways and move beyond the expression of personal feelings and beliefs to "a more articulate and explicit formulation of this intuitive knowledge" (p. 104). For Strike, this is the beginning of ethical reflection, and his goal is to engage students in activities and conversations that cultivate such reflection and help them "make principled moral decisions" (p. 116) about their work as teachers. I share Strike's goals of formalizing intuitive knowledge about the familiar, awakening the recognition of moral and ethical nuances of teaching, and compelling the thoughtful reflection about and adjudication of ends and means in terms of their moral and ethical desirability; I also share his experience relating to the transformation of students' enhanced awareness when they consider examples of real practice as filtered through a lens of moral and ethical sensitivity.

My course adopts two broad and intersecting approaches: the use of case study pedagogy and the examination of research literature on a series of relevant themes. Strike (1993), again, notes:

> Cases provide material for discussion of moral principles that can be selected or crafted to serve the purposes of instruction. It is important not to claim too much for cases. They are not the be all and end all of moral learning. What they are is a useful way to teach specific moral concepts to novices in classroom settings. (p. 112)

Discussing cases develops students' capacity to talk about fairness, honesty, trust, caring, respect, and other principles as they are either upheld or challenged in very specific examples of problematic school-based and classroom-based situations that confront teachers with difficult decisions. The first 45 minutes of each 3-hour class I teach is devoted to case study work, in which students discuss a case in small groups. One student per group acts as the facilitator of the session. The facilitator chooses a case from a collection of case studies; the cases are usually one to three pages long, and they depict a range of authentic scenarios (if necessary, the cases are adapted or updated to be more relevant to specific contexts most familiar to the students). Normally, each group will have the opportunity to read and analyze eight to ten different cases during the course, with the role of facilitator alternating among the students. Each facilitator guides the discussion by focusing on the possible moral implications of the dilemma or situation depicted, ways to resolve it, and likely consequences of actions and inactions, while highlighting the underlying ethical principles. Students are encouraged to use an ethical, decision-making framework to aid in the analysis of the case and to make conceptual connections between theoretical points addressed in the course's scholarly readings and the practicalities described by the case. The goal is to push students beyond generalized discussions of personal and intuitive belief and feeling to grounding their perspectives in more formal philosophical wisdom and professional knowledge.

Before initiating the case study component, I introduce students to ethical codes and other formalized policies and regulations governing professional conduct in their jurisdiction. I also provide them with a range of ethical frameworks and brief philosophical overviews of various moral and ethical theories such as deontology, teleology, utilitarianism, virtue ethics, ethics of justice, rights, and care, in order to distinguish between making decisions for action or dilemma resolution on the basis of anticipated good and bad consequences and on the basis of a nonconsequential respect for duties and principles. The frameworks, while differing in structure and detail, follow a similar conceptual pattern. They usually involve a series of steps that require students to:

1. Identify the dilemma and explain why it is ethical in nature
2. Clarify the relevant facts and circumstances of the case and consider one's first instinctual reaction

3. Identify the various stakeholders
4. Consider alternatives that could be taken to resolve the situation
5. Apply ethical resources (e.g., differing moral theories, policies, codes of ethics, general maxims, principles, exemplars of others' judgments) to the alternatives to determine ultimately the best course of action

I have found that the students enjoy case study analysis, and the more deeply they engage with the language of ethical principles, the more likely they are to discover layers of moral and ethical complexity that they may have overlooked at first.

As the course progresses, there is a heightened expectation that students relate their deliberation of practice—both practice as described in the cases and in observations of their own and others' practice during their clinical teaching experiences—to the theoretical concepts addressed in the relevant body of scholarship on the moral and ethical work of teaching. This expectation extends not only to in-class discussions, but also to their written assignments; their major culminating essay requires them to write their own case study and analyze it using course resources and literature that addresses a range of thematic issues.

Themes covered in class include consideration of the teacher as a moral agent, and what this means in terms of daily responsibilities, curricular work, and formal and spontaneous interactions with students. While these themes largely address ethically positive aspects, other themes grapple with the ethically complicated life of teachers—their dilemmas and tensions, the collegial stresses, the problems exacerbated by administrative policies and regulations that challenge teachers' moral sensibilities as they strive to make good choices within complex environments. A further area of discussion relates to the contentious question of how to deal ethically with controversial issues in the classroom, and how much teachers should reveal about their own perspectives on them, socially, politically, and ideologically. These themes raise questions of moral and ethical significance; they demand that teachers examine both their motives and their actions in terms of integrity and what is fair, honest, responsible, trustworthy, empathetic, respectful, and caring. They also stimulate lively debate and disagreement.

Differing interpretations of the moral work of teachers are suggestive of a central theoretical impediment in the instruction of applied ethics; it is the propensity for students, and indeed teacher educators, to slide into an implicit form of moral relativism in part as a consequence of the nature of case study deliberation as well as the acceptance that there may be no one right answer. However, to recall the physical therapist and social work educators quoted previously, there are "better" answers—not everything is equally good from an ethical point of view. Reflection, discussion, and indeed argumentation around complex philosophical and practical ideas do not mean that right and wrong are merely subjective and situational. Such a misconception undermines the point of ethics education and removes the rationale for having professional ethical standards and for defining the professional work of teachers as being essentially moral work. This is something I try to be vigilant about by using the language of ethical principles and virtues as applicable to teacher practice, and by resisting any justification for conduct based solely on instrumental reasoning when it tends to obscure such principles and virtues. However, it is a challenge.

CONCLUSION

Strike (1993) concedes that teacher education programs are inevitably limited in their capacity to produce ethical practitioners: "Character is the product of years, not credit hours" (p. 107). Nonetheless, as he continues, the goal of instruction in the ethics of teaching is not to "make students saints or sages, but it can help them to conduct their professional lives in a more responsible way" (p. 107). In order to enable this, teacher educators must first ensure that their students understand that teaching is not merely an academic or technical endeavor, but that it is infused with moral and ethical expectations, responsibilities, and complexities that take form in the manner in which teachers conduct their work.

Borrowing from the stated intended practices of professional educators in other disciplines, this chapter has argued that teacher education would benefit from similarly highlighting the ethics of teaching as a core and explicit component of its programs. While traditionally not seen as an obvious priority, ethics education that facilitates a deeper appreciation of the moral aspects of teaching may be best developed by the following actions:

1. Making applied professional ethics a clear and identifiable programmatic element, not an infused, embedded, additional, optional, assumed, implicit, or irrelevant topic of study that one needs to search the program to find
2. Recognizing that while professional ethical standards or codes are only a part of the wider picture, students still need to know them and learn to apply them
3. Using a moral language that privileges ethical principles and virtues, grounded in theoretical rigor and practical applicability
4. To this end, using examples of genuine situations as exemplars of the moral work of teaching—case studies, empirical data from relevant research, experiential accounts of practice teaching
5. Exploring ways to work closely with field-based professionals to showcase exemplary ethical practice

Ethics education and enhancing the appreciation of the moral nature of teachers' work are not about making bad people good. They are about making good people aware that their choices and actions have the potential either to uplift and advance or hinder and thwart the emotional and intellectual well-being of the students in their care. Ideally, most student teachers strive to make right choices that achieve the former and prevent the latter from occurring. Teacher education should be committed to engaging them intentionally and explicitly in this mission toward becoming ethical professionals.

NOTES

1. I gratefully acknowledge the Social Sciences and Humanities Research Council of Canada for its support of this research project, entitled "The Cultivation of Ethical Knowledge in Teaching," 2005–2008.

2. Unless otherwise noted, quotations in this chapter represent previously unpublished interview data from the same research project cited above: Campbell, 2005–2008.

REFERENCES

Bullough, R. V., Jr. (2011). Ethical and moral matters in teaching and teacher education. *Teaching and Teacher Education, 27*(1), 21–28.

Campbell, E. (1997). Connecting the ethics of teaching and moral education. *Journal of Teacher Education, 48*(4), 255–263.

Campbell, E. (2003). *The ethical teacher*. Maidenhead, UK: Open University Press.

Campbell, E. (2008). Preparing ethical professionals as a challenge for teacher education. In K. Tirri (Ed.), *Educating moral sensibilities in urban schools* (pp. 3–18). Rotterdam, Netherlands: Sense Publishers.

Campbell, E. (2011). Teacher education as a missed opportunity in the professional preparation of ethical practitioners. In L. Bondi, D. Carr, C. Clark, & C. Clegg (Eds.), *Towards professional wisdom: Practical deliberation in the "people professions"* (pp. 81–93). Farnham, UK: Ashgate.

Hansen, D. T. (2001). Teaching as a moral activity. In V. Richardson (Ed.), *Handbook of research on teaching* (4th ed., pp. 826–857). Washington, DC: American Educational Research Association.

Jackson, P. W., Boostrom, R. E., & Hansen, D. T. (1993). *The moral life of schools*. San Francisco: Jossey-Bass.

Richardson, V., & Fenstermacher, G. D. (2001). Manner in teaching: The study in four parts. *Journal of Curriculum Studies, 33*(6), 631–637.

Sockett, H. (1993). *The moral base for teacher professionalism*. New York: Teachers College Press.

Sockett, H. (2009). Dispositions as virtues: The complexity of the construct. *Journal of Teacher Education, 60*(3), 291–303.

Sockett, H. (2012). *Knowledge and virtue in teaching and learning: The primacy of dispositions*. New York: Routledge.

Sockett, H., & LePage, P. (2002). The missing language of the classroom. *Teaching and Teacher Education, 18,* 159–171.

Strike, K. A. (1993). Teaching ethical reasoning using cases. In K. A. Strike & P. L. Ternasky (Eds.), *Ethics for professionals in education: Perspectives for preparation and practice* (pp. 102–116). New York: Teachers College Press.

Strike, K. A., & Ternasky, P. L. (1993). *Ethics for professionals in education: Perspectives for preparation and practice.* New York: Teachers College Press.

Willemse, M., Lunenberg, M., & Korthagen, F. (2008). The moral aspects of teacher educators' practices. *Journal of Moral Education, 37*(4), 445–466.

CHAPTER 4

Teaching Moral Responsibility

Practical Reasoning in a
Pedagogical "Wonderland"

Barbara S. Stengel

Approximately 30 sophomores enter the classroom on the first day of Foundations of Modern Education at Millersville University in South Central Pennsylvania.[1] These sophomores are bright young men and women who want to be teachers. Most of them have known this ambition for years. Nearly all were inspired by a particular teacher who had a significant impact on their lives. They imagine themselves inspiring others in the same way.

Despite their enthusiasm for teaching, they know little about what is involved. They do not typically think of teaching as a profession that is both morally and intellectually demanding. Nor are they are cognizant that teaching is a craft to be developed. They imagine that once they know mathematics or English or science, they will know how to teach it. For them, teaching is talking, the transmission of information. Doing it well is a matter of personality, not of intellect. It requires enthusiasm but not judgment. My aspiring educators think they themselves will be different from the ineffective teachers they have known because they will care about their students as those teachers did not. They will take their responsibility as teachers seriously. As they enter my classroom, they are not sure why they are there or how I can help them achieve their professional ambitions.

I begin by reading to them from *Alice's Adventures in Wonderland* (Carroll, 1865/1993), featuring Alice and the Caterpillar. We spend time determining which is the right (right or left? right or wrong?) side of a mushroom. We follow that by thinking aloud about point of view and perspective and the limits of human vision as a metaphor for human judgment. I hand them several news articles and editorials about the federal government's decade-long incursion into basic education,

No Child Left Behind. Each article represents a different institutional and political point of view. I ask the students to read and, with two other classmates, interpret what is going on.

We come back together as a class to begin the task of articulating the layers of and players in the educational system in this country. They see only themselves as teacher. I push them to see policy makers, state officials, school board members, superintendents, principals, taxpayers, parents, students—and to see all, especially their students, as persons worthy of their attention and regard. I ask them, "Who decides what you will do in the classroom? Who will benefit from what you do?" When they offer an opinion, I ask for evidence. I interrogate, but do not denigrate, the values they assume. I suggest that schools and classrooms are sites of power relations, contestable and often contested. They don't understand what I mean—yet. They leave the room without a syllabus and with a sense that they have wandered into Wonderland.

The course they will run over the next several months is intended to teach *pedagogical responsibility*. My persistent use of the language of responsibility is intentional. It functions to shine light on two realities of teaching:

1. Teaching is a moral endeavor, a relational practice of response and responsiveness that both requires and gives rise to responsibility.
2. Responsibility, moral and professional, can be cultivated in the development of the practical judgment teachers cannot avoid.

These are the themes explored in this chapter.

In what follows, I alternate between articulating theoretical assumptions and describing my own teaching practice, and musing about what both might mean for broader conceptions of moral responsibility, professional judgment, practical reasoning, and our understanding of the relation between liberal arts and professional preparation in teaching. I begin by addressing the concept of responsibility, examining its relation to practical reasoning, and explaining why I find this to be a useful tool in shaping students' experience of teaching as a moral endeavor. I describe some aspects of Foundations of Modern Education, representing some of the interactions, assignments, and events that intentionally create a layered experience which students must take in and sort out. After that, I think back and link back to questions about the nature and importance of professional judgment, the sense of pedagogical responsibility, the possibilities for practical reasoning understood as the deliberation that leads to ethical action, and the places in the undergraduate course of study where judgment, responsibility, and reasoning emerge. At the end, I return to what it might mean to teach responsibility.

VISIONS AND VERSIONS OF PEDAGOGICAL RESPONSIBILITY

Aspiring teachers are typically responsible (young) men and women. They faithfully attend classes, complete assignments and interact appropriately. They are responsible within the limits of an educational system whose rules and mores they have mastered. That system has clearly defined roles and behaviors for teachers and students. Teachers set the agenda, students comply, and those two functions can be clearly delineated.

This achievement of responsibility is both an accomplishment and a limitation. It is an accomplishment because it represents moving beyond self to the recognition that being and doing for and with others is worthwhile. It is a limitation because the teaching self is shaped by a single narrative of schooling as society's "balance wheel," a narrative that incorporates but also hides the normalizing function of schooling. That narrative distinguishes fact from value, content from method, curriculum from child, teaching from learning, and educational practice from the democratic functioning that some imagine to be its *raison d'etre*. "Appropriate" power relations in schools are more likely to be imagined as a benevolent dictatorship than an authoritative democratic interaction. That dominant economic interests should operate on school and curriculum is taken for granted.

This course we run together enacts a different vision and version of responsibility. In the version I limn for my students competing defensible narratives abound, fact and value are mutually constitutive, and schooling has a constructive, creative capacity that challenges its taken-for-granted normalizing function. The roles of teacher and student take shape and evolve based on the authority and need of both parties, at least in principle. The moral—that is, that which is *worth doing*—is messy. Democratic education—the development of future democracy-capable citizens in and through educational contexts that are democratically conceived—is the guiding value and vision because it is the only value that frames respect for the competing cultural and individual values held by various stakeholders.

The cultivation of moral and professional judgment seems unnecessary in my students' educational worldview. Their own goodness and purity of intention is taken for granted. The teacher who knows a lot and tells what she knows richly and accurately is an effective teacher—if she has the right personality, of course. And being "effective" is the goal. But professional judgment is a critical, complex element (perhaps *the* critical element) in an educational world marked by competing defensible narratives and intertwined facts and values. To become aware that the truth of a matter is contestable while still maintaining professional focus and momentum is a challenge of high order. I have found this understanding of responsibility—in which responsibility becomes a form of moral and professional inquiry—useful in the education of future teachers.

This understanding can be fleshed out by using a trio of cognate terms: *response, responsive,* and *responsibility. Response* represents the reality that educators are always responding to pedagogical situations only partly of their own making;

they *must* respond, but they can *only* respond. Control is a regulative ideal perhaps, but never a real possibility.

Responsiveness invokes the relational nature of all teaching and learning. Teachers and students stand in relation to one another and the quality of their interactions is determinative of the quality of their shared understanding. This is not the simplistic point that if teacher and student get along, the student will learn more. Rather, it implies that the way in which they interact shapes the substance of possible learning.

Responsibility acknowledges that persons are accountable for their actions. However, accountability is not to be understood retroactively, in terms of blame and punishment, but prospectively, in terms of who I now am in the world and what you can expect of me in the future. This is the understanding of responsibility that animates teaching as a moral practice and also animates the course I teach.

The understanding of responsibility I have come to adopt has its roots in the thinking of John Dewey (1922) and H. Richard Niebuhr (1963). With Dewey, I accept that "action is response" and that response can be more or less intelligent, more or less effective, more or less sensitive to the other and to the environment, more or less indicative of the self who acts. From Niebuhr, I borrow his central synecdoche: that the root structure of moral action is neither deontological (discover-obey) nor teleological (means-end) but responsive (interpret-respond). Judgment's ever challenging mandate is to enact the right response, that is, the response that the situation demands. Dewey calls this a "vibrating response"; Niebuhr refers to it as the "fitting response."

Practical reasoning is the process of thinking into action. As Niebuhr makes clear in the context of ethics, deciding what to do cannot be merely a matter of following rules or protocols, though these may be useful. It cannot be merely a matter of setting goals and identifying the action whose consequences will contribute to goal achievement, though this tack has utility as well. It is both of these and more. It is the sensibility to recognize and identify the action of the other who shapes my perception and prompts my response. It is the capacity—and the will—to interpret what is going on generously and thoroughly—that is, from multiple perspectives, adequately framing the source of difficulty, confusion, or discomfort. It is the ability to imagine potential responses and to anticipate the consequences of each possibility for all affected. It is the recognition that any response will in turn prompt a counter-response in the communities of agents who share my social worlds, constituting and framing the domain(s) of my action. And it is an acknowledgment that, in the end, every response takes shape in the light of personal value commitments, commitments that are a complex function of feeling, thought, and past practice.

Consider a simple example: an 11th-grade English teacher in an underfunded urban school who must prepare her students for state reading and writing assessment tests set for the spring of the year. The curriculum says, "American Literature"; the principal says, "Improve test scores." She is unsettled. She feels as though she can't do both. What should she do? She could set aside one day a week for "test prep" and follow her regular curriculum the rest of the time. She could have students read one piece of American literature each week and develop from that a series of reading checks and writing prompts that will develop the skills the testing demands. She could tell the principal that she is working on skills and teach literature as usual. She could reconstruct her curriculum so that it integrates test skills with the regular American literature content. She could teach the first semester as she has in the past and start a full-time test prep program in January. She could collaborate with other English teachers to determine a common plan. She could ask the principal to provide coaching to improve her ability to work with her students on test skills. This array of actions, singly or in some combination, is open to her. There are certainly other possibilities as well. But it is important that she do *nothing*, that she make no response, until she has first asked herself, "What is going on here?" This is the interpretive question. It is a question that expert teachers often ask and answer invisibly, leaving outsiders and novices with the mistaken impression that the question of what to do is the only critical one.

So our English teacher asks herself, "What is going on?" Knowledge of the theory and practice of teaching English to high school students and of this urban district and its social and economic realities will shape what she looks for and what she sees. And it is not merely a matter of what she sees now, in this moment, but also how she has attended over time to her students and their circumstances.

- What do the tests demand?
- Are her students generally unprepared? Or unprepared in some specific, targetable ways?
- What interests her students? What do they need?
- What is the principal saying?
- Why is the district under the gun regarding the tests? Are these concerns legitimate?
- What materials are at her disposal—regarding test preparation and/or American literature?
- How much time does she have?
- Why does she feel that she can't do both? Is that accurate? Who might be able to help her think this through?
- Are there other considerations besides these particular tests? For example, will those students taking college entrance exams be disadvantaged if they don't get a full measure of American literature?
- Can test prep be done through independent study? Is there home support to make this feasible?
- Can test prep be accomplished in this school year?

These are not merely prudential questions; each one can be answered in ways that privilege and deny attention to diverse others. Only when our teacher takes seriously the questions of recognition and interpretation will she be able to act, to respond, in a fitting way, that is, in a morally defensible way. Too often interpretation gets short shrift.

It is the interpretation that points the way to (one or more) likely hypotheses and narrows the range of possible responses. And that interpretation involves valuation. That is, what our teacher sees in her students and her own circumstance will be a function not only of what she knows about American literature, the teaching of writing, 11th-graders, and the reality of high-stakes testing, but also what she and they take seriously, what is valued. If, for example, she values literature as a tool for self-understanding, she may opt for minimal test prep because she believes that literature study will have a greater impact on her students' futures. If she values being a "team player," she may believe it is her duty to focus on test preparation. And if she likes a challenge, she may opt to rewrite her curriculum in an integrative way.

This understanding of action as response provides a heuristic for making sense of educational situations in which more than one person, more than one good, more than one goal, and more than one rule or principle are always at work. I find that I can *structure* students' thinking without *determining* it. That is, a response framework pushes them to do three things:

1. To consider all factors (or as many as their level of sophistication presents) in identifying the challenge at hand
2. To imagine and test possible responses
3. To act in concert with their own value commitments rather than mine, but also be cognizant of the value commitments that mark teaching as a social practice and as a profession

My particular concerns in Foundations of Modern Education are the first and third of these elements. I turn now to a limited example of how we take this up.

FOUNDATIONS OF MODERN EDUCATION: A SYLLABUS REVIEW

If you followed my students to the course website, you would encounter this:

We begin the semester with a set of "essential questions" to guide our learning together:

1. How are teaching and learning, schooling and education related? What is the responsibility of the teacher? The purpose of schooling in 21st-century America?
2. What is the structure of our educational system? How does it work? How is power generated? How does it flow in that system? Can/should that structure be changed? (The political question)

3. Who pays the bill? Who benefits? Is there equal educational opportunity? Is it fair? (The economic question)
4. Is there one "American culture"? Whose knowledge, culture, and way of life are privileged and preserved in contemporary schooling? Is it better to be White than Black? Male than female? Christian than any other religious persuasion? Can schools construct an American culture while respecting the cultural background kids bring to schools? (The sociocultural question)
5. How did we get the educational system that we have? Which individuals, events, social forces, and common values shaped our educational system? (The historical question)
6. What is the purpose of schooling in a democracy and how should it be carried out? How has this question been answered in America, and how would YOU answer it? (The philosophical question)

Our primary goal is "pedagogical responsibility." That is, I will help you acquire and develop a critical, moral perspective regarding every aspect of the profession of teaching and the domain of schooling in 21st-century American democracy. That perspective is a key element in the responsive and responsible decision making that marks the effective educator.

We will reach our goal by reading, responding to, and exploring in depth several classic and contemporary educational texts and by critically reflecting on your experience in the schools in light of these texts. . . . At the end of our time together, you will be knowledgeable about schooling in America and your knowledge, enlivened by the critical, moral perspective noted above, will guide your perceptions and actions as a teacher.

Foundations of Modern Education is taught together with another course, Psychological Foundations of Teaching, and an urban field experience. With the introduction above, I explain to my students why this course and the bloc of which it is a part are *foundational*. "Foundations" courses in any field are often viewed as "the basics," the simple things one must learn before moving on to the complicated stuff. This is not the case here, as multidisciplinary issues linked to "critical, moral perspectives" are anything but simple. "Foundations" courses also suggest the acquisition of knowledge that will later be applied in teaching practice. Again, this is not the case here. The structure of the course rejects the epistemological assumption that knowledge acquisition precedes knowledge use, opting instead for an epistemic view that focuses on thoughtful (and carefully guided) practice as the vehicle for knowledge acquisition. Both Foundations of Modern Education and its companion course are foundational because they address the "interpretive" moment in the "interpret-respond" relation. These courses make use of theory, research, and contemporary reporting to enable students to "see" more clearly and completely the macroscopic (social foundations) and microscopic (psychological foundations) dimensions of teaching and learning in the schools in which they do their practica. Seeing generates the data that frames and names the problem prompting a response.

For example, a student who reads Horace Mann's "Twelfth Report to the Massachusetts Board of Education" (Mann, 1848/1957), while reflecting on his own educational experience, will be more likely to detect and name the goal conflicts in the urban high school where they are prepping students for state standardized tests. Similarly, a student who is asked to gather observational data about the middle school students she is tutoring will be able to "read" those students more richly when asked to make sense of the data against the background of several developmental theories.

Subsequent study and practice will focus on the "response" moment in the "interpret-respond" frame, developing students' capacity for imagining possible pedagogical responses and determining which action is the "vibrating" or "fitting" response in a given set of circumstances within the community of agents that has education as its intention. Just as interpretation takes shape in light of concepts, theory, research, and experience, so too does response.

But for now, I am teaching my students to see more richly, more clearly, and more faithfully so that the problem they name is likely to generate a response that is pedagogically and morally defensible. Because this sight is new to my students, the greeting above makes little sense to them when they first read it. My hope is that it will make sense at the end of the semester, at the end of our time together, when the evidence of class meetings and various readings and school experience and independent inquiries come together in a comprehensive reflective exercise known to the students as the "bloc book."

Because each essential question functions as a center of gravity drawing and organizing material and activity from throughout the semester, I will use just one here—#3 school funding and its link to equal opportunity—as an example.

Who Pays? Who Benefits? Is It Fair?

Future teachers should be able to "read" the differences between school districts as, in part, a function of economic difference. To do so, they need to know that schools are funded differently in different states, that in the state of Pennsylvania, for example, funding is increasingly local, and that wealthy localities have the economic power to offer schooling of a different kind than their poorer neighbors. They also need to know that federal mandates for special education or ESL instruction are underfunded, thus further disadvantaging those poor districts that also enroll a large number of students with special needs. All this requires some understanding of SES, or socioeconomic status, and its link to geographic location. SES sparks consideration of the sociopolitical concept of meritocracy, the equal protection clause of the Fourteenth Amendment, and the question of equal educational opportunity. The addition of high-stakes tests with both state and federal consequences to the educational landscape further complicates things.

To get all this, students need to wrestle with the economics of school finance: property values, tax rates, and the factors that improve or harm a district's financial position. But they also need to tangle with state and federal politics, special interest group concerns, the mistrust of the educational establishment that has fueled the high-stakes testing movement, the reality of social status, and the question of what schools are for in a capitalist economy and a democratic polity. Only then can they ask themselves why we maintain a system in which some children are well educated and others are not. Only then can they judge what professional and/or political action is the best, the most ethical, response. Will I teach in a poor urban or rural district because I am needed, despite the pressures of diminishing resources and increasing social disruption? Or will I recognize the differences and choose the district that will support my professional efforts with resources and respect? Future teachers who hope to make an informed and thoughtful judgment about this very first question—where will I teach?—will think through more than one discipline, more than one value perspective.

How do I prompt this interdisciplinary and multifocal wrestling? In the case of school funding and equity, there are at least ten elements:

1. Students read Chapter 4 of Jonathan Kozol's *Savage Inequalities* (1992). Chapter 4 compares Camden and Cherry Hill, New Jersey—places many of my students have been and seen. Kozol's graphic description of the differences between the two districts and their environs rings true and hits home.

2. Students explore a school finance tutorial located on the state Department of Education website that describes the mechanics of school funding and provides an array of economic statistics that enable students to see how the system works.

3. Students gather specified information (demographics, SES, property values, tax rate, test scores, and so on) on a school district of their choice using various web-based sources. They bring the information to class, and we construct a comparative portrait of 25 to 30 school districts.

4. Students read news articles about No Child Left Behind and the state assessment tests. Then they go into schools and participate in "teaching to the test."

5. Students take pictures during their field experience. The photographs capture the physical, social, cultural, and economic realities of the schools where they assist. Students mount and label their photos and bring them to class to compare to those of students who observed in other buildings. I also ask them to compare them to the school districts they attended.

6. Students use concept-mapping software to construct a flowchart of the U.S. system of schooling. On these charts, they are asked to plot the flow of money as well as the flow of influence.

7. Students attend a school board meeting. They are encouraged to attend to the elements of school finance and the board's role in insuring adequate funding.
8. Students participate in a brief exercise that illustrates the school practice of tracking, especially in high schools. Their participation reveals the ways in which economic and cultural biases alter decisions made about students' educational and economic futures.
9. Students send messages to the class e-mail list reflecting on equal educational opportunity as it is in evidence in the school and classroom where they are spending their time.
10. I provide in-class and individual explanations as needed and referee the processing of all this data.

Some of this work occurs in class, and some of it involves independent or group effort outside of class. It is possible to view my explanations (though perhaps not my refereeing) as the least important element in the quality of the students' learning. By the time students have carried out the tasks outlined above, my explanations become supplementary, if not superfluous. I note this partly because the opposite is often true—that student work is supplementary to the instructor's explanations—but also because this approach is central to the acquisition of practical reasoning. Students learn to reason well about matters of practice by reasoning about matters of practice in circumstances where the reasoning is framed and guided by a knowledgeable mentor. There is no substitute.

The Bigger Picture

Each essential question is explored over time through a similar set of activities. As noted earlier, the tasks the students undertake are designed to inform more than one question. For example, each of the tasks that illuminate the question of school finance also contributes to an understanding of the structure and politics of the system. The Kozol (1992) reading, the school finance tutorial, the school district information sheet, the news articles, the field experience visual record, the flowchart, the school board meeting, and the tracking exercise are all part of a bigger picture.

From this layered pattern of guided activity over time, understanding emerges and is checked against the emerging understanding of peers and my constructive guidance. This understanding enables the future teachers to recognize values conflicts, political disputes, institutional structures, and power relations and to locate themselves in that landscape. This is moral work as well as academic work.

From the outset, I encourage students to bring themselves to the task of learning to interpret and respond to educational challenges. The most obvious example of this is the required conference with me during office hours, completed before the 6th week of the semester. These meetings are informal and generally unstructured; I follow where students lead me as we both reveal something of our backgrounds and goals. I pay attention to them; I invite them to pay attention to me. The only structured moment occurs when I ask students to rate themselves on a list of seven dispositions that can contribute to the development of the responsible teacher. In this way, future teachers are asked to recognize that who they believe themselves to be shapes the kind of teacher they can become.

At the end of the semester, three complementary activities serve to consolidate, integrate, and extend the insights students have already achieved:

1. A "roll-the-dice" final exam in which one of the six essential questions becomes the sole essay question
2. A portfolio, or "bloc book," in which all work from both bloc courses and field experience are organized around seven broad program outcomes, and through which students are challenged yet again to make sense out of the interpretive foundations of teaching and learning in its relation to the broad field of responsible school teaching
3. A self-assessment essay in which each student describes and analyses what he or she knows and can do now but could not do when the course began, realizing that they have been spending time developing powers of recognition and interpretation.

Each of these assignments prompts students to organize what they know in ways that will allow that knowledge to figure as a resource in future instances of the practical reasoning that I have termed pedagogical responsibility. That is, insights lead to an expanded field of vision, richer moral perception, more accurate characterization and interpretation, and, ultimately, more fitting response.

The end of the course brings us back to the beginning, more knowledgeable and more able to make sense of what we have done. The first class session described at the opening of this essay sets an agenda that students can barely glimpse. The essential questions the syllabus limns typically provoke interest but little understanding. It is only *after* the experience of the course run that students, through the process of summative essay, portfolio development, and self-assessment, come to understand the essential questions, the thematic outline, and the purpose of the course.

This way of teaching has a rich payoff but one significant peril as well. The payoff will be discussed in detail below. The peril is linked to the level of substantive ambiguity and psychological uncertainty built into the structure of the course because it is built into the nature of teaching as ethical work. Overlapping questions without easy answers, assignments that aren't obviously related, and themes that seem intertwined challenge students' preconceptions that a course should make sense at each step along the way. When the loose ends get the better of them, students can become frustrated. The psychological uncertainty generates a different kind of frustration. Students who are accustomed to having others (teachers) tell them when they are good enough often don't want to take on the task of evaluating themselves—no matter how much time is put into unpacking the practice in order to clarify the criteria for evaluation or how much guidance is provided in the process. They want grades assigned at regular intervals so they know how they are doing.

Too much frustration, whatever its source, can block student learning. The peril I face is losing students to this learning-inhibiting frustration. It is my task to recognize this frustration as it arises, and to respond with regular interaction, individual support, and thoughtful relationships with all students. Establishing this is admittedly a challenge, but it is also a source of significant satisfaction. Still, the payoff is not personal gratification, but the real change in students' ability to recognize relevant factors and to make moral sense of what they see. What is this change? What do my students know after navigating this course of study with its layered construction and multiple narratives?

In a sense, the structure of the course *is* the lesson, the point of the journey. My students recognize that they are entering a professional domain—the school system—that is itself layered. It is what Barbara Benham Tye (2000) calls a "loose-ly coupled system" where competing narratives (e.g., No Child Left Behind and Nel Noddings's *Caring* [1984]) coexist. They recognize that they are agents with choices but not control, responding to, for example, both diversity and homog-enization, praise of equality and lack of equity, liberating ideas and standardized tests. They recognize that education is intellectual work and that intellectual work carries value at every turn. They recognize that interpretation grounds response and that only interpretation based on defensible evidence will lead to a fitting, morally defensible, pedagogical response. They learn all this because they experi-ence the layeredness, the choice without control, the value conflicts, and the search for evidence. They are invited to pay attention and to name these experiences, thus making professional and personal sense of them. They exercise practical reason-ing—the interplay of interpretation and response in the context of a professional, ethical community—to interpret the evidence they gather and to determine po-tential and actual responses to pedagogical challenges.

Do they all get it? No. But they do all get that there is more to it than they thought. Even those who never quite make sense of the overload of data, ideas, and challenges I offer recognize that there is something to be interpreted, something that requires response, as they proceed on their path toward the profession of teaching.

REFLECTIONS ON PRACTICAL REASONING AND TEACHING RESPONSIBILITY

While my teaching is intended broadly to open my students to their own powers of practical reasoning, the primary focus of Foundations of Modern Education is just one facet of this process: to recognize rightly that which requires response. To recognize is not merely perceptual and never simply delimited. It is affective and conceptual as well, rooted in the desire to attend to and understand the other and in the acknowledgment that one can only see what one knows to look for.

This attention to attention is, I contend, an underappreciated aspect of practical reasoning, of pedagogical responsibility. The press to action without thorough attention to recognition and interpretation can easily result in a response that is less than fitting, that fails to account for the moral dimensions of teaching. As I noted earlier, the practical reasoning of expert teachers appears to the uninitiated to skip the interpretive step, focusing instead on the elements of response. In educating future teachers, it is important to make every aspect of professional practical reasoning transparent.

Because I view knowledge *use* as a vehicle for knowledge *production* (or learning), I employ a "pedagogy of practical reasoning" to achieve this transparency. Nine elements, evident in the syllabus referred to above, mark this approach: recognition, time, evidence, relation, habit, perspective, power, courage, and context.

- *Recognition* is the process of percept and concept coming together. The future teacher who doesn't understand the concept of "vested interest" won't recognize it in the school board's insistence that test scores must improve at the expense of any other consideration, and thus will not be able to respond constructively. There is, of course, a kind of serendipity involved in the conjunction of percept and concept. This is why teaching that juxtaposes consideration of concepts with participation in practice is useful.
- The development of professional judgment, of pedagogical responsibility, is a process of formation that occurs over *time*. I offer students related tasks, issues, and challenges that accumulate data over time, and in time those data take shape as judgments about interpretations and judgments about responses. A desire for efficiency can defeat the development of this kind of practical reasoning. My course is designed to give students the time they need to look and see, to test ideas, to make mistakes, to misunderstand, to keep searching for the interpretation that makes sense and that will point to a response that fits.
- To make a judgment implies that one has considered *evidence*. Judgments rely on evidence of all kinds: research data, observations from experience, accepted concepts and theories, the opinions of acknowledged authorities, even gut feelings. But having evidence at hand isn't enough; one has to be willing and able to think through the evidence. I choose the phrase "think through" carefully and intend it literally. The evidence enables the thinking. It is the medium in which it occurs. Thinking it through, reaching a defensible judgment in action, depends on thinking through it.
- Pedagogical responsibility is a *relational* process. The interpret/respond structure implies interaction with at least one other and within a community of others who frame the sense of any action. My students

respond to me and to the agenda I set within the university program and the domain of school teaching. That agenda demands their further response to each other and to the teachers and students with whom they work in their field experience. The nature of these relations will have a direct impact on their development of practical reasoning.

- The practice of pedagogical responsibility is a *habit*. It is acquired quite deliberately at first and becomes apparently instinctive once acquired. Students follow my guidance by completing the tasks I set, answering the questions I pose, and following the steps I suggest. In time, those questions and steps are internalized; students may even, ironically, forget the process exists as they become more competent practical reasoners. There is more than one irony here. Practical reasoning is where one turns when professional routine breaks down, when a challenging situation renders habit (what Dewey called "habituation") powerless. If practical reasoning is itself a habit, can it too break down? Can there be a professional challenge that defies practical reasoning? The answer is yes, if we allow practical reasoning to be distilled into a protocol rather than a practice. This kind of habituation must be avoided. A view that understands practical reasoning as a rhythm of interpretation and response in context provides both guidance and flexibility.

- *Perspective* emerges as an important element in two distinctive ways. First, one's standpoint affects what can be seen and recognized. It is difficult to grasp the dilemma faced by the 11th-grade English teacher described earlier when one's own education has occurred in well-funded schools where educated parents provide whatever is needed for effective education. To see it requires the ability to shift positions imaginatively, perhaps by reading Kozol's descriptive text *Savage Inequalities* (1992). Even then, the impact is muted. Second, one's standpoint is a function of one's story, a life narrative that shapes self and value. Because judgments always reflect one's values, differences in standpoint or perspective may well mean differences in reasoning and judgment.

- No one can reason for another. To encourage practical reasoning is to encourage freedom. To encourage freedom of thought and action is to encourage democracy as a "mode of associated living." The voice of each is heard precisely because each has a voice, formed and strengthened as practical reason develops. Thus pedagogical responsibility alters *power* relations. Domination or power over becomes difficult to maintain; power with/to takes precedence. Conversely, authoritarian educational experience makes it less likely that practical reasoning can develop.

- Pedagogical responsibility is indeterminate. The teacher who seeks the fitting response will never know for sure when they have hit it. There is always ambiguity, always doubt, always risk. Learning this brand of practical reasoning is itself a risk-laden process since there is no substitute

for finding one's own way (though admittedly, a good guide can make the
risks minimal). As a result, practical reasoning requires *courage*.

- It may be unnecessary to highlight *context* as a topic of pedagogical
responsibility. Perhaps it is clear from the inclusion of relation and
perspective and evidence and recognition that context matters.
Nonetheless, I state it here to counter a tendency in our "folk theory"
about teaching that a good teacher is a good teacher wherever he goes.
Many assume that the teacher who can respond well in an 8th-grade
algebra class in a suburban school supported by a professional learning
community can also respond well in a 12th-grade calculus class in a small
town where he is on his own and unsupported. The expectation is that his
judgments will be just as acute and astute. While I don't doubt that there
are some for whom this would be true, I also know from long experience
that many teachers effective in one context are not able to make the
transition to another. And I also know that some who are ineffective in
one place can be magically rendered effective with a transfer to a different
setting. Pedagogical responsibility may not be context-bound, but it is
avowedly context-sensitive.

A brief glance at the nine topics I have enumerated here—recognition, time, evidence, relation, habit, perspective, power, courage, and context—suggests a star-
tling link not only between the development of professional judgment and the
development of ethical character but also between professional teacher education
and the ideal of a liberal arts education. These nine elements of practical reasoning
might just as well function as the topics for a program in both moral education
and liberal arts!

I have long insisted that the quality of any teacher's encounter with the liberal
arts—through both general education and the academic major—played a critical
role in his or her professional and character development, but I am not sure I ever
understood so clearly *why* I know this to be true. In the process of pedagogical responsibility, and in the interpretive moment in particular, a teacher's ability to make
sense of recognition, time, evidence, relation, habit, power, perspective, courage, and
context will determine the power of action in response. The liberal arts educate this
as assuredly as my professional course does. The teacher educator would do well to
attend to the quality of general education that candidates experience.

PRACTICAL REASONING FOR TEACHERS =
PEDAGOGICAL RESPONSIBILITY

Practical reasoning is a concept with a long history, with its recognized roots
in the ethical work of Aristotle. Aristotle's powerful formulation of practical

reasoning was reincarnated in Dewey's pragmatic idiom. Here I extend Dewey's view through H. Richard Niebuhr's focus on response as the central metaphor for thinking into action. Throughout this essay, I have used "practical reasoning" and "pedagogical responsibility" interchangeably to express my understanding that the practical reasoning of teachers is a pattern of interpretation and response. Pedagogical responsibility implies the ability to respond well, to be responsive, to take responsibility in a particular pedagogical circumstance. This can occur only when the circumstance has been fully recognized, fully interrogated, fully interpreted.

Foundations of Modern Education is not the only vehicle for developing teachers' pedagogical responsibility. Any course, any practicum, any residency can enable teachers to attend and respond to this ineluctably moral practice *if designed to do so*. The experience I describe here is designed to introduce future teachers to interpretation and response. It opens them up to things they have never seen and ideas they have never considered. It forces them to make sense of odd juxtapositions and unexpected events. It requires a response that taps mind and heart, fact and value to shape character as well as practice. In a semester-long encounter that is often as unsettling as Wonderland was to Alice, they are invited to take on their own powers of practical reason, professional judgment, and moral responsibility.

NOTE

1. This essay portrays and analyzes a course taught when I was a professor of Educational Foundations at Millersville University in Pennsylvania. References to the artifacts of the course and this teaching make sense with reference to that location. I have recently changed institutions and no longer teach a course of this kind to undergraduate students.

REFERENCES

Benham Tye, B. (2000). *Hard truths: Uncovering the deep structure of schooling.* New York: Teachers College Press.

Carroll, L. (1993). *Alice's adventures in wonderland.* Mineola, NY: Dover. (Original work published 1865)

Dewey, J. (1922). *Human nature and conduct.* New York: Henry Holt.

Kozol, J. (1992). *Savage inequalities.* New York: Harper.

Mann, H. (1957). Twelfth report to the Massachusetts Board of Education. In L. Cremin (Ed.), *The republic and the school: Horace Mann on the education of free men* (pp. 79–112). New York: Teachers College Press. (Original work published 1848)

Niebuhr, H. R. (1963). *The responsible self.* New York: Harper & Row.

Noddings. N. (1984). *Caring: A feminine approach to ethics and moral education.* Berkeley: University of California Press.

CHAPTER 5

Building an Ethical Self

Awareness of Many Modes of Ethical Thinking and Acting

Donald Blumenfeld-Jones, with Don Senneville and Mary Crawford

James B. Macdonald (1995), one of our most important curriculum theorists, asserted that there are only two questions worth asking in education: What is the meaning of human existence? and, How shall we live together? He further asserted that not only were these the only two questions worth asking, we answer them every day in the ways we organize education. The content and activities we choose indicate to learners what kinds of materials and experiences are meaningful and what we leave out indicates what is not important (on the selective tradition, see Raymond Williams, 2011). Macdonald's second question is the ethics question, dealing with what we deem to be appropriate interactions and behaviors in ways of living together. This question is also answered every day in schools in the ways we organize, monitor, and control student-to-student and student-to-teacher and student-to-administrator interactions. In this organization we have in mind a particular kind of person, an ethical person, whom we are attempting to shape into existence. We can see this occurring in our classroom management/classroom discipline schemes, the monitoring and controlling of passing times (on the way to lunch and recess, between classes), how one enters the school itself in the morning and leaves in the afternoon. In short, everywhere in schools we address how to live with each other, and our surroundings are a location where ethics lives. This dimension of the curriculum we call the "hidden curriculum" (Jackson, 1990).

As teacher educators, we must be aware that what our learners know about living ethically occurs not only within this hidden curriculum but also within the culture that permeates education through what our learners bring into schools from their lives outside of schools. Messages on what is moral and proper, found everywhere in the media, are absorbed every day (even if we, as a society, often decry those messages) as we are presented with multiple ethical positions. I write "positions" to assert that our present world is comprised of multiple ethical ideas grounded in multiple ethics systems that conflict with each other and yet appear side by side in the very way we think about any issue. This confusion of positions that are really confusions of various ethics systems challenge us as we attempt to act ethically.

Turning to public discourse about education can give us a view of these confusions. Several years ago two graduate students and I (Blumenfeld-Jones, Harrison, & Turner, 2008) performed a study in which we analyzed articles on No Child Left Behind (NCLB) found in three major national weekly news outlets (*Time, U.S. News and World Report,* and *Newsweek*). Our task was to reveal what we termed the "underlying ethical architecture" supporting the discourse about this legislation. We argued that any author under review was likely unaware of such architecture but that through the deployment of certain kinds of rhetoric, the author was appealing to particular ethical positions aligned with particular ethics systems that could secure agreement by the readership to the points being made. The articles were offered either as pure reportage of a situation or as reportage melded with some op-ed qualities. In our analysis we pointed to the confusions that marked the discourse within the articles and saw these as markers of a more pervasive confusion within our society.

As a public, we argued, our ethics are well-grounded in what is termed *consequentialism* (or *utilitarianism*—briefly discussed below). As consequentialists we attempt to maximize an agreed-upon moral good, having the most people as possible possess that moral good; in this case the most children succeeding in school. However, we also often call ourselves a "pragmatic" people. *Pragmatism* involves engaging in group deliberation using imaginative renderings of possible ethical scenarios until the group arrives at a consensus about what should be our ethical response to a situation, not necessarily maximizing the good (LaFolette, 2010). Pragmatism is at odds with consequentialism, and yet we found claims of pragmatism alongside consequentialist ideas and language. We argued that people tend to use *pragmatism* as a stand-in for being practical and that consequentialist views are seen as eminently practical. Here there is a confusion of who we want to be.

Beyond this kind of confusion, we also discovered that while consequentialism is the most obvious ethical system in play, it does not entirely dominate our discourse. There is a strong presence of what is termed *deontological theory* in play, an ethics dedicated to finding the universally right thing to do, no matter the consequences. NCLB is strongly deontological, as it focuses on nonnegotiable positions such as high standards and highly qualified teachers, which are fundamental to fairness and just the right thing to have. Proponents argued that to reject these as always true was to engage in a "soft racism of low expectations." Racism was positioned as fundamentally wrong, not because of its consequences but simply because it is wrong. This mélange of consequentialism and deontology (along with a smattering of virtues ethics language, appealing to the good character of teachers, for instance, to stay the educational course even though teaching is a difficult profession) reveals the confusion in which we live.

This condition of living within a confused stew of ethical ideas suggests, educationally, that our first task as teacher educators is to reveal the existence of this congeries of ethical positions for our preservice teacher students and for our teachers who study with us in master's programs. In revealing the presence of a variety of ethical standpoints within our everyday thinking, we can also help them tease apart the positions and their associated ethics systems. In so doing they can come to understand how each system works in the world, the implications of such workings, and how we might reach for a world that is more clear about its ethics rather than the happenstance situations in which we presently find ourselves.

This constitutes the grounding context from within which my teaching of ethics occurs. In the rest of this chapter I describe how I teach many modes of ethical thinking and action and describe the experiences of my students.

TEACHING MANY MODES OF THINKING AND ACTING ETHICALLY

One of my major ethics-teaching purposes is to liberate our teachers from this world of what I term *shadow ethics* (hidden and yet directing our actions). I have taught this approach to ethics education for many years: in a summer institute for practicing classroom teachers and in a social studies methods class for preservice teachers. The initial goal in both programs is to help each participant confront him- or herself as thinking/acting in ethically conflicting ways (an inevitable situation in our current culture) and, in the case of the classroom teachers, to provide ways of thinking about how to allow their students to experience themselves as conflicted ethical thinkers/actors. I provide didactic avenues for understanding the following selection of systems of ethics:

- Deontology from Immanuel Kant
- Divine command theory
  - A variant of deontology
  - The source of choosing rules is not reason but the Divine commanding us to act in particular ways[1]
- Virtue ethics
- Utilitarianism/consequentialism—three variations:
  - Act consequentialism (the act is evaluated for consequences)
  - Rules consequentialism (rules that will predictably yield valued consequences)
  - Ethical egoism (maximizing one's own version of good)
- Pragmatist ethics

- Communitarian ethics
- Care ethics
- Buberian/Levinasian ethics, which I term *humility ethics* (discussed later in this chapter)

I see our ethical duty as teacher educators to be providing as much information as possible about the ethics systems. We must present them not just as theory but as real ways of thinking and acting in the world. We must also present the conflicts between them. I ask my students to craft their own ethical selves rather than telling them what ethical selves they should be. I, and my colleagues, ask ourselves:

- How can we expect anyone to act ethically if the person is unaware of options for acting ethically in a more clear way?
- How can we expect to build an ethical world if our citizenry has no idea about how to think ethically for him- or herself?

In what follows I describe the ethics education I and my colleagues offer to practicing classroom teachers and I offer to undergraduate teacher preparation students. I finish with a section devoted to humility ethics.

Summer Institute for Teachers: Building an Ethical Self

In the Summer Institute for Teachers I work with Don Senneville, director of Foothills Academy in Scottsdale, Arizona, and Mary Crawford, assistant principal at the same school. We take the participating teachers through a set of activities designed to sensitize them to their own status as ethical thinkers/actors for the purpose of their choosing and developing a self-aware ethical self that is grounded in knowledge about the ethics options. We work toward their understanding how they may teach to these options in their own classrooms. We do activities that teach not only about a variety of ethics systems but how these systems can address real classroom situations. We emphasize the idea that for learners to become ethical thinkers they need to experience thinking in ways particular to each ethics system. We guide the teachers toward understanding how each ethical system structures ethical thinking and action and can translate into structuring classroom interactions and classroom discipline systems, which in turn construct classroom communities that honor each system.

We use three means for teaching the ethics systems:

1. A choice-making activity in which participants begin to see how they align themselves around specific ethical ideas (without yet connecting those ideas to ethics systems)
2. The didactic method of lecture/conversation about the various systems

3. Small-group discussion using the various systems to adjudicate ethical
    dilemmas in real-world classrooms (asking how a consequentialist or
    deontologist or care ethicist might act in a particular situation)

It is important to note that the participants often attend the Institute with the
idea that we will give them specific disciplinary strategies for getting their learners
to "act ethically." Instead we present the classroom as a place of ethical confusion
with many systems in play in one space. The students are now seen as living under
particular ethics systems. The classroom behaviors the teachers desire are grounded in perhaps different ethical systems. All people act out of specific, although
unnoticed, ethical desires. We want them to exit the institute with the resources to
understand the full array of options available to them and their students.

We start our Institute with Mary Crawford presenting a number of diametri-
cally opposed ideas. We divide the large group into evenly sized groups randomly
through taking colored sticks from a hat. Each group is randomly assigned one of
the dyads below. Then a particular group physically stands on a line in the room,
one end of which is one end of a dyad and the other end is the other end of the
dyad. We use the following dyads as prompts for this activity:

- Ethics as natural vs. ethics as learned
- Ethics as absolute vs. ethics as relative to situations and culture
- Ethics intuited/emotions vs. ethics as rational
- Ethics as absolute vs. ethics as evolving
- Individual choice vs. group determined
- Ethics for happiness vs. ethics for protection
- Ethics area specific vs. ethics general
- Ethics as useful vs. ethics for its own sake
- Learning ethics a responsibility at school vs. learning ethics the
   responsibility of family

After a group has placed itself along the line, we ask each participant to "explain" her or his choice. This is inevitably illuminating for them as often they report to us that they hadn't known there was an "option" to their point of view or
that this was even a point of view they held. They also see that they might want to
reconsider a hard and fast idea about what constitutes "being ethical." They struggle with seeing themselves no longer as "correct" but rather as just one legitimate
option among others. They report that this helps them as they may be able to see
their students as holding legitimate but opposing points of view. Their tolerance
for ambiguity is increased. This is important as we want them to understand that
ethical life is often murky.

In our didactic teaching we offer the basic tenets of a limited number of systems
including how one needs to think from within a system in order to live that sort of

ethical life. Don Senneville, who teaches this portion, limits the systems to consequentialism in general, deontology, communitarianism, care, virtue, and humility ethics. Then, in small groups, the teachers confront real classroom situations and examine how each system might be used to resolve the situation in an ethical manner:

- How might a deontologist deal with this issue?
- How might a consequentialist deal with this issue?
- How might a care ethicist deal with this issue?

The teachers are able to experience how the selfsame situation looks quite different depending on the ethical stance one takes, and they see that no one stance is more correct than another. Each is ethically defensible. Don emphasizes that, in order for their learners to become ethical beings themselves, they should be engaged in "solving" the ethical dilemma before them. Rather than the teacher employing a system to achieve peace in the classroom or an ethical classroom, he or she teaches all the members of that society how to reason and act ethically on her or his own. The students are helped to become ethical thinkers rather than receivers of others' ethics. We also spend time on teaching ethics through subject matter, exploring how the ethical dilemmas of scientists or historians or writers or business people might become part of the subject matter curriculum.

The overall response from the teachers is very interesting. They report feeling opened up by the process. The intellectual character of the Institute along with the various activities in which they were engaged—some of which they intend to use in their classrooms—leaves them feeling rejuvenated as teachers. One particular outcome has been very fulfilling. A teacher attending the Institute was inspired by the activity of making a Talking Stick (based on the Ojai Institute's promotion of a deliberative practice called Council; see Zimmerman & Coyle, 1991) for talking with each other in a way that allows each person to be heard more fully than is usual. She took this idea back to her 6th-grade classroom the next school year. They began the year with making a Talking Stick to build their community. Soon the stick became an important part of their classroom life. Groups of students would approach the teacher with a dilemma that was occurring between them. They would ask to take the stick and go in the hallway to work out the problem on their own. This activity was witnessed by other teachers in the school and fairly soon other teachers approached our participant to ask about this practice. It was producing such civil results and lasting solutions to problems, they wanted to know what she was doing in her classroom that was so different from their classrooms. This is but one example of how this Institute produces results that are about individuals learning how to deliberate together around ethical life and achieve something of sustainability.

Undergraduate Preservice Teachers

For my undergraduate students, who do not have very much classroom experience, I take a somewhat different approach. I begin with a lecture/conversation format for communicating the details of various ethics options available to them. For them, I offer the full array of ethical systems listed earlier. I also present examples for each system from inside classrooms that concretize the system. As they don't have much teaching experience, rather than an activity exploring actual classroom ethical dilemmas, I ask them to create a Personal Ethics Statement. In their writing they must elaborate the ethical system's tenets, describing how they will organize a classroom to reflect that ethical stance and how they will educate their students to think and act ethically on their own. I ask each person to choose one system. Sometimes I will allow two but never more than two. When I allow this, the person must show how the two systems might augment each other rather than cancelling each other. The requirement to write on how they will educate for the learners to become ethical beings is very important. I emphasize, as I do with the experienced teachers, that for me the ideal is allowing the learners to experience all of the systems in order to make an informed choice themselves as to how each of them would like to live. I put forward the idea that if we value freedom in our society, freedom is a matter, in part, of each person having access to a wealth of ideas from which he or she may craft a life. Anything less is, in my estimation, miseducational.

Asking the students to stay with only one system (and at most two) is difficult for them. They have a tendency toward eclecticism, liking parts of many of the systems. They would simply like to mix them together. I inform them that in so doing it is likely that one system will cancel the others out. I report on my research in ethical architecture supporting public discourse (Blumenfeld-Jones et al., 2008). I describe how this "canceling" works and ask them to choose the one system that most fits. I find that even when a person chooses two, as I request a rewrite of the statement (and a rewrite is always needed), I have to point to how the systems involved are incompatible and ask the student, now, to choose just one, the one that feels best. I point to the idea that the simplicity of one is misleading in that it's not simply simple-minded but the system gains in power of resolving social/ethical conflicts. They see how their choices both limit and enable. They struggle with this but report, in the end, that it allows them to focus more firmly on being ethical in their own lives.

HUMILITY ETHICS

In this section I present one of the systems which I teach to my undergraduates and which Don, Mary, and I teach to practicing teachers. I have three reasons for doing so. First, Don, Mary, and I agree that this system is particularly meaningful for teachers, as it touches upon something that goes beyond cognitive understanding to a stance about what it is like to "be ethical." Second, it is always taken up by the learners as a profound moment for them to experience themselves in a new way. Third, as I will argue, unlike the other systems, this approach does not collide with them as it constitutes what Emmanuel Levinas (1969) called "first philosophy." He meant by this that it is the origin of ethics rather than being a particular system of ethics. It is the undergirding of being ethical in the first place.

To begin, unlike the above systems, which are grounded in the development of rationality and cognitive understanding, humility ethics is grounded in the work of Martin Buber and Emmanuel Levinas. Their ethics are based in accounts of how we live together and what it means to exist together (ontological concerns), rather than a cognitive, epistemological approach (knowing about various systems and how to act from within them—as these systems are grounded in rationality, it makes sense to teach them in this way). The appellation "humility," as will be discussed in more detail below, derives from the humility we have when we recognize that we do not know another person.

In the ethics systems described above, we begin in what we do know and what we can determine. To review, pragmatism relies on conceptualizing a set of alternative scenarios, including their possible outcomes; determining in a group what scenario to undertake, undertaking it, and deliberating over the desirability of what has unfolded. Deontology requires the use of reason to determine what to universalize. What you determine doesn't have to feel good (a tenet of moral intuitionism; see LaFolette, 2010) because feelings are not a guide to ethical life and, in fact, get in the way of ethical life. Consequentialism requires performing what is termed a *social calculus* to estimate what ethical good should be maximized and how one will maximize it. All of this is rationally based. As will be shown, below, humility ethics begins in what we do not know and cannot determine, thus having a humble attitude about our capacity to be ethical. This distinguishes it from the above systems as they rely upon considering what constitutes the good and then acting on what is concluded.

Departing from the Rational

Rationality as a basis for determining what is ethically proper has been called into question by Mark Johnson, among others. In *Moral Imagination* (1993), Johnson argues that ethical reasoning is only useful in situations in which the ethical dilemma is clear-cut and the ethical decision is already quite clear. Johnson asserts that most ethical dilemmas are murky rather than clear; no outcome is particularly "good" in the ethical sense of that word. In this situation rationality is of no use. Johnson argues that there is good evidence from cognitive science that people employ their imagination to determine what to do. While pragmatism certainly parallels this, in moral imagination a person does not rationally compare one scenario to another, but imagines/feels the scenarios and, based on feelings that some might consider inarticulate, makes a decision about how to act. Johnson further suggests that in order to cultivate a moral imagination we might consider educating for artists' dispositions, as artists do their work as a way of cultivating imagination in general, and moral imagination is a specific variant of imagination in general. My task as an educator, then, is to provide my learners with aesthetic experiences that parallel the artist's dispositions referenced by Johnson. I will discuss my approach to this after detailing what constitutes humility ethics. Such a description is necessary for the reader to understand why I do what I do with my learners.

Humility ethics is an ethics steeped in this sort of noncognitive "feeling in the world." Humility ethics is not about the formulation of rules to live by as are the cognitive approaches, but rather how to be in relation to another. It has similarities to care ethics, but unlike care ethics humility ethics is not about rational determination of what is needed in a particular care situation. Care ethics depends upon determining another's condition and what you might do, in all care, to attend fully to that other person. Humility ethics, on the other hand, begins before you know what the other needs. Humility ethics is a kind of "natural" initial connection with another that precedes active caring for another. It is what Levinas (1969) terms a *metaphysical desire* that functions as the source of why you care at all, rather than being the source of a specific care. This is what makes humility ethics nonrational and what makes caring more or less rational. While some might consider this a fine distinction, I am suggesting that it is, at the very least, one necessary to consider. Allow me to elaborate this nonrational basis further.

Entering the Imaginary and Felt Life

Martin Buber in his iconic *I and Thou* (1923/1958) teaches that there are two primary words we speak to live in the world: *I-It* and *I-Thou*. We cannot do without either primary word. Buber is not prescribing one word or the other to live ethically. They are both necessary. Buber sees himself as describing, not prescribing, human life. I-It positions us to see the world around us as a set of "its" (resources/things/objects/people even) at our disposal to craft our lives. There is the "I," and there is everything else. This is a natural state of affairs, not one to be bemoaned. The other primary word, *I-Thou*, reveals that we are not alone in the world, that the world is always made of two, is dialogical in character in a fundamental way. For Buber, the unit of analysis to understand society is not as a set of individuals but as people connected to each other in mutual ways of care and making the world. To the degree that we do not experience this connection as basic to our lives, to that degree cannot live ethically. To the degree that we know this (not only cognitively but emotionally, sensorially) in a deep way, to that degree, feeling our connection to another, we will always have the false divides drop away and the truth of the world (we are in connection to each other at all moments) will be the truth by which we live. An I-Thou experience is not constant. That is, for day-to-day life we dwell in the I-It status and for the most part that is how we experience life. However, there are moments when the truth of the I-Thou is revealed to us, in an intimate bodily moment which Buber describes as "feeling from the other side":

- Two men fighting suddenly feel the blow delivered as if it had been received (Buber, 2002b, p. 114)
- Two men who are naturally friends find themselves as enemies but embrace and feel the world's categories fall away and experience the true meaning of friendship (Buber, 2002a, pp. 6–7)

I-Thou is the source of ethics. These experiences are fleeting. We cannot make them occur. But we can be available to their possibility, available to this dimension of human life that is often eclipsed in the day-to-day world by I-It. Again, it is not wrong to dwell in the I-It; it is inevitable. But we live only half a life if we do so exclusively. In teaching toward this possibility, I share with my students (both my classroom teachers and my teacher preparation students) Buber's writing on this. I ask my learners to remember/consider moments in their lives when the categories they used to make sense of another (smart person, shy person, mean person, rich person, poor person, and more) fell away and they only saw "a person." In those moments, I teach them, they were experiencing how categories used to label some-one turned that someone into only a resource for the person and how, when they moved beyond such labels, a very different being appeared before them. I also ask them to remember moments in their own lives when they felt labeled and knew they were more than their labels.

As with Buber, Levinas sees all ethics occurring between two people. (Although Levinas rejected parallels between his work and that of Buber, I am unconvinced and proceed as if they are similar and supplementary to each other.) In *Totality and Infinity* (1969) Levinas provides a phenomenology of how the self comes to be. He establishes that human beings have a fundamental desire for connection with some-thing beyond the self, which he terms *metaphysical desire*. This desire for connection functions as a background driving force behind our actions and decisions. In craft-ing a self, the human being sees the world as a set of resources he or she marshals in order to become a self and to make connections. This in-gathering into the home of the self (Levinas's metaphor) is accomplished through fitting the world into lan-guage which we use to categorize experience. This move, however, is in direct con-tradiction to the desire to be connected to something outside oneself. Why is this? By making sense of incoming experience through already established categories, the self makes what was different from her or him into something that is like her or him or, as Levinas terms it, making "other same." This making "other same" defeats the desire to make connection with something other than oneself. As it turns out, this process of appropriating the world to craft a self is not entirely successful. Some of the world can be made to fit into the language system of the self and nourish it; some of the world cannot be made to do so and is never noticed. And some of the world refuses such a move and yet remains present to the self. That "thing" that refuses to be subsumed to the categories of the self is another human being. In the moment of recognition that one can never make that other being into oneself the possibility of connection is made, metaphysical desire is enlivened.

As already stated, some "things" refuse to be transformed into someone else's categories. Levinas terms this encounter an *infinity*. It is infinite because I am unable to categorize it. Subsequently another world beyond my control, an infinite world, is uncovered. With this recognition of infinity comes another recognition: The Other (he capitalizes the word to show graphically its difference from the usual other things in my world) is simultaneously fragile and needs to be cared for. In this moment responsibility for the Other is born as the Other calls out to me to make the world safe for the Other. I want to do so, in this state, because I recognize that the infinity exceeds all that I can know and I can experience my own infinity simultaneously. At last I feel my connection to something outside of myself.

How might we attain such a moment of responsibility and ethics? Levinas uses the image of "face" to concretize this moment. In the face of the Other, now not known to me, I can experience an innocence calling for my responsibility. Levinas is quite serious about this: If a person can see that he or she does not know the Other, can see past the categories he or she was using just a moment ago to understand the Other, the Other becomes the face of youth and innocence. The experience of this occurs, so Levinas asserts, in prelinguistic moments, before the Other congeals into known categories, into male/female, raced, aged, abled, and so forth.

Educating for Humility Ethics

I approach educating for humility ethics in several ways, bringing together Johnson's notion of moral imagination, Buber's ideas about I-Thou, and Levinas's notion of infinity as the face.

- I present Mark Johnson's ideas about imagination, read Buber's words on I-Thou, parsing them as I do so, present Levinas's notions, some through his words and some through my own presentation of his ideas, and present some of my own published work on the experience of labels and categories as a diminishment of self and on the spontaneous arising of responsibility for another that I have felt (Blumenfeld-Jones, 2012a).
- I ask the group, in pairs, to share stories of when each person felt diminished by categories and labels. I use the phrase "I am more than that" to get at the feeling of infinity that all of us possess, a feeling connected to our using labels ourselves about ourselves that we know cannot capture the whole of us.
- I ask each individual to think of a time when he or she suddenly felt responsibility, remember it in detail (what was the person doing, what was the other person doing, what was the context of the experience, what were the attendant bodily as well as mental experiences).

- Through guided movement experiences, we attempt to acknowledge others without speaking. I have everyone move through the room and focus on seeing the whole body of the person. The movement can be anything and I ask each person to move in whatever way he or she wishes, no restrictions. Students must both move and see others moving. In that state of dual awareness (awareness of the self, awareness of the other) each person can notice that he or she is being seen by others and is seeing others. In this, individuals can also notice that they have thoughts about who the others are as they make all kinds of movements and know simultaneously that no one can actually know what they are doing or being at that moment. I then remind the group that we can notice beings around us prior to making sense of them, that this prenoticing is the location of connection to the infinite. I want them to notice what they see/feel just before they make sense of what they see/feel (just before their seeing/feeling becomes words in their minds).

What are some of the results of this teaching? First, when I do the story sharing experience, both participants in the Institute and undergraduates see immediately that they could share the ideas with their own students (tailoring it for the age group in question) and could easily have students learn how to share such stories and live in an awareness of being available to an I-Thou moment and the possibility of seeing beyond categories. Second, in terms of the movement experiences, I teach them to trust sensation as much as cognition. Students report that they now feel others in a way they had not entertained previously. Really paying attention to the physical presence of the other changes their ability to notice the other. The students report that they are, for a moment, noticing how others are noticing them and in that moment perhaps noting the pureness of the Other for a moment. I imagine that in reading this you may feel it is a bit mystical, but I would argue it is actually quite concrete, as reported by my learners.

I want to emphasize that to do this work people do not have to be special. Anyone can feel in her or his body this awareness described above. Having the correct understanding of the implications of those sensations is the place in which the work must be done. While this returns us to cognition as an important component of ethics, the cognitive remains secondary to the experiences; without the experiences the cognitive understanding would not be useful. Words are only a prescaffolding for the real work of remembering and recognizing what words cannot capture (Blumenfeld-Jones, 2012b, in press). My students tell me they recognize this. As Zen Buddhism attempts to cultivate a "beginner's mind," so here I ask people to enter into the spirit of the presence of the Other before you know the Other to be something specific.

How can humility ethics carry over to the preservice teachers' classrooms? Students learn what it means to be present to the possibility of the I-Thou relationship so that, should it occur they are already open to it. The students, in their availability to the "face" of the other, will be better able to see each other as a "face" as Levinas suggests. Thus they are more likely to remember that they must see others with humility (that they are humbled by the infinity of the Other and always stand in a state of awe and service to that Other). These availabilities and dispositions are cultivated for the sake of creating a community that is steeped in a form of responsibility borne out of a desire for connection with Others. In such classroom communities learners can begin to understand human relationships prior to living through whatever ethical system (or systems) is (are) in place in the classroom.

To accomplish the above, there must be some direct teaching of these ideas. The experience of sharing stories, having the movement experiences, and studying these ideas sets the ground for these students to carry this approach to ethical life forward into their own classrooms. Having had these experiences in their preservice study, they are provisionally equipped with the necessary knowledge/experience to move humility ethics forward into their teaching. They can, in turn, guide their learners in the ways of humility ethics, thus cultivating in their learners the remembering of not being known themselves and the disposition of humility of "not knowing." Concretely, when a dispute arises in a classroom, the student, now teacher, can remind their learners:

> What of the face of the Other did you remember just before you had that dispute? There was someone who wasn't someone who had done something wrong but *just someone* in all the infinity that that notion indicates. Did you remember that? This won't excuse another's actions, but we will be able, by so remembering, to separate the actions (unacceptable) from the human being (always acceptable). Did you remember that?

Through such questions they and their learners are reminded of our relationships. It is in these ways that humility ethics can work.

I have written that humility ethics does not necessarily displace any other form of ethics that an educator might wish to employ. One might engage in consequentialist thinking from this humility base, becoming less "sure" of the outcomes that are desirable and thus having greater flexibility and less reliance on rules, more ability to see the specific life of the Other in front of you. Deontologists, focused as they are on human dignity, would have some affinity to humility as rationality becomes but one guide, not the exclusive guide. Kant's *The Critique of Pure Reason* (1781/1966) was an exploration of the limits of reason, not an exploration of how to use reason or a validation of reason as the only way of knowing. Care ethics, already supple in this area, could have a greater range of response and, just as we have learned that sometimes caring means listening and not suggesting, acting, or saving of another, so humility ethics can remind the caregiver of being wary of assumptions. Virtue ethics might see the cultivation of humility as an important addition to its list of virtues and might even see it as a prime virtue. In short, humility ethics is offered as both a way of living ethically, a way of understanding our motivations for acting ethically, and as a ground out of which our ethics systems can be developed.

CONCLUSION

In this chapter I have shared the approach that I and my colleagues take to teaching how to create ethical communities in classrooms. We do not direct them in a specific direction even though both groups initially expect we will tell them strategies for getting their learners to act ethically in the ways they want the learners to act. Rather we open up the interesting and complex world of ethics and show them a way to educate that, in our estimation, truly leads to an ethical world: People act out of self-understanding and confronting the possibilities of what it means to be an ethical person and make active choices to live that life in as explicit a manner as possible.

In my own work with students I remind myself that the undermining of surety on the part of teachers is an important educational goal. Educating may be a science, but we should remember that the best scientists always function from skepticism and openness to disproving their own ideas. My students (both practicing teachers and preservice undergraduates) may come in sure of what they think, but they leave realizing that ethics is not a matter of yes and no, but rather a matter of parsing always unclear situations and doing the best we can under the circumstances. As noted in the response of classroom teachers to our Institute, this rejuvenates them, knowing that they have options. It also allows them to appreciate that their learners are also ethical beings prior to being their students and that these ethical beings (their students) just as much as they (the teachers) need a breadth of understanding if they are to fulfill their potential as ethical beings. My preservice students appreciate that I offer them the opportunity to think for themselves in this domain and the activities are a revelation of their own potential as ethical educators. With that, I leave you with this thought: Trust your own ability to embrace this confusion as an exciting adventure and trust that, just as my students are not special beings but can do the movement and story work, so you can with your students foray into this way of ethics, knowing there are no "right" answers but only more questions that lead to a more ethical existence.

NOTE

1. While U.S. schools have assiduously excluded religious teaching from the schools, it should also be noted that many people have a strong religious life outside of school that, for them, provides their moral compass. I have chosen to include divine command theory

to enable my learners to live more coherent, integrated teaching/personal lives. At the same time, I note that they must not proselytize but must find how their basic tenets can be translated into classroom life.

REFERENCES

Blumenfeld-Jones, D. S. (2012a). *Curriculum and the aesthetic life: Hermeneutics, body, democracy, and ethics.* New York: Peter Lang.

Blumenfeld-Jones, D. S. (2012b). Democracy, moral imagination and the development of responsibility: New cornerstones for teacher education. In *Curriculum and the aesthetic life: hermeneutics, body, democracy, and ethics* (pp. 101–105). New York: Peter Lang.

Blumenfeld-Jones, D. S. (in press). Johnson, Levinas and sensibility: An aesthetic avenue to ethics? In T. Costantino & B. White (Eds.), *Aesthetics, empathy and education.* New York: Peter Lang.

Blumenfeld-Jones, D. S., Harrison, E., & Turner, T. (2008). *Curriculum, education discourse, civic responsibility, and humility ethics: Changing how we talk and think.* Paper presented at the annual meeting of the American Educational Research Association, New York.

Buber, M. (1958). *I and thou* (2nd ed., R. G. Smith, Trans.). New York: Scribner. (Originally published in German 1923)

Buber, M. (2002a). Dialogue. In *Between man and man* (R. G. Smith, Trans., pp. 1–45). New York: Routledge. (Originally published in German 1929)

Buber, M. (2002b). Education. In *Between man and man* (R. G. Smith, Trans., pp. 98–122). New York: Routledge. (Originally published in German 1926)

Jackson, P. (1990). *Life in classrooms* (2nd ed.). New York: Teachers College Press.

Johnson, M. (1993). *Moral imagination: Implications of cognitive science for ethics.* Chicago: University of Chicago Press.

Kant, I. (1966). The *critique of pure reason.* New York: Anchor Books. (Originally published in German 1781)

LaFolette, H. (Ed.) (2010). *The Blackwell guide to ethical theory.* Oxford, UK: Blackwell.

Levinas, E. (1969). *Totality and infinity: An essay in exteriority* (A. Lingis, Trans.). Pittsburgh, PA: Duquesne University Press.

Macdonald, J. B. (1995). *Theory as a prayerful act: The collected essays of James B. Macdonald* (B. J. Macdonald, Ed.). New York: Peter Lang.

Williams, R. (2001). Base and superstructure. In (Ed.) J. Higgins, *The Raymond Williams reader* (pp. 158–178). Oxford, UK: Blackwell.

Zimmerman, J., & Coyle, V. (1991, March/April). Council: Reviving listening. *The Utne Reader,* 79–85.

CHAPTER 6

Nurturing a Moral Stance in Teacher Education

Catherine Fallona and Julie Canniff

Currently, public conversation regarding teacher education programs focuses on graduates' impact on student achievement. This emphasis on measuring teacher effectiveness in terms of student achievement negates the impact teachers can potentially have on the development of students' moral and intellectual virtue. At the University of Southern Maine (USM) the teacher education faculty is committed to ensuring that graduates leave our program with the dispositions, skills, and knowledge to act as moral exemplars in their classrooms. We have spent several years articulating our stance on the moral and intellectual development of teacher candidates and infusing this stance into our mission, curricula, and assessments.

In this chapter we share the infusion of the moral into USM's teacher education program. We describe our context and moral base, the processes by which the faculty actualize our moral stance, and cases of graduates who exemplify the moral and intellectual virtue we strive to foster. Finally, we conclude with implications for nurturing the moral stance of future teachers.

THE MORAL BASE OF USM'S TEACHER EDUCATION PROGRAM

The teacher education program at USM consists of a yearlong, graduate-level internship and coursework. There are two primary pathways: the undergraduate-graduate Teachers for Elementary and Middle Schools (TEAMS) Program and the postbaccalaureate Extended Teacher Education Program (ETEP). All students participate in the same graduate-level internship, complete the same shared assessments, and meet the same standards for program completion.

Like most teacher education programs, we have a Conceptual Framework that articulates our mission. Our mission is captured in a single sentence that expresses the ethical obligation to which we dedicate our energies:

We seek to foster respectful and collaborative learning communities, well-informed decision-making, valid reasoning, and a concern for equity and social justice in the fields of education and human development.

Our work is driven by a moral stance that our teacher candidates leave our program committed to equity. To express this commitment, the faculty constructed an "Equity Framework for Teacher Educators and Intern Teachers."

Depending upon one's point of view, a commitment to equity may or may not be a moral commitment. In the case of our teacher education program, we ground the definitions and practices articulated in the Equity Framework in moral and intellectual virtue. Virtue ethics serves as our moral base because the best human life requires the exercise of virtue (MacIntyre, 1984). The exercise of virtue is important because, like Aristotle (trans. 1985), we believe, virtue comes about as a result of habit. The moral agent rather than a set of moral principles is the primary source of moral knowledge (Prior, 1991), and it is within the context of important relations to others that children acquire the characteristics of mature virtue (Sherman, 1997). In the context of our teacher education program, we are interested in two relationships that have the potential for fostering moral and intellectual virtue. The first is the relationship between the teacher educator and the teacher candidate, and the second is between teacher and student. Recognizing the significance of the exercise of virtue in the context of these two relationships, the question of what virtues need to be exercised in teaching and teacher education becomes important. Because equity is at the heart of our mission, our work is most particularly rooted in the virtues of justice and wisdom.

In the tradition of Aristotle (trans. 1985), justice is virtue "toward others" and is especially concerned with the public good. In other words, it is a social virtue that consists of treating equals equally and unequals unequally in proportion to their relative differences. The just teacher has an ethical commitment to be fair and foster a just community. This means that all students are sufficiently supported, as needed, in their paths to success, and teachers develop a climate inclusive of all individuals and worldviews. Teachers are morally obligated to foster mutual understanding and celebration, but in order for this to happen, teachers must understand that each person has cultural identities and intelligences that are multidimensional and dynamic. Teachers must honor the learning strengths and experiences each of their students brings to the classroom.

Teachers who honor students, make them feel safe and cared for, and provide them with a sense of belonging have the wisdom to foster empathetic relationships that are a necessary foundation for healthy learning communities. Wise teachers have extensive knowledge and the ability to integrate epistemological and technical content through reflexive practice, perspective, intuition, and judgment (Peterson & Seligman, 2004). They are able to assess students' knowledge, skills, and dispositions in order to respond to learners' needs and give formative feedback. Wise teachers apply principles of universal design and strategies for differentiated instruction to provide challenging work for all students with levels of support as needed, contextualizing lessons and units using student interests and strengths and the experiences and skills they bring from home and community.

Additionally, wise teachers' practice reflects normative aims of education. They know and understand the most important goals and values of life and how to teach students how to reach these goals (Nozick, 1989). They help students understand human actions and motives, including what is appropriate when, and how to improve oneself and one's relationships with others or society. The teacher's depth of wisdom regarding these matters supports her ability to model moral and intellectual virtue.

The wise and just teachers we work to prepare have the knowledge, skills, and dispositions described above to support all learners. They also have an explicit moral stance that embraces the teacher's ethical responsibility to be a model of moral and intellectual virtue. To develop this stance, our faculty explicitly articulate the moral language of teaching and model moral and intellectual virtue.

NURTURING A MORAL STANCE AMONG TEACHER CANDIDATES

Nurturing a shared, explicit moral stance among teacher candidates that attends to what it means to be a just and wise teacher takes time, effort, and commitment. Therefore, we have spent the last several years trying to actualize our Equity Framework to ensure that USM teacher candidates leave our programs committed to expressing the virtues of justice and wisdom in their practice. The application of USM's Equity Framework depends on admitting high-quality teacher candidates and on making virtue explicit in the teacher education curriculum and assessments.

Admissions

The faculty's work in selecting new educators who demonstrate the moral and intellectual virtues of justice and wisdom begins with an examination of their application essay, and a subsequent interview to enter the program. The application essay prompt is framed around the program's Equity Framework and asks applicants to respond to the following:

> How do you see yourself providing equitable learning opportunities for your students? Illustrate your thinking by using specific examples.

Faculty who evaluate these essays read for the applicant's reflexiveness in describing experiences with learners where the author's personal assumptions or biases were challenged and/or extended. For example, one applicant described her prior experience as a new educational technician in a setting where she was asked to work with children with autism. She told a story of encountering one young man who was mute and unresponsive to the teachers. The teacher applicant decided to begin reading stories out loud that featured individuals who had overcome great obstacles to achieve their goals. When she began, the child was sitting in her vicinity but did not appear to be listening. By the end of the first quarter, the child was actively participating in the story, verbalizing his dismay at setbacks and visibly moved when the protagonist triumphed. The teacher applicant reflected at length on her initial assumptions regarding this child's potential and her discovery that every child has something to learn and contribute to his or her community. She is an example of how our admissions process delves into candidates' dispositions toward students. Through candidates' essay responses, we make initial judgments regarding candidates' ethical commitment to be fair and foster a just community where all students are honored for the strengths and experiences they bring to the classroom, included as members of the learning community, and supported in their paths to success.

Following the paper screening of the applications, selected candidates are interviewed and asked a series of questions to draw out the applicant's capacity for describing and reflecting on equity in educational contexts. One question requires the applicant to read a scenario of an interaction between a culturally and linguistically diverse student and a teacher. The candidate's predisposition for justice is revealed in his or her assessment of the student's capacities and struggles, as well as the applicant's awareness of his or her own cultured position, of privilege, and of bias in the setting, the curriculum, or the school policies.

Another question requires the applicant to identify a big idea or concept in the field of math, science, English, or social studies, and to describe how he or she would teach this idea or concept to students. The faculty listens for a candidate's wisdom represented by his or her understanding of the complexity of the content. The faculty pays particular attention to the quality of the candidate's reasoning regarding how he or she would have students apply their knowledge.

Because of the faculty's consensus on the need to embed the virtues of justice and wisdom into every phase of our work, they have become adept at probing the beliefs and dispositions of applicants to ensure that these virtues are stable and consistent. As teacher educators, we know that we can provide candidates with theoretical knowledge related to equity issues in education and that we can teach them strategies to differentiate instruction to address the needs of all learners. However, in most cases our collective experience has taught us that we cannot take teachers who are not predisposed to be just and wise teachers and make them so, but if we admit candidates who already possess the capacity to express moral and intellectual virtue, we can foster those virtues and support candidates in learning how to express them in their practice.

Curriculum

In order for faculty to implement the equity framework in the context of the preparation experience, they needed to develop a program curriculum that requires teacher candidates to interact with that framework. Curriculum in this sense is synonymous with the structural, moral, and intellectual components of the program and is closely aligned with the virtues of justice and wisdom.

The first important curricular aspect of the program is the cohort, as the context for developing a culture of collegiality. Through group norming processes, weekly seminar meetings, and building-based collegial clusters, teacher candidates develop their professional identities within a community of practice (Wenger, 1998). The internship cohort, which is led by a university faculty cohort coordinator, is the primary source of learning and support for interns. The intent is for the cohort seminar to be a model for the kind of moral classroom we hope the teacher candidates will construct as teachers. Specifically, our goal is for the cohort to be a just learning community where all students are sufficiently supported, as needed, in their paths to success. The cohort coordinator must get to know each teacher candidate's cultural identities, intelligences, strengths, and experiences and honor them. Among the cohort, the coordinator must create a sense of belonging, foster mutual understanding, and nurture empathetic relationships as the foundation for the development of a learning community. For the cohort, the coordinator also models the wisdom of practice, demonstrating extensive knowledge of teaching and learning and the ability to integrate that knowledge into practice. The cohort coordinator assesses the teacher candidates' knowledge, skills, and dispositions in order to respond to their needs and give formative feedback and support, as well as appropriate challenges.

The second core curricular aspect of the program is the immersion of teacher candidates into the daily life of a classroom for two semesters in partnership districts, and the integration of university courses into this internship. Through this experience, teacher candidates observe the moral dimensions of teaching daily and reflect upon their observations and their practice in relation to what it means to be a teacher who is just and wise. For example, teacher candidates are asked to attend to the fair and equitable treatment of students. This includes developing an inclusive climate that is responsive to students, providing them with challenging work, and supporting them as needed to achieve success. The cohort coordinators, mentor teachers, and internship supervisors all provide interns with feedback on the degree to which they model the virtues of justice and wisdom in their relationships with students and in their classroom instruction.

The third core aspect of the program's curriculum is the coursework. Equity is a strong theme running through the courses in the program. Particular emphasis is placed upon integrating the principles and practices of culturally responsive pedagogy (CRP; see Gay, 2010) and Universal Design for Learning (UDL; see Rose & Meyer, 2002) into the courses. Of course, neither CRP nor UDL is moral by their nature. Rather, we use these frameworks and the strategies embedded within them to provide teacher candidates with concrete ways in which they may respond to the diversity of learners in their classrooms and express the virtues of justice and wisdom in their practice.

Assessment

A foundational feature of the program is a performance-based teacher candidate assessment system. Through a set of program assessments, each teacher candidate is required to provide a body of evidence for achieving mastery of the USM Teaching Standards. Evidence for these standards documents the teacher candidate's competence in knowing about the diversity of child and adolescent development and culturally responsive practice, as well as his or her pedagogical content knowledge, facility in integrating technology into practice, competence in planning, and use of multiple instructional strategies and forms of assessment. The teacher candidate must show evidence of professionalism, skills in collaboration, and commitment to professional development. The cohort coordinator, mentor teacher, and internship supervisor evaluate this evidence at three points during the yearlong internship, confirming that the teacher candidate has achieved a proficient level of these standards by the end of the internship.

At the beginning of the internship, the teacher candidate assembles a profile. This profile is multifaceted, requiring teacher candidates to collect data and closely analyze them to understand the learners in his or her classroom as well as the communities in which they live and go to school. The teacher candidate gathers data related to learners' communities, personal and familial backgrounds, learning preferences and intelligence strengths, work habits, social interactions, interests and aspirations, academic skills, and prior knowledge. The data are collected through surveys, interviews, inventories, pre-assessments and examination of student work, conversations with mentors, and observations. The resulting profile is one of the first concrete measures of a teacher candidate's moral stance toward equity. For example, the classroom profile that the teacher candidate constructs conveys whether the teacher candidate believes that each student brings valuable learning strengths and experiences to the classroom or whether the teacher candidate views students through a deficit model.

Following the profile, teacher candidates are required to design, implement, and assess a major teaching unit. A unit is operationally defined as a topic, theme, or project that is substantial enough to warrant both ongoing formative assessments and a culminating, or final, assessment of student learning. The unit must relate to topics in the grade-level curriculum, pay special attention to applicable Maine Learning Results and/or Common Core Standards, and use a backwards-planning methodology. An analysis of resulting student work and a reflection on instructional implications are expected as part of the finished product. Through the lesson plans and unit reflections, the teacher candidate's moral stance is assessed. This assessment is based upon the teacher candidate's commitment to supporting all students' learning. For example, does the teacher candidate plan and carry out a unit that contextualizes lessons using student interests and strengths and the experiences and skills they bring from home and community, and does the intern differentiate and apply the principles of Universal Design for Learning in his or her planning and instruction?

Another shared program assessment that offers insight into a teacher candidate's moral stance is his or her classroom management plan and implementation. As a part of this plan, the teacher candidate is required to construct the classroom environment, establish a classroom community, and manage behavior. The teacher candidate's moral stance is evident in whether he or she models the behaviors expected of students and whether he or she fosters an inclusive classroom environment where all students feel safe, cared for, and like they belong.

The teaching philosophy is also an important program assessment. Teacher candidates compose their first teaching philosophy, drawing on their experiences in coursework and in the classroom. Throughout their internship year, they reflect, revise, and refine their teaching philosophy to indicate their individual approach to the teaching profession. The teacher education program standard is that the teacher candidate can clearly communicate his or her beliefs about teaching, learning, and the role of education in ensuring access and equity for all students.

The core formative and summative program assessment is a standards review. At multiple points during the year, teacher candidates are assessed on their progress toward meeting the USM Teacher Certification Standards. Teacher candidates are rated on whether they are proficient in each standard, based on the program assessments just described and a wealth of evidence from observations and course assessments. For example, Table 6.1 displays USM Teaching Standard 1, which has to do with the knowledge of the diverse ways in which people learn, and the assessment evidence that allows teacher candidates to demonstrate their expertise in this area. The virtue of justice is at the heart of this standard's focus on equitable and culturally responsive practices that provide all students with opportunities to learn.

Table 6.2 displays USM Teaching Standard 2 related to content knowledge and USM Teaching Standard 7 on instructional planning and implementation. The virtue of wisdom in each of these can be seen through the emphasis on preparing teacher candidates to approach content with a deep understanding of the big ideas, the modes of inquiry, and the critical questions. Teacher candidates who are able to plan curriculum by attending to the needs of the learners and the diversity of perspectives on factual and procedural knowledge, and carefully evaluate the effectiveness of their planning on their students' learning are demonstrating the virtue of wisdom.

The teacher education faculty has devoted significant time and scholarship to bringing a strong moral and intellectual coherence to our program. As the program assessments show, the teacher education faculty has developed a program that represents a commitment to nurturing a moral stance toward equity that is rooted in a teacher's expression of the moral and intellectual virtues of justice and wisdom. The results are teacher candidates who understand their potential for influencing students' moral development. They are conscious that they must model

Table 6.1. USM Teacher Education Department Equity Framework, Teaching Standard 1, and Assessment Evidence

Equity Framework	Teaching Standard	Assessment Evidence
Justice: Responsiveness to students and providing opportunities to learn	*Standard 1. Diversity of child and adolescent development, learner needs, equitable and culturally responsive practices:* The teacher demonstrates knowledge of the diverse ways in which students develop and learn by developing expertise around learning opportunities that support students' intellectual, physical, emotional, and social development.	• Community profile • Learner profiles • Curriculum and setting barrier analysis • Lesson plan modifications based on classroom and barrier analysis profiles. • Lesson plan reflections • Cohort journals and seminar discussions • Teaching unit: Final reflections • Philosophy of teaching

moral and intellectual virtue if they intend to influence the moral development of students.

MORAL WORK OF TEACHER CANDIDATES AND GRADUATES

The program and faculty's success in nurturing a moral stance among its teacher candidates and graduates is determined by the stance the graduates take when they become teachers. Some of the teacher education faculty research at USM includes longitudinal studies of graduates from ETEP to document the endurance of their beliefs and practices in their teaching. These studies extend the teacher education faculty's relationship with students and support our graduates in continuing to reflect upon the moral nature of their work. Almost without exception, those individuals who have remained in the classroom continue to describe their teaching in the language of moral and intellectual virtues. For example, Canniff conducted three sets of focus groups with ETEP graduates who had been teaching more than 5 years. Her objective was to understand the core beliefs that led them to enter ETEP in midcareer, the degree to which those core beliefs were fostered in ETEP, and the extent to which those core beliefs have endured during their professional careers. The following case studies of Heather, Tim, and Ian provide examples of how they brought moral and

Table 6.2. USM Teacher Education Department Equity Framework, Teaching Standards 2 and 7, and Assessment Evidence

Equity Framework	Teaching Standards	Assessments Evidence
Wisdom: Pedagogical content knowledge, inquiry, and scholarship	*Standard 2. Knowledge of subject matter and inquiry:* The teacher understands the framework and standards of the subject matter she/he teaches. She/he uses the discipline's tools of inquiry, central concepts, and teacher candidates structure, and makes interdisciplinary connections to promote learner's inquiry.	• Curriculum maps, instructional teaching units and lesson plans based on essential questions, enduring understandings, content standards, and assessments for and of learning • The integration of technology tools into the design of lesson plans and units and into the students' use of these tools • The implementation of critical thinking and decision-making assignments into the units and lesson plans • The implementation of inquiry-based units and lesson plans
Justice and Wisdom: Pedagogical content knowledge, opportunity to learn, inquiry	*Standard 7. Instructional planning and implementation:* The teacher plans and evaluates instruction based on knowledge of the learner, subject matter, community, intended content standards, and curriculum.	• Lesson plan modifications based on learner profiles and curriculum or setting barrier analysis • Lesson plan reflections incorporate what was successful, what was adapted, and what needed to be changed . • Reflection on the lessons/units' responsiveness to students, effectiveness of planning, and use of instructional strategies • Final unit reflections evaluate what was learned in planning, teaching, and assessing the unit

intellectual virtues into their classrooms, their curriculum, and their interactions with colleagues.

Heather was a member of an ETEP cohort in 2003–2004. She completed her ETEP year with a provisional certificate to teach English at the secondary level and subsequently acquired a second certification to teach special education. Heather taught English from 2004 until 2010 in a moderately affluent high school that was part of a single, municipal school district near a midsized city on the Maine coast.

Tim was a member of an ETEP cohort in 2002–2003. He completed his ETEP year with a provisional certificate to teach English at the secondary level. Tim taught in a consolidated high school in a low-income rural district that is part of three counties, with six different towns in each county, "in the middle of nowhere."

Ian was a member of another ETEP cohort in 2002–2003. He also completed his ETEP year with a provisional certificate to teach English at the secondary level. Ian taught in a consolidated high school in a low-income rural district that included three different towns. However, Ian's high school was explicitly designed to be a Coalition of Essential Schools high school and the physical structure of the school, the curriculum, and professional norms have remained consistent to this vision for over a decade.

Heather, Tim, and Ian were typical secondary ETEP candidates during their internship year. They each had a strong work ethic while in the program and were hired immediately into full-time teaching positions. Each of them completed their Master's of Science in Education: Teaching and Learning within 5 years of completing their certification year. Their "typicalness" is important in that there was nothing especially "exceptional" about any of them. However, the moral virtues common to Heather, Tim, and Ian were found in their strong stance for justice, fairness, and respect for differences. Each of these teachers confronted their assumptions about their students' potential for academic and personal success on a regular basis. Yet they continued to draw on the curricular skills and knowledge introduced in ETEP to assess, modify, and accommodate their instruction so that all of their students knew how to be successful.

The intellectual virtues they held in common built on the same curricular and assessment knowledge base. Heather, Tim, and Ian used the state learning standards to identify the key concepts, skills, and factual knowledge their students needed. They selected a few big ideas that energized student inquiry into the literature they were teaching, and they found ways to connect the students' personal lives and interests to these big themes. ETEP's strong emphasis on using essential questions, including moral essential questions, to focus student discovery is something our candidates practice again and again.

Personal Moral and Intellectual Stance

Heather described herself as a "working-class Maine kid," who grew up "not speaking good proper English with her extended family and neighbors because they wouldn't understand what I was saying." However, Heather also graduated from Bowdoin College, one of the elite, "baby Ivy League" colleges, and the experience brought social class distinctions into sharp focus for her. Heather stated that her experiences growing up and attending college shaped the kind of English teacher she is:

> In my senior class, [we] spend a lot of time looking at sociocultural ideas. So in order to get at those, I talk a lot about social class or ways of talking and accents. I think the way that I am around kids works really well for me. I feel connected to them—like "we're from the same place, so I understand you."

Tim grew up in an affluent coastal Maine community and attended the University of Maine. Tim's identity is strongly rooted in his ability as an athlete and his love of coaching. His coaching experiences with young people of all backgrounds allowed Tim to transcend the cultural dissonance he encountered at his high school and motivated him to learn about his students and the communities in which they lived.

> The school is located in a region I had never been to before or had much connection with. It's completely outdoorsy—everybody hunts. I would be surprised if there were more than three students who don't hunt. It is also a community with some pretty severe poverty. It's brutal, to be perfectly honest with you. I have quite a few foster children in the classroom—students who move from house to house to house, who don't have parents, who live with the grandparents. A couple of years ago, six kids had parents die from cancer in the same year. I have had to understand what their strengths are, but it's worked out well because it shows that I'm a learner as well.

Ian grew up in rural Maine, attended a large, consolidated high school, and eventually graduated from Springfield College in Massachusetts with a degree in English and business. He came into teaching by spending a year substitute teaching while trying to promote his rock band. Ian described himself as someone who liked school and was successful at meeting school expectations. Nonetheless, he was aware that some of the students who were not in the "level-one" tracked classes had a different experience with teachers and administrators. Ian made a brief attempt as a senior in high school to push back at administrators who, he perceived, deliberately targeted students who were nonconformists; however, it wasn't until he began teaching at his current high school that he discovered how important it was to be a vocal advocate for students.

> I've always known that if I really am opposed to something, I can fist it. The teachers do a fist-to-five thing, so, if the whole faculty does a big vote, I can put up my fist. Of course, that means I need to explain exactly why [I voted

the way I did], and I need to commit myself to help the process. But having that power and voice is empowering, really.

In this brief introduction, Heather, Tim, and Ian revealed a strong alignment with the ETEP equity framework. Heather was intellectually driven to understand the strengths and limitations of social class on her own and her students' opportunities to learn in a conventional American high school. She made the hidden codes of social class explicit to her students without denigrating their experiences or their aspirations. Tim used the common language of sports to help him navigate the cultural differences between his background, that of his students, and the communities in which they lived. He learned to be culturally responsive, while also holding his students to the kind of expectations that would be recognized by any postsecondary institution. Ian deliberately chose to teach in an environment that did not track students into artificially constructed academic silos. He actively contributed to the school's institutional systems that valued layers of collaboration, and he has always taught his content as part of a two-person humanities team that integrates literature, English language arts, and social studies.

Moral Responsibilities to Students

Heather, Tim, and Ian all talked about the ways ETEP shaped their thinking about their moral responsibilities to students, the way they delivered instruction, and their commitment to working with others in leadership roles. During their internship, they were required to observe, survey, interview, and connect with their students on many different levels. The data were used to differentiate the way a topic was delivered, the ways in which technology facilitated an individual's engagement with the content, and the choices students had for demonstrating what they knew and were able to do. The data were also used to modify the physical environment, the pacing, the way students were grouped, and the timing of when content was delivered in order to accommodate student learning modalities and preferences. Not only did this focus on students' opportunities to learn require an inquiry stance from interns, but it set the norm for why and how teachers must respond to the needs of all learners in their classrooms.

Heather's commitment to making a positive impact on her students, along with the unique features of the space in which she teaches [a major hallway bisects her classroom], continually requires her to deliberate about her curriculum, her pedagogy, and her assessments.

> This year, I thought one of my classes was just going to be unteachable, especially in this space. I had to change what I was doing and so I've been teaching them completely different all year; I've been putting them in different places, and it has changed the way I taught. Now they're all learning the same things, but they wouldn't have learned if I had tried to teach it in the same way.

Ian expresses the impact ETEP made on his thinking about heterogeneous versus homogeneous classrooms.

> ETEP was nothing like the schooling I had at O.H. which is right down the road. What I saw with ETEP was a whole new way of looking at [teaching]. I teach in a heterogeneous classroom, and the kids in my class don't only see kids in practice on the football field; they're in the same room with them all the time. I remember feeling like cliques happen in schools so you get these groups, but half of it is because of the structure of the school. I think those bigger ideas definitely influenced me as a teacher.

The community in which Tim teaches presents a conflicted stance on the role of schooling in their definition of success. From the beginning, Tim took a stance in which he respected the right of his students to hold different perspectives on the value of school or the value of his curriculum, but in his classroom he consistently holds high academic expectations for them, and he models his expectations for them as stewards of their school environment.

> I think respect would be the biggest thing I use in the classroom. It's an everyday occurrence. I can't have a day go by without having to think or use respect in some class. For instance, I took it upon myself and redid the landscaping in front of the school. I spent the entire summer with another man and we made this nice garden with all these walkways. So the kids are now policing it themselves—I'm on the second floor and [the front of the school] is right outside my window and I hear kids saying, "Get off that. Don't do that."

The virtues of justice and wisdom are represented in these three accounts. Heather and Tim work to understand the cultural identities and intelligences each student brings into the learning environment. Their respect for and responsiveness to their students' emotional needs creates a safe and caring environment for them. Ian wisely recognizes the value of having all kinds of students in his classroom—not only for the intellectual give-and-take when discussing difficult ideas, but for the message it sends that neither social nor intellectual cliques are welcome in his classroom.

Intellectual Responsibilities to Student Inquiry

The content methods courses in ETEP connect content with pedagogy and with academic standards for mastering the content. In these courses, interns are introduced to strategies for how to teach their content that set high expectations for learners all along the standards' continuum. The following examples reveal the efforts Tim and Heather went through to construct their curriculum in a manner that justly met the needs of all students.

Like many high school English teachers, Tim found his curriculum was constrained by an increasing level of accountability. He was constrained by the resources in his school that could give him access to literary formats in digital or visual forms. But he was especially constrained by the students' lack of appreciation for how English benefits them. As a result, Tim planned his curriculum using analogies that were meaningful to his students, while continuing to hold high expectations for their performance.

> You know, there is an intrinsic motivation in the students who are on a ski slope or on a basketball court—they want to be there. And telling a student "this matters" is . . . students need to have the "it matters" come naturally. There needs to be something that you have that they want. [Like being] on the ski slope, they must want to learn more, to want to know what's happening, or want to understand it. I can tell them how important it is, but if they don't want it, then you're never going to get that ski slope or basketball court feeling. It needs to come from that intrinsic motivation of what they want. What we have to find are the hooks to hang things on so it does matter to them.

Heather took a similar approach with her English students. She worked hard to articulate a "big idea" that would energize student inquiry throughout the year, and then began developing her curriculum so that it continually pulled students back to examine that idea.

> Actually, Julie Canniff had a big impact on the way I conceive of the whole year. I'm a whole-to-part thinker, so I really like looking at "What is the purpose of this year? Why are they here?" And I use that to help me revise my curriculum every year. The senior year they study the sociocultural perspective. We're looking at cultural values, and we're kind of acting like sociologists. To me, that really gave the curriculum some power. Using some of the principles I learned from ETEP of "Where am I trying to get them by the end of the year, and what are the essential questions," as Julie would say, I came up with some "throughlines" that stuck with me all year. No matter what we were doing, I kept coming back to those ideas. I think it adds a lot of coherence, and I'm really proud of the work I've done. I know it's because of what I learned about curriculum in ETEP.

The virtue of wisdom is revealed in Tim's ability to tap into his students' intrinsic curiosity about topics that matter to them and connect them to some of the universal themes in the literature he asks them to read. He reminds them that practicing the skills of effective communication is just as important as practicing the skills of downhill skiing. When he inspires a genuine willingness to inquire, he knows he has hooked them. The wisdom of Heather's curriculum is revealed in the ways she infuses a moral essential question into her yearlong planning.

She demands that students engage with messy, complex themes from a variety of perspectives, anchoring their ongoing inquiry in the essential question. Tim and Heather have refined the pedagogical content knowledge skills gained in their teacher preparation program because their stance on intellectual virtues is to hold all their students to high expectations.

Collaboration and Collegiality

The internship cohort seminar knits all of these experiences together setting high expectations for reflection on virtually every aspect of the teaching experience. The seminar socializes the interns into a mind-set that all teaching is dependent on collaboration and collegiality.

Ian still values the emphasis that ETEP placed on being a reflective and reflexive practitioner. Unlike Heather and Tim, Ian teaches in a school culture that was a seamless transition from the ETEP cohort/internship into his Humanities Department. Ian's high school is inherently learning centered, where teachers learn from other teachers as much as students learn from teachers and one another. Moral and intellectual virtues are expressed in the school governance structure, the curriculum, the standards, and the continual process of reflection on what is working and what is not.

I did far more thinking, reflecting, real learning, and appreciating learning in ETEP than I ever did anywhere else. We were required to draw from our own experiences, our own strengths, and recognize our weaknesses. I think that's the learning I like best. I like looking at, "Okay, what intrinsic things do people have that they can offer?" And then almost exploiting those and see how far you can take it. It takes a lot of talking and thinking and reflecting, but I think grad school was where I really opened up to it.

I like the pod structure, even though it is hard to take planning time, and actually get to work; it's a constant collaboration. From a teacher perspective, having my whole team all around me means we can talk about this kid right now. We can throw meetings together quickly. Teachers talk it out, work it out; teachers have a lot of control over what happens. We have so many amazing teachers at my school. They are so passionate, and they model how to just go for it, mix it up, and do the school culture that I can see every day. I like that modeling; breaking stereotypes.

The virtues of justice and wisdom are expressed in the daily work of these three teachers. They are not a set of lofty, abstract concepts, but are internalized beliefs and practices—many of which were initially fostered through their preparation program. The practices of these three teachers are consistent with ETEP's Equity Framework and represent a moral and intellectual stance that assumes all students deserve the opportunity to learn.

IMPLICATIONS FOR TEACHER EDUCATION

As teacher educators, we learn from studying cases of our teacher candidates like Heather, Ian, and Tim. We use them to revise and improve our programs to achieve our goal of preparing teachers who have a moral stance based upon equity. Over the course of the last several years, we have used cases of our teacher candidates to revise aspects of our admissions process, to delve more deeply into teacher candidates' dispositions, and to further develop our teacher education curriculum and assessments so they better align with our goals for the kinds of teachers we hope to prepare. We continue our work in this vein and have a lot more to learn, but we believe that what we have learned can inform other teacher educators who are interested in making the moral more explicit in their work.

The first implication that we have to offer is our recognition of the importance for teacher educators in a program to develop a shared moral stance. Developing the moral stance of teacher candidates requires that teacher education faculty have a moral stance themselves. Like most teacher education faculties, we come from various disciplinary backgrounds, have different perspectives on teaching and learning, and often use different language. At times, the differences in our language and our theoretical and disciplinary backgrounds have been a barrier. However, through hard work and conversation, we have been able to overcome most of the barriers associated with our differences and develop a shared moral stance. The development of this stance has been important to helping us clarify the kinds of teachers we hope to prepare. It sustains our program's mission in times when we are all individually working with our cohorts as well as when we are challenged with questions about what we do and why. Therefore, we recommend that teacher education programs truly interested in nurturing the moral stance of their teacher candidates begin with nurturing the moral stance of their faculty.

It is our faculty's moral stance that it is the teacher's responsibility to model the moral and intellectual virtues of justice and wisdom. Being a model requires that teachers know and understand the moral and intellectual dimensions of teaching and how they are expressed in practice. Therefore, the second implication of our work is that teacher educators need to make virtue explicit. Teacher educators need to consistently and intentionally use their moral stance as guides in admissions, curriculum, and assessment. Teacher education programs need to intentionally prepare teachers to consider their craft from the perspective of moral and intellectual virtue and the potential influence that their expression of virtue can have on the moral development of their students.

Understanding a teacher's moral influence is an important line of inquiry for teacher education programs. It is important for teacher educators to understand whether their efforts to foster a moral stance endured following graduation. Therefore, a third implication of our work is that teacher educators must engage in inquiry related to whether their graduates' moral stance persists throughout their professional careers. In our case, we have some evidence that our graduates have a moral stance related to teaching, but because our focus has been on how the teacher models moral and intellectual virtue, we have little understanding of students' perspectives on their teachers' expression of virtue or how their moral development has been influenced by their teachers. This is an important next step in our own line of inquiry and one we encourage other teacher educators to examine.

If teacher education faculty commit themselves to moral inquiry, make the moral nature of their work explicit through their language and actions, and create programs with coherent standards and outcomes related to moral and intellectual virtues, then we believe teacher education will have a significant impact on the profession of teaching. The teachers who graduate from teacher education programs with a strong moral stance will express moral and intellectual virtue in their practice, and although the relationships between teachers and students are complex, we believe those expressions will nurture students' development as morally and intellectually virtuous human beings. Thus the explicit development of the moral in teaching and teacher education is a worthy endeavor.

REFERENCES

Aristotle. (1985). *Nicomachean ethics* (T. Irwin, Trans.). Indianapolis, IN: Hackett.

Gay, G. (2010). *Culturally responsive teaching: Theory, research, and practice* (2nd ed.). New York: Teachers College Press.

MacIntyre, A. (1984). *After virtue* (2nd ed.). Notre Dame, IN: University of Notre Dame Press.

Nozick, R. (1989). *The examined life: Philosophical meditations.* New York: Touchstone Press.

Peterson, C., & Seligman, M. E. P. (2004). *Character strengths and virtues: A handbook and classification.* New York: Oxford University Press.

Prior, W. J. (1991). *Virtue and knowledge: An introduction to ancient Greek ethics.* London: Routledge.

Rose, D. H., & Meyer, A. (2002). *Teaching every student in the digital age: Universal Design for Learning.* Alexandria, VA: Association for Supervision & Curriculum Development.

Sherman, N. (1997). *Making necessity of virtue: Aristotle and Kant on virtue.* Cambridge, UK: Cambridge University Press.

Wenger, E. (1998). *Communities of practice: Learning, meaning and identity.* Cambridge, UK: Cambridge University Press.

CHAPTER 7

Let the Theory Be Your Guide

Assessing the Moral Work of Teaching

Lisa E. Johnson, Jonatha W. Vare, and Rebecca B. Evers

Inherent in the moral work of teaching is a disposition focusing on humanistic, equitable actions. Educators must be open to varying perspectives, flexible in instructional approaches, and democratic in managing diverse classrooms. In the preparation of future teachers, the National Council for the Accreditation of Teacher Education (NCATE) mandates assessment of two professional dispositions, those of fairness and the belief that all children can learn (NCATE, 2008). To operationalize such morally grounded dispositions, teacher preparation programs must decide how to best cultivate the development of these and other dispositions in its candidates, and how to assess the demonstration of dispositions in daily classroom activities. As faculty at Richard W. Riley College of Education (Winthrop University) have wrestled with these and similar challenges during the past few years, a theoretical, data-based framework has emerged to guide our efforts (Johnson, Evers, & Vare, 2010).

Our college's mission is aligned with the National Network for Educational Renewal's continuing agenda of excellent education for all students in a democratic society (Sirotnik, 1994). Building democratic moral communities in schools where school-university partners collaborate to achieve educational equity, provide nurturing pedagogy, and engage in responsible stewardship forms a focus for our work (Fenstermacher, 1999). In response to NCATE's (2010) recent charge to strengthen the clinical preparation of teacher candidates, groups of partnership faculty have redesigned teacher education in innovative ways that will prepare candidates to meet the needs of an increasingly diverse array of students who attend our nation's schools. This newly designed program promotes the dispositional development of teacher candidates through an experience-based curriculum, opportunities to solve problems that arise in ill-structured contexts, frequent guided reflection, and continuing dialogue with teachers, peers, and university professors.

The redesign of our teacher preparation program provided a unique opportunity to construct a comprehensive model for promoting and assessing the morally grounded dispositional development of our teacher candidates. Recently our college adopted a framework that defines four cognitively based dispositions and aligns each with behavioral indicators of appropriate judgments and actions (Johnson et al., 2010). The four dispositions are Fairness, Integrity, Commitment, and Communication. Using a matrix of dispositions, judgments, and actions, assessments are designed that link to particular dispositions, with assessment data easily aggregated to track candidates' development over time. In this chapter we focus specifically on the disposition of Fairness as a direct parallel to the moral work of teaching and use examples of assessments to show how faculty can establish a longitudinal record of candidate performance.

A THEORETICALLY GROUNDED FRAMEWORK TO GUIDE INSTRUCTION AND ASSESSMENT

Our view of the moral work of the teacher is grounded in a developmental framework that integrates the perspectives of John Dewey and Lawrence Kohlberg with those of Nel Noddings and Carol Gilligan. Following Dewey's view of the moral self, we see the teacher as one who must at times disregard personal gain, or what might best serve the self, and seek what is best for the common good (Bergman, 2005). In Neo-Kohlbergian theory, this shift reflects a move from egocentric, personal interest to postconventional reasoning based on principles derived from an ethic of justice (Rest, Narvaez, Bebeau, & Thoma, 1999). Also central to the care theory of Gilligan (1982) and Noddings (2002, 2003) is development of an ethic of responsibility to self and others. According to Noddings (1999), a conception of fairness based on an ethic of justice is inherently inadequate as a sole guide to moral thinking because it attempts to achieve equity through the application of sameness. We agree with Strike (1999) who recommended a pluralistic stance that accommodates the complexity inherent in moral decisions. Therefore, our framework integrates ethics of both justice and caring within an approach to teacher preparation.

A primary challenge for teacher educators is helping candidates develop dispositions of reflection, inquiry, ethical judgments, and orientation toward the multifaceted needs of students whom they teach. Our view of dispositions is a cognitive one (Dottin, 2009) that enables measurement with behavioral evidence, as recommended by Damon (2007) and NCATE (2008). Following the early lead of Katz and Raths (1985), we define *dispositions* as trends of a teacher candidate's judgments, behaviors, and reflections over time. This supports our focus on collecting performance data in particular contexts.

Teacher Candidates' Stages of Moral Reasoning

Our framework applies Neo-Kohlbergian theory to the development of teacher candidates' moral reasoning about issues of equity in schools and classrooms. Candidate reasoning on moral dilemmas can be characterized by three developmental schema:

- *Personal Interest* is an exclusive focus on how a teaching-learning situation affects oneself.
- *Maintaining Norms* stresses keeping in line with the conventional status quo in schools and classrooms or a view of fairness as treating all students the same.
- *Postconventional* views actions based on convictions as an educational change agent or a view of equity as treating students fairly by considering differences (Rest et al., 1999; Vare, Evers, & Mensik, 2008).

According to this framework, candidates make moral judgments through schemas, and subsequent actions are congruent with principles embedded in the judgments. Judgments and actions are behavioral indicators of dispositions, and the teacher education curriculum is designed to help candidates develop increasingly complex dispositions that are based on the principle of fairness.

The Importance of an Ethic of Care

Within our framework, we incorporated a pluralistic stance that recognizes the importance of caring to the disposition of fairness. As a moral approach to relationships, caring provides an ethical basis for actions that are grounded in responsibility to self and others (Gilligan, 1982). Teacher candidates first possess a sense of responsibility to self, then a sense of responsibility to others, and last a view that integrates responsibility to self and others (Brown & Gilligan, 1992; Taylor, Gilligan, & Sullivan, 1992). The starting point of caring is the teacher-student dyad, a reciprocal relationship of the one-caring and the cared-for (Noddings, 2003). To employ an ethic of care, teacher candidates must develop abilities to focus on another rather than the self, to recognize the needs of others and become motivated to assist, and to engage in genuine dialogue, a form of two-way communication that exists when the conversation is truly open and has no predetermined agenda (Noddings, 2003). A caring teacher candidate demonstrates the ability to take a student's perspective, receptivity to the needs of a student, and persistence of caring when a student does not respond overtly. Through appropriate interaction, the teacher candidate establishes and maintains a caring relationship that enables trust to develop. Trust, receptivity, and other-directed motivation form the relational basis for judgment and actions upon which the disposition of fairness is dependent.

ASSESSMENT WITH INDICATORS OF JUDGMENT AND ACTION

The purpose of constructing our framework was twofold—to select and define professional dispositions and to provide a basis for their assessment. Furthermore, to assess teacher candidates' dispositions, we needed to specify observable behaviors that were associated with those dispositions. Our work began with identification and definition of key professional dispositions that should characterize the daily work of teacher candidates. In 2009 a university-wide task force of ten faculty members selected four dispositions that were aligned with core principles of Winthrop University, the National Board for Professional Teaching Standards, and the National Network for Educational Renewal. The four dispositions and their definitions are:

- *Fairness:* Assumes responsibility for the learning of all students in the classroom in a caring, nondiscriminatory, and equitable manner and persists in effective learning for all students
- *Integrity:* Demonstrates a recognition of and adherence to the moral, legal, and ethical principles of the university and the profession
- *Communication:* Interacts in ways that convey respect and sensitivity regarding the perspectives, experiences, and expertise of others
- *Commitment:* Embraces the complexity of the work of teaching through reflective practice and professional growth

The task force also identified appropriate judgments and actions as observable indicators of each disposition (Johnson et al., 2010). As Kohlberg and others have noted in their study of moral development, judgments do not always lead to corresponding moral actions (Rest & Narvaez, 1994). Therefore, we recognized the importance of collecting performance data to provide evidence of both aspects of teacher candidates' dispositional development. Judgments are reflected in work samples such as reflections, case studies, dilemma responses, and lesson plans, while actions are documented through performance assessments like observations of teaching. Sample indicators of *judgments* representing the disposition of fairness include:

- Has a positive view of others, believing in the worth, ability, and potential of all children
- Takes into account a variety of learners' needs when planning instruction and assessments
- Acknowledges existing structures or practices that promote inequity
- Views issues from perspectives of marginalized persons and groups

Similarly, we have identified specific, observable *action* indicators:

- Modifies instruction and/or assessment based on a variety of learners' needs
- Monitors and adjusts when presented with ill-structured problems
- Sets high expectations for all learners, providing scaffolding for success
- Teaches by invitation—invites students to increase the challenge or decrease the challenge based upon performance
- Uses authentic, relevant assessments to measure student understanding
- Advocates for marginalized students and families
- Challenges inequities of existing structures
- Addresses the behavior, not the child
- Supports equitable access to knowledge in the school, district, profession, or community

In our model, faculty can incorporate indicators of judgments and actions within scoring rubrics for particular course assessments, and data can then be aggregated by indicator to track the development of each disposition over time.

Pilot Assessment Studies

To illustrate how the indicators of judgment and action can be used to assess dispositions, the task force piloted two unitwide assessments: a revision of the Admission to Teacher Education Program Essay and a perception checklist. Each assessment had a specific purpose and with implementation provided significant direction in how to move our work forward. We begin by describing each assessment and then share lessons learned.

Admission to Teacher Education Program Essay. Within the current requirements for existing students to enter teacher education, they must submit an essay describing their past learning and future goals as an educator. A pilot study was conducted revising the essay to use actual teacher candidates' journal responses to create classroom-based scenarios. Instead of having candidates submit an essay, they would respond to prompts about one of the scenarios. Candidates volunteering to be part of the pilot study registered to come to a computer lab at which time they were given a case study and directions for completing a 3–4 page response. The response required a description and analysis of challenges in the case study related to the four dispositions followed by a reflection on how the candidate as a teacher would have addressed the challenge.

Faculty selected indicators from the dispositions matrix and used them to create a scoring rubric for the essay with three descriptive levels—beginning, emerging, and leading—and corresponding indicators for each of the four dispositions. At the beginning level, a response related to fairness is characterized by a lack of awareness of structures or practices that promote inequity. For example, one candidate reflected on the case study, "Michael considered writing assignments to be boring and does not have the self-control to stay in his seat during class discussions or independent writing activities." This candidate did not acknowledge the possible impact of the class structure on the student's behavior. At the emerging level, reasoning suggests maintaining existing school or classroom structure. This is evident in a candidate response describing a classroom rule, "He was not giving the respect to the teacher by not raising his hand and getting called on." Finally, reasoning at the leading level challenges existing structures or practices that may hinder student learning, "Instead of treating Michael like talking in class is prohibited, the teacher should encourage his high verbal ability and teach Michael when it is and is not okay to use it."

Faculty involved in the pilot study agreed the essay was an appropriate assessment of dispositions; however, data from the scores assigned to the essays (two faculty scored each essay) revealed lack of interrater reliability. It was difficult to achieve consistency between rubric levels, especially at the beginning and emerging levels. Discussions revealed differences in how the rubric indicators were interpreted and assessed in the essay responses. In addition, some faculty discussed whether the responses were providing a true picture of candidate judgment or whether the responses were more of a regurgitation of course content.

Perception Checklist. In addition to the essay pilot, a perception checklist was developed that could be used by faculty in any course. This checklist has been used by individual faculty to facilitate goal-setting conversations with candidates that faculty believe lack appropriate professional dispositions. For example, an instructor gives the candidates a paper copy of the checklist to complete, reflecting on indicators such as, "Demonstrates behaviors that are consistent with the belief that all students can learn" and "Demonstrates the ability to listen and be respectful of divergent viewpoints." Then during a personal conference, the faculty member and candidate compare their responses. When there is disagreement, they discuss the issue and work to resolve the problem. Finally, at the end of the conference, the candidate is asked to set goals for the remainder of the semester. As the semester progresses, faculty and candidate discuss progress toward meeting the goals.

Two administrations of the checklist were conducted. Faculty in one methods course and one core education course volunteered to ask students in their courses to self-assess their dispositions, while the faculty member conducted the same assessment on each student. Data gathered on the self-perceptions of candidates related to the moral disposition of fairness indicated candidates have high perceptions of their disposition for fairness. On a scale of 0 (no opportunity) to 3,256 (67%) of the 380 candidates rated themselves as level 3; 120 (32%) candidates rated themselves as level 2. Faculty perceptions of candidates' dispositions differed from the candidates. Of the 12 faculty who participated, four (33%) rated the majority of candidates as level 3, and eight rated them as level 2 (67%). While faculty overall rated candidates lower, neither faculty nor the candidates themselves administered a rating of "1."

Lessons Learned from Pilot Studies

The Perception Checklist provided an opportunity to assess where candidates saw their dispositional strengths and weaknesses and how this was parallel or incongruent with faculty perception. The purpose for assessing candidates' dispositions with the checklist was not to dismiss those whose dispositions were found lacking, but to use the data to help candidates set goals to improve their dispositions and assess our ability to have an effect on candidates' growth toward being fair and equitable teachers. Although it was only in use for one academic year, we believe that the use of the checklist by individual faculty and candidates can provide a valuable opportunity for dialogue and personal reflection. These opportunities to talk with candidates about what it means to be fair, ethical, and equitable are very important growth experiences. However, having faculty rate candidates they only know for a short period of time and in a very specific context may not provide an opportunity to support those candidates most in need of disposition development. This was evident in the absence of any rating below a 2. Because the checklist seemed geared more toward program evaluation than individual assessment, it needed to be transformed to provide the data needed to support candidate growth.

Lessons learned from piloting a revised Teacher Education Admission Essay centered on areas of success and issues that must be resolved in rubric construction and scoring as well as integration of such activities in courses rather than a high-stakes checkpoint (Johnson, Evers, & Vare, 2011). A successful aspect of the assessment method derived from the use of familiar material to construct the scenario and instructions in the prompt. Data from exit interviews with teacher candidates indicated that the content of the scenario resonated with their experiences in field-based settings and that the wording of the instructions represented a task with which they were familiar (i.e., analyzing morally based concerns such as how issues of fairness arise in a classroom event). As suggested by Johnson (2008), in order to reduce the possibility of regurgitation, similar assessments should be embedded in particular courses rather than in an abstract admissions process far removed from actual curricular experiences, particularly when the assessment process occurs prior to admission to teacher education.

The pilot study also revealed several issues that faculty explore as we continue to develop dispositional assessments. A key concern involves reliability in scoring. In the pilot study, use of many faculty members from university-wide departments made the achievement of sufficient reliability in scoring unnecessarily complex. Scorers must share an understanding of the meaning of the indicators, and this may be best achieved by connecting assessments to courses in which teams of instructors create assignments and scoring rubrics. Collaboration that involves frequent dialogue about key terms and phrases in the indicators is more likely to produce the shared understandings necessary for reliability in scoring.

A challenge for our faculty is the creation of scoring rubrics that appropriately reflect teacher candidates' progression in dispositional development, especially related to the moral dimension of fairness. We realize that one purpose of the teacher preparation curriculum is to nurture and scaffold the development of appropriate professional dispositions. Accordingly, we want to create levels of judgments and actions within rubrics that reflect the current level of candidates' dispositional development, acknowledge an expected level of attainment at particular points in the teacher preparation program, and do not penalize them unfairly. In the pilot studies we attempted to write indicators that reflect a progression from beginning to emerging and leading performance of dispositional development. Upon reflection, we see that the progression from beginning to leading involves a great deal of change in dispositions, and we are not yet satisfied with our description of the levels of development. Construction of sound rubrics is an iterative process that involves continuous application, analysis, and revision, and we see ours as a work in progress. What we also learned from the pilot studies was a need to move deeper than the creation of dispositional assessments. We needed to start at the foundation—the teacher preparation curriculum—to examine how we were providing opportunities and experiences for candidates to develop an understanding of the moral work of teaching.

ASSESSMENTS FOR A REVISED CORE CURRICULUM

Armed with our "lessons learned" from the pilot assessment studies regarding dispositional development in core content and assessments, we proposed a plan to revise our teacher preparation curriculum to be grounded in field-based experiences aimed at preparing graduates to meet the diverse needs of all learners. In 2009 we were awarded a federal grant to plan and implement such a transformation that has at its core the moral work of teaching.

Revised Core Curriculum

Using our cognitive stance on dispositional development in the moral domain, our new core acknowledges candidate transitions through schematic stages of change related to how they reason and act upon ill-structured events (situations in which a multitude of perspectives exist in how to address issues). Utilizing these theoretical foundations, we established four phases of teacher candidate growth:

- *Phase I: Observation, Analysis, and Self-Reflection on Teaching and Pedagogy*—Engages in metacognitive and contextual awareness as *student*; challenges perspectives from own school and childhood experiences

- *Phase II: Understanding Learners, Implementing Interventions, and Examining Results*—Moves from *student* to *professional*; makes a dispositional commitment by embracing new perspectives and developing asset views of learners
- *Phase III: Management, Instruction, and Assessment*—Internalizes what it means to be a *professional* educator; successfully balances simultaneous implementation of multiple facets of classroom dynamics and engages in action research that leads to evaluation and critique of practice
- *Phase IV: Understanding Classrooms, Communities, Schools, and Systems*—Displays *professional* understanding of education as a democratic system; exhibits generativity (Ball, 2009) by continuously applying new knowledge to existing frameworks.

Within each phase are carefully designed, field-based experiences to promote development of the moral disposition of fairness. Movement to more complex levels of moral reasoning and action evolves from interactions within contexts in which one encounters moral dilemmas accompanied by the opportunity to reflect upon and analyze the experiences with others (Reiman & Johnson, 2003). No longer is our core characterized by the traditional sequence of education courses, but it is guided more toward fostering what William James referred to as "additional endowments" (Hamachek, 1968, p. 205)—moving beyond knowing subject matter and child development theory and internalizing what it means to be a democratic, equitable educator using such information. We used the Four Component Model (FCM) originally designed by Rest to support the structure and assessment of specific course content aimed at developing the moral and ethical disposition of our teacher candidates. As described by Rest et al. (1999), the interaction of the four components "together give rise to the outwardly observable behavior" (p. 101).

- *Moral Sensitivity*—identifying and interpreting the moral and ill-structured aspects of a situation and the various perspectives from which the situation can be viewed and addressed; considering the cause-and-effect nature of solutions and how each course of action might impact those involved
- *Moral Judgment*—of the various courses of action possible, choosing that which is most morally justifiable while taking relationships and contextual factors into account; considering what is right for persons other than those with whom one is in a direct, caring relationship (Rest & Narvaez, 1994).
- *Moral Motivation*—commitment to following through on a moral course of action; valuing the moral over other values and accepting personal responsibility for the chosen action

- *Moral Character*—persistence to achieve a moral task; having the courage, competence, and confidence to resolve an ill-structured, ethical dilemma regardless of distraction or discouragement
- The FCM is not order specific—we do not see candidates as achieving moral sensitivity then moving to judgment, motivation, and finally character. Rather, their behavior is a manifestation of how they are able to engage in an integrated framework of all four components. As described in the phases, we have constructed the teacher education experience to be developmental; candidates continuously engage in the four components as they have experiences with and construct knowledge about diverse learner needs. Note that we have purposefully chosen the word *ethical* over *moral* throughout the curriculum to imply direct connection to the teaching profession, as in Bebeau (1994).

Phase I Courses

- EDUC 101: Developing Observation and Analysis Skills—Teacher candidates observe diverse P–12 settings in order to increase sensitivity (awareness) of diverse learner needs and the impact of teacher behavior. In conversations about observations with course instructor and mentor teachers, candidates engage in ethical judgment discussions. [Note the purposeful word choice of *ethical* versus *moral* throughout the curriculum to imply direct connection to teaching profession as in Bebeau (1994).]
- EDUC 200: Developmental Sciences and the Context of Poverty—Candidates study patterns of change in learners, recognizing development occurs in different ways, at different rates. They establish a meaningful relationship with a learner living in poverty to foster understanding of contextual factor influences. Candidates implement effective strategies for working with learners living in poverty and begin to develop a sense of ethical motivation through a professional responsibility to meet the needs of all learners (Bebeau & Monson, 2008).

Phase II Courses

- EDUC 220: Assessment to Meet Diverse Learner Needs—Assessments should be valid and reliable in diagnosing and measuring individual understanding. Candidates implement multiple assessments following principles of Universal Design for Learning and ethically use the assessments to guide instruction.
- STAR Rotation courses—EDUC 201: Supporting the English Language Learner; EDUC 202: Supporting the Learner with Special Needs in the

General Education Classroom; EDUC 203: Supporting the Learner Identified as Gifted—STAR (Study, Teach, Analyze, Reflect)—Rotation courses provide candidates with an opportunity to implement assessments to diagnose and measure understanding of an individual in the general education classroom with a diverse need. Through working with individual learners and their families, candidates continue to develop ethical sensitivity, explore judgments related to diversity, and refine their professional identity.

Phase III Courses

- EDUC 305: Technology in the Classroom—Candidates implement lessons using technology as a tool to solve a specific teaching/learning challenge and meet the principles of Universal Design for Learning. Ethical principles of access and use are a focus of the experience.
- EDUC 306: Teaching Methods for the Inclusive Classroom—After working with individuals and small groups, candidates explore methods for engaging an entire class of diverse learners. Candidates reflect upon judgments made during implementation of multiple instructional strategies.
- EDUC 350/1: Examining and Establishing Positive Classroom Climate— Candidates study, then implement, a positive behavior support plan through a tiered approach to meeting social and emotional needs. Candidates examine their ethical character for sustaining a democratic process for classroom management.

Phase IV Courses

- EDUC 401: Understanding Contextual Factors—During the first semester of a yearlong experience, candidates investigate the learning-teaching context of their internship classroom noting specific academic, environmental, and social influences on individual learners. They examine their professional responsibility to meet the needs of all of the learners in their class.
- EDUC 402: Assessment and Instruction—Candidates use knowledge of contextual factors to design and implement a learner-centered, standards-based unit of study that includes evidence of learner growth in defined goals and objectives. They discuss the necessary character and perseverance needed to support all learners.
- EDUC 410: Education in a Democracy, Broadening Professional Perspectives—Candidates explore the moral and ethical domains of the broader educational field through the context of their internship classroom, school, district, and state.

Sample Assessments

In designing assessments of the fairness disposition that is so prevalent throughout the core curriculum, we maintained a foundation in the Four Component Model. Although the courses have varied foci, the content covered ties directly to the candidate field experience. Thus instead of creating assessments for each course, we developed protocols for use throughout the teacher preparation program. We learned through our pilot essay that the assessment needed direct alignment with the experiences candidates were having and should be embedded within courses. Teams of faculty who teach a specific course can apply the protocols to the specific focus of the course (e.g., learners living in poverty, technology access, and so on). Such a model has multiple benefits for the candidates as well as the college. Candidate exposure to the protocols at multiple program points cultivates a sense of familiarity, providing a level of comfort and openness to engage in ethically grounded conversations. For the college and for the candidates, data gathered longitudinally can be used to measure development over time. Information is shared with candidates throughout their experience through the structure of the course and can be used to make critical decisions related to program progression.

Three assessments illustrating assessment of the fairness disposition are discussed below. First, a protocol for dilemma discussions emphasizes sensitivity to the ill-structured events that characterize classroom teaching and the process of reasoning through the various strategies for resolution. Next is a rubric for assessing the moral components of a written lesson plan. Finally, a list of moral action indicators highlights data collected during candidate teaching episodes.

Dilemma Discussions. Throughout Phase I and Phase II of the revised core curriculum, candidates are observing teachers through virtual and field-based experiences. To highlight the moral aspects of classroom teaching, we use the following protocols to structure dilemma discussions. The purpose of the protocols is to expand candidates' ethical sensitivity toward ill-structured classroom events and consideration of multiple means of problem solving. Candidates explore the impact of instructional decision making, as they propose a course of action that promotes equity and fairness.

- Accessing Prior Experiences—Write about (or create) a classroom dilemma you remember that highlights the impact of teacher behavior on _____ (*instructor can complete the sentence according to course focus*). Using the event, address the following prompts:
  - Describe at least three different ways of addressing the dilemma (one way can include how the teacher actually addressed the dilemma).
  - For each suggested strategy, what are the benefits and costs to each person involved?

- Which strategy do you think is the most ethical course of action? Why?
- Classroom Observations of Mentor Teachers—Describe a dilemma related to _____ (*instructor can complete the sentence according to course focus*) that occurred during the observation. Using the event and your contextual knowledge of the classroom, address the following prompts:
  - Describe at least three different ways of addressing the dilemma (one way can include how the teacher actually addressed the dilemma).
  - For each suggested strategy, what are the benefits and costs to each person involved?
  - Which strategy do you think is the most ethical course of action? Why?
- Self-Reflection of Teaching Episode (A similar protocol is used for candidates to reflect upon their own teaching. This occurs starting in Phase II and continues through Phase IV.)—Describe a dilemma related to _____ (*instructor can complete the sentence according to course focus*) that occurred while you were teaching. Using the event and your contextual knowledge of the classroom, address the following prompts:
  - How did you address the dilemma? What was the impact on each person involved (including you)?
  - Considering the impact of how you addressed the dilemma, would you change the strategy you used? Why or why not?
  - If someone disagreed with you regarding how to address the dilemma, how would you decide which course of action to take?

A matrix of fairness judgment indicators (see Table 7.1) aligned with the three moral judgment schema levels measures candidate responses to the dilemma discussions (Johnson & Reiman, 2007; Vare et al., 2008).

Instructional Strategy Plan Rubric. As candidates move into Phases III and IV, lesson planning becomes a targeted skill. We modified the assessment tool used for dilemma discussions (Table 7.1) to highlight specific instructional components but continued the alignment with the judgment schema and fairness indicators. Faculty in various content areas can integrate the Instructional Strategy Plan Rubric shown in Table 7.2 (adapted from Evers & Spencer, 2011) with the specific lesson plan elements required by the specialized program (e.g., secondary mathematics, middle-level science, special education, and so on).

Observations of Candidate Teaching. While the Dilemma Discussions and Strategy Plans focus on candidate judgment, the Observation of Candidate Teaching assesses how ethical actions manifest during instruction. Table 7.3 illustrates assessment of

Table 7.1. Dilemma Discussion Rubric

Developmental Level	Candidate Judgments
Self-orientation (Exclusive focus on self, egocentric orientation)	• Defines "on task" behavior as being when learner is actively working on assignment given by instructor • Sees role as an authority in the classroom/relationship • Views rules as needed to maintain order • Has an orientation toward need for learner conformity • Considers only personal stake in reference to action • Sees dilemmas as having only one solution
Maintaining structures (Maintaining the conventional status quo, view of fairness as equality)	• Presents ideas based only in working within existing classroom/school structure • Gives some consideration to learner perspective or internal motivation • Considers the main purpose of rules and norms is to provide safety, stability, and equality • Views fairness as equality (same for all) rather than equity (based on individual needs) • Views the school in terms of its hierarchical structure (principal-teacher; teacher-student)
Advancing equity (Change agent character, view of equity as treating students fairly by considering differences)	• Realizes multiple perspectives exist for achieving equity • Considers the ethical implications of instructional choices • Views dilemmas from perspectives of marginalized persons or groups • Takes into account a variety of learner needs when planning instructional strategies • Views rules as being designed to protect certain rights • Considers rules as alterable and relative • Plans actions that support equitable access within classroom, school, district, community, and profession

Table 7.2. Instructional Strategy Plan Rubric

Performance Components	Self-Orientation	Maintaining Structures	Advancing Equity
Impact on learners of lesson tasks and skill requirements	• Views curriculum holistically versus a set of necessary tasks • Considers curriculum accessibility the responsibility of the learner versus the teacher	• Includes tasks and skills presented in established curriculum materials • Considers impact on groups of learners versus individuals	• Views curriculum from multiple perspectives • Considers impact of tasks and skills on individual learners
Instructional procedures, learning activities, and assessment	• Plans focus on teacher control • Instructional strategy is teacher-centered, lecture-based • Learners presented as a "class" versus individuals • Information presented directly from prescribed text • Assessment occurs at end of lesson and is used for grading purposes only	• Plans aimed at keeping all learners at equal pace throughout lesson • Main instructional strategies are teacher-centered with some opportunity for learner interaction • Standards and textbook provide primary basis for instructional strategies • Assessment occurs mainly at the end of the lesson and is the same for all learners	• Plans learner-centered lessons that encourage decision making and problem solving • Incorporates interactive instructional strategies • Integrates motivational characteristics of learners • Considers various viewpoints in conventional social situations • Suggests multiple strategies for teaching content • Includes assessment at various points in lesson to provide instructional cues • Incorporates assessment that is authentic and relevant • Considers assessments that vary by learner need

Table 7.2. Instructional Strategy Plan Rubric (continued)

Performance Components	Self-Orientation	Maintaining Structures	Advancing Equity
Accommodations	• Suggests generic accommodations lacking connection to content or individual need • Relies on one accommodation to meet various learner needs	• Accommodations chosen from a given "menu" • Suggested accommodations represent least disruption to classroom structure	• Suggested accommodations are specific to lesson tasks and individual learner • Research/best practice is used to justify chosen accommodations
Lesson analysis	• Considers success of lesson in terms of performance on summative assessment • Learner engagement and "on task" behavior defined as the learner quietly working on assignment given by instructor • Views learners as responsible for mastering material • Suggestions for future teaching or reteaching include repetition of same instructional strategy	• Reflection focused on how well learners achieved stated objectives and followed lesson structure • Assessment used to consider continued needs of individual learners • Additional teaching occurs using same strategy but in a different setting (small group, one-on-one, and so on)	• Considers multiple strategies for making curriculum accessible for learners not achieving mastery • Views success as learner ability to achieve objectives, considers multiple problem-solving strategies, *and* engages in decision-making processes • Uses assessment data to make instructional modifications

candidate ethical actions. Similar to Tables 7.1 and 7.2, fairness indicators are aligned with the three ethical schema specific to pedagogical categories. Again, content areas integrate the indicators with other criteria specific to the discipline.

Tables 7.1, 7.2, and 7.3 illustrate sample assessments of candidate judgments and actions in the moral disposition of fairness. They provide an opportunity for

Table 7.3. Observation of Candidate Teaching Rubric

Performance Components	Self-Orientation	Maintaining Structures	Advancing Equity
Content knowledge and connections	• Establishes self as only content expert • Maintains presentation of information in one content area at a time	• Uses materials reflecting classroom diversity • Aligns presentation of content with curriculum manuals • Makes connections to teaching in other disciplines	• Presents content in ways that support personal connections for learners • Open to questions about and contributions to content coverage from learners
Learning environment	• Measures "on task" through behavioral observations only • Takes more of a controller role in the classroom/relationships • Becomes easily bothered by socially defiant behavior • Creates rules without learner input • Takes challenges to rules personally • Shows no sensitivity to learners' emotional needs	• Establishes rules that are categorical, clear, and uniform • Expects learners to obey rules and norms out of respect for the social system • Works to maintain the established order in the classroom and school setting • Attempts to address behavior, not the child	• Makes extensive use of cooperative learning activities • Takes more facilitative than presenter role • Shows tolerance of socially defiant behavior • Encourages learners to take part in rule making
Instruction	• Makes instructional decisions without regard to learner perspective or internal motivation • Gears actions to meeting personal needs or interest	• Uses formulas and other proven methods to solve problems • Attempts to try new and varied instructional strategies, although they are not part of repertoire • Uses same strategies for all learners • Recognizes need to monitor and adjust during instruction	• Modifies instruction based upon consideration of individual learner needs • Encourages decision making in learners • Employs more interactive instructional strategies • Considers various viewpoints and multiple problem-solving strategies

Table 7.3. Observation of Candidate Teaching Rubric (continued)

Performance Components	Self-Orientation	Maintaining Structures	Advancing Equity
Instruction			• Shows a willingness to help students understand and reason about ill-structured problems • Monitors and adjusts when presented with dilemmas (i.e., learners understanding more or less than expected) • Models ethical character through persistence to ensure all learners master content
Assessment and data use	• Uses only generic instructional and assessment modifications (not based on individual learner needs) • Single assessment used by all learners	• Designs and uses various assessments • Engages all learners in same assessment • Primarily uses assessment data to communicate school and district achievement goals	• Uses assessment modifications specific to individual learner needs • Designs and uses authentic, relevant assessments • Effectively and ethically communicates assessment information to learners, parents, guardians, colleagues, and administrators
Professionalism	• Sees role as teacher focused on benefits to self • Questions ability of specific learners to master curriculum • Possesses need for learner conformity • Considers self as authority	• Sees role as teacher defined by classroom and district policies • Works to maintain hierarchical structure of classroom and school • Considers how to make classroom experience the same for all learners	• Shows high levels of ethical conduct in classroom and school commitments • Demonstrates resolve to care about learners, curriculum, and school • Advocates for marginalized learners and their families

longitudinal data collection over the course of the teacher preparation program, easily integrated with course and program specific requirements related to the revised core curriculum. The assessments represent an evolution in our thinking about how to assess the moral work of teaching in our teacher candidates.

CONCLUSION

For at least the past 5 years, we have been working through pilot studies, task force meetings, action research, and curriculum transformation to develop a theoretically grounded model of dispositional development and assessment. Beyond the requirements of accreditation agencies to promote and assess the dispositions of fairness and the belief that all children can learn (NCATE, 2008) is our own moral imperative to provide opportunities for teacher candidates to develop judgments and actions characterized by equity, openness, and humanism. Such a task is far from simple, yet holds many implications for educator preparation programs aimed at moving toward a focus on the moral work of teaching.

First, we caution against the "patchwork" mind-set. To integrate the moral aspects of teaching into current courses and assessments characterizes the work as more of an afterthought than a foundation. Candidates are likely to regurgitate what instructors want to hear versus engaging in the cognitive development toward advancing equity for all learners. It took several years and multiple case studies for us to realize that we needed to stop trying to add to existing structures, but change the structures in their entirety. We needed to look at how the curriculum itself needed to change to reflect our moral imperatives before trying to develop and implement assessments. Our work in transforming the teacher education core curriculum was successful through a strong theoretical framework and shared understanding of the dispositions candidates needed to promote equity in today's diverse classrooms.

As we learned from multiple pilot studies, integrating instruction and assessments with actual field experiences provides an authentic environment through which development can occur and allows candidates opportunities to engage in real-life learning tasks. We attempted to move in this direction with the admission essay pilot and found candidates responded favorably to the case studies taken directly from situations reflected upon in early coursework. This point was extended when we transformed the core curriculum to be the actual foundation for teacher preparation. Candidates need direct, multiple, and varied experiences upon which to develop moral sensitivity, judgment, motivation, and character. The case studies upon which they are reflecting need to be their own, removing little chance of regurgitating what they think instructors want to hear.

As members of the National Network for Educational Renewal, we have as part of our mission to build democratic moral communities characterized by educational equity, nurturing pedagogy, and responsible stewardship (Fensterm-acher, 1999). We are committed to developing candidates, through a field-based, ethically centered curriculum, who will meet the ill-structured and diverse nature of today's classroom with the disposition that all children can learn.

REFERENCES

Ball, A. (2009). Toward a theory of generative change in culturally and linguistically complex classrooms. *American Educational Research Journal, 46*(1), 45–72.

Bebeau, M. J. (1994). Influencing the moral dimensions of dental practice. In J. R. Rest & D. Narvaez (Eds.), *Moral development in the professions* (pp. 121–146). Hillsdale, NJ: Lawrence Erlbaum Associates.

Bebeau, M. J., & Monson, V. E. (2008). Guided by theory, grounded in evidence: A way forward for professional ethics education. In L. P. Nucci & D. Narvaez (Eds.), *Handbook of moral and character education* (pp. 557–582). New York: Routledge.

Bergman, R. (2005). John Dewey on educating the moral self. *Studies in Philosophy and Education, 24*(1), 39–62.

Brown, L., & Gilligan, C. (1992). *Meeting at the crossroads: Women's psychology and girls' development.* Cambridge, MA: Harvard University Press.

Damon, W. (2007). Dispositions and teacher assessment: The need for a more rigorous definition. *Journal of Teacher Education, 58*(5), 365–369.

Dottin, E. S. (2009). Professional judgment and dispositions in teacher education. *Teaching and Teacher Education, 25*(1), 83–88.

Evers, R., & Spencer, S. (2011). *Planning effective instruction for students with learning and behavior problems.* Boston: Pearson.

Fenstermacher, G. D. (1999). Agenda for education in a democracy. In W. Smith & G. Fenstermacher (Eds.), *Leadership for educational renewal* (pp. 3–27). San Francisco: Jossey-Bass.

Gilligan, C. (1982). *In a different voice: Psychological theory and women's development.* Cambridge, MA: Harvard University Press.

Hamachek, D. E. (Ed.). (1968). *Human dynamics in psychology and education.* Boston: Allyn & Bacon.

Johnson, L. E. (2008). Judgment level or regurgitation: Analyzing the moral disposition of teacher candidates. *Journal of Moral Education, 37*(4), 429–444.

Johnson, L. E., Evers, R., & Vare, J. (2010). Disconnection as a path to discovery. In P. C. Murrell, M. E. Diez, S. Feiman-Nemser, & D. L. Schussler (Eds.), *Teaching as a moral practice: Defining, developing, and assessing professional dispositions in teacher education* (pp. 53–72). Cambridge, MA: Harvard Education Press.

Johnson, L. E., Evers, R., & Vare, J. (2011). *Developing capacities of moral agency and ethical practice in teachers and teaching.* Symposium presentation at the annual meeting of the American Association of Colleges for Teacher Education, San Diego, CA.

Johnson, L. E., & Reiman, A. J. (2007). Beginning teacher disposition: examining the moral/ethical domain. *Teaching and Teacher Education, 23*(5), 676–687.

Katz, L. G., & Raths, J. D. (1985). Dispositions as goals for teacher education. *Teaching and Teacher Education, 1*(4), 301–307.

National Council for Accreditation of Teacher Education (NCATE). (2008). *Professional standards for the accreditation of teacher preparation institutions.* Washington, DC: Author.

National Council for Accreditation of Teacher Education (NCATE). (2010). *Transforming teacher education through clinical practice: A national strategy to prepare effective teachers.* Washington, DC: Author.

Noddings, N. (1999). Care, justice, and equity. In M. C. Katz, N. Noddings, & K. A. Strike (Eds.), *Justice and caring: The search for common ground in education* (pp. 7–20). New York: Teachers College Press.

Noddings, N. (2002). *Educating moral people: A caring alternative to character education.* New York: Teachers College Press.

Noddings, N. (2003). *Caring: A feminine approach to ethics and moral education* (2nd ed.). Berkeley: University of California Press.

Reiman, A., & Johnson, L. E. (2003). Promoting teacher professional judgment. *Journal of Research in Education, 13*(1), 4–14.

Rest, J., & Narvaez, D. (Eds.). (1994). *Moral development in the professions: Psychology and applied ethics.* Hillsdale, NJ: Lawrence Erlbaum Associates.

Rest, J., Narvaez, D., Bebeau, M. J., & Thoma, S. J. (1999). *Postconventional moral thinking: A Neo-Kohlbergian approach.* Mahwah, NJ: Lawrence Erlbaum Associates.

Sirotnik, K. A. (1994). Equal access to quality public schooling: Issues in the assessment of equity and excellence. In J. I. Goodlad & P. Keating (Eds.), *Access to knowledge: The continuing agenda for our nation's schools* (pp. 159–185). New York: College Entrance Examination Board.

Strike, K. (1999). Justice, caring, and universality: In defense of moral pluralism. In M. C. Katz, N. Noddings, & K. A. Strike (Eds.), *Justice and caring: The search for common ground in education* (pp. 21–26). New York: Teachers College Press.

Taylor, J. C., Gilligan, C., & Sullivan, A. (1992). *Between voice and silence: Women and girls, race and relationship.* Cambridge, MA: Harvard University Press.

Vare, J., Evers, R., & Mensik, M. (2008, March). *Conceptions of equity and social justice: Developing a rubric to assess teacher candidates' dispositions.* Paper presented at the annual meeting of the American Educational Research Association, New York.

Part III

TEACHING MORALITY

Complementing the chapters from Part II, the chapters of Part III primarily speak to preparing and supporting teachers in *teaching morality*—drawing primarily upon psychological views of the moral development and functioning of students, and how to support those processes, within teacher education.

In Chapter 8 Daniel Lapsley, Anthony Holter, and Darcia Narvaez present their analysis of three approaches to preparing teachers for the moral work of teaching (MWT). The authors ultimately advocate the third of those presented: Intentional Moral Character Education. That approach integrates the first two, making explicit the moral content in each, and adding focused attention on treatments that foster the development of moral qualities such as virtue. This approach is then illustrated in a postbaccalaureate teacher certification program that has characteristics of both the infusion of the moral work of teaching across the curriculum as well as specialized courses that focus on that moral work as part of best practice instruction in classrooms.

Chapter 9 comes from Marilyn Watson, Karen Benson, Lana Daly, and Joy Pelton. The chapter provides an overview of the extensive, well-documented work of the Child Development Project's program of social and moral development for elementary classrooms, and examines efforts to integrate its materials and practices into two teacher education programs at California State University, Sacramento. The account highlights many of the challenges teacher candidates face in developing a teaching practice consistent with the program's recommendations, and the ways teacher educators helped them meet those challenges within their teacher education programs.

Chapter 10, from Larry Nucci, draws upon his experience at the University of Illinois, Chicago, and the University of California, Berkeley, in teacher education programs that developed a strong focus on preparing candidates for the MWT. Based upon student work products, exams, and surveys, along with experiences working with faculty, Nucci argues for the importance of infusing the MWT throughout teacher education programs, in much the same way that moral education is to be infused in the K–12 curriculum. This model follows a Brunerian spiral curriculum, in which candidates have repeated opportunities to extend their understanding of the MWT, and gain skills in applying that understanding in analyzing and responding to classroom situations.

In Chapter 11 David Shields, Wolfgang Altoff, Marvin Berkowitz, and Virginia Navarro describe the systematic initiative to infuse character education throughout their teacher education curriculum at the University of Missouri–St. Louis. Their description of this initiative focuses primarily on their program and professional development efforts related to their evolving taxonomy of character education competencies and their approach to implementing these competencies throughout their teacher education program. Their recommendations focus on the need for collaboration, leadership, professional development, salient goals, integration, accountability, and contextual fit.

CHAPTER 8

Teaching for Character

Three Alternatives for Teacher Education

Daniel Lapsley, Anthony C. Holter, and Darcia Narvaez

The concern over the proper induction of the younger generation by the older into the norms and canons of good conduct is probably a universal of the human experience. For this reason the work of character development is a broadly shared goal that animates the work of socialization agents in every contextual setting that involves children, but most especially in classrooms and schools where youngsters and teens spend most of their time outside of the family home. The development of character has been an explicit aim of education ever since the emergence of common schools and the rise of systems of public education (McClellan, 1999). How well schools have come to discharge this mission is broadly contested and the source of periodic but intense national dialogue (Goodman & Lesnick, 2001).

The status and efficacy of moral character education is the target of several recent reviews (Berkowitz, Battistich, & Bier, 2008; Lapsley & Narvaez, 2006; Lapsley & Yeager, 2013). In this chapter we attempt to link what is known about effective character education with strategies that might serve as a basis for teacher preparation. As everyone knows, nothing much happens in educational reform unless teachers do it and principals enable it. How teachers and principals organize classrooms and schools to deliver effective character education will hinge importantly on how moral character education is understood.

Some theorists are alarmed at the present status of moral character education in educational policy debates. Kristjansson (2002) points to a crumbling of belief in direct moral character formation in schools, which is either a cause or consequence of moral concerns being sidelined from mainstream educational discourse. In his view, the duty of schools to cultivate the character of children has been marginalized in the Western world. Perhaps we have lost our nerve or else lost contact with resources that would justify explicit moral character education in terms that do not excite intractable culture wars about "whose values" are taught and for what ends.

We contend that the case for moral character education is simpler than has been supposed. There is little need to invoke the litany of alarm about the rising tide of youth disorder or to engage in tendentious historical analysis of who is responsible for allegedly purging character from the curriculum. Instead, as the chapters in this book make clear, the case is made by pointing to the fact that moral values are immanent to school life and that instruction in values is inescapable and inevitable. Values are infused in every interaction of teaching and learning, from selection of topics and insistence on high standards and respect for truth, to expectations and modalities of community and discipline that govern school life (Carr, 1991). Indeed, the classroom environment is saturated with moral values and ripe with opportunities to engage students' moral character formation. It is not "if" character education should be taught in the classroom, but rather "how consciously and by what methods" (Howard, Berkowitz, & Schaeffer, 2004, p. 210).

Moral language—the language of right relation and what is worth doing—has never been absent in schools and continues apace. How best to prepare teachers to speak well the language of morality and, indeed, for recognizing occasions that require it, is a significant challenge for teacher education. This is a task that many teachers and educational leaders feel ill equipped to undertake, and it is also one that is underrepresented in many preservice teacher formation programs (Schwartz, 2008).

In the first section of this chapter we propose three strategies to prepare teachers for moral character education. We call these strategies (1) Best Practice Education, (2) Broad Character Education, and (3) Intentional Moral Character Education. As we will show, there is something quite positive to be said about each approach, although we will come down in favor of the third option but on the proviso that constructive Best Practice animates it. Then we provide an example of a teacher education program based on the third approach and close with implications for teacher education.

MORAL EDUCATION IN TEACHER EDUCATION

The relative neglect of moral character education in the formal preservice teacher curriculum has at least two proximal causes (Narvaez & Lapsley, 2008). The first is the daunting surfeit of training objectives that already crowd the academic curriculum of teaching majors. When faced with the reality of finite credit hours available for teacher education, along with the demands of external accreditation and state licensing requirements, many teacher educators assume that the preservice curriculum leaves little room for formal training in moral character education. Research suggests that the focus on other and more pressing federal requirements, such as adequate yearly progress, effectively squeeze out other important programs from the official school curriculum (Schwartz, 2008). The second cause is that often it is not at all clear what it would mean to equip preservice teachers to take up the mission of moral character education, even if there was an intentional commitment to do so in preservice teacher training programs.

How can we equip preservice teachers with the skills to take up their task as moral educators? What would training for character and ethical development look like? If moral character education is to be formally and optimally integrated into the classroom, then much is required in the preparation of the teachers who are the architects of these learning environments. Narvaez and Lapsley (2008) originally proposed two options that they termed a "minimalist" and "maximalist" approach to the preparation of teachers for moral character education.

What we previously called the minimalist approach to character education (Narvaez & Lapsley, 2008) was an undifferentiated blend of Best Practice and Broad Character Education. This minimalist perspective asserted that "the knowledge base that supports best practice instruction is coterminous with what is known to influence the moral formation of students" (Narvaez & Lapsley, 2008, p. 158), meaning that a substantially larger or different tool box of instructional practices is not necessary for becoming an effective character educator. We take up this view first.

Best Practice Education Perspective

Best Practice views character education as immanent to best practice instruction. Character formation is an outcome of good education (Berkowitz & Bier, 2005). Consequently there is little need for specialized instruction or design of distinctly "moral" education curriculum. Rather, character development is an outcome of effective teaching. It is a precipitate of best practice instruction. In order to be assured that the moral formation of students will be in good hands, the teacher educator need only ensure that preservice teachers are prepared to be outstanding teachers.

In many ways this is already the default stance in schools. Schools marked by pervasive best practice have students who want to be there, who feel a strong sense of connection to teachers, and who experience school as a caring community.

There is now substantial evidence that building students' connection to caring school communities has the most pervasive and strongest relationship to a range of outcomes of traditional interest to character educators. Payne, Gottfredson, and Gottfredson (2003) showed, for example, that schools characterized by communal organization—mutually supportive relationships among teachers, administrators, and students; a sense of collaboration; and commitment to common goals and norms—tended to have students who reported attachment to school, a sense of belonging, and belief in the legitimacy of rules and norms.

Indeed, youth who feel connected to school are less likely to be delinquent, use substances, initiate early sexual activity, or engage in violent behavior. They are more likely to report higher levels of academic motivation and lower levels of physical and emotional distress (Battistich, 2008; Elias, Parker, Kash, Weissberg, & O'Brien, 2008; Hawkins, Guo, Hill, Battin-Pearson, & Abbot, 2001). And the benefits of school connectedness have longer term effects. Data from the National Longitudinal Study of Adolescent Health showed that the sense of belonging to school predicted less depressive symptoms, social rejection, and school problems; and greater optimism and higher grades *1 year later* (Anderman, 2002). Loukas, Ripperger-Suhler, and Horton (2009) report similar findings. In their study middle school adolescents who reported low levels of school connectedness showed increases in conduct problems 1 year later. Low connectedness in late middle school was also associated with greater anxiety, depressive symptoms, and marijuana use in high school and 1 year after high school (Bond et al., 2007). School connectedness can also buffer the negative effects of poor parenting (Loukas, Roalson, & Herrera, 2010).

And what promotes connection and community? According to a report of the National Research Council (2003), it is not anything exotic or even curricular. It involves educational practices well within the wheelhouse of best practice education, including not separating students into vocational and academic tracks, setting high academic standards for everyone, giving all students the same core curriculum, creating small-size learning communities, forming multidisciplinary education teams, and providing opportunities for service and experiential learning and community service. Moreover, the Best Practice approach is underscored by several of the 11 principles for effective character education promoted by the Character Education Partnership (CEP; Beland, 2003). It aligns with:

- Principle 4, regarding caring school communities
- Principle 6, on the importance of rigorous academic curriculum
- Principle 7, with respect to fostering intrinsic motivation to do the right thing by building a climate of trust and respect, by encouraging autonomy, by building shared norms, and by class meetings and democratic decision making

In short, the Best Practice approach endorses a set of well-attested pedagogical strategies that are considered educational best practice, including cooperative learning, democratic classrooms, and constructivist approaches to teaching and learning. It endorses practices that cultivate autonomy, intrinsic motivation, and community engagement (Beland, 2003). It requires authoritative leadership in the classroom much like authoritative parenting in the home (Wentzel, 2002). And it has the added virtue of requiring no significant alteration of preservice teacher training.

However, the problem with this approach is that while it *foregrounds* best instructional and educational practice it *backgrounds* intentional values education, and so is susceptible to the charge that it is content to remand moral character education to the *hidden* curriculum. But the Best Practice moral education strategy is the first in this continuum of strategies precisely because it is the foundation for effective education in general and a requirement for more intentional training in moral character education. In our view a teacher is an effective moral educator to the extent that he or she is an effective educator, and this requires expertise in pedagogical content knowledge (Shulman, 1987), including content knowledge specific to moral education.

Broad Character Education Perspective

Lapsley and Narvaez (2006) drew a distinction between broad and narrow character education and character education conceived as a treatment or an outcome. Often the case for character education is made on the basis of troubling epidemiological trends on adolescent risk behavior. On this account character education is needed because there is an epidemic of poor academic achievement, school dropout, cheating, premarital sex, adolescent pregnancy, and substance use. Showing disrespect, using bad language, and attempting suicide are forms of irresponsible behavior (Brooks & Goble, 1997). Presumably these risk behaviors bear the mark of poor moral character. Consequently, any program that drives down these trends—that is, programs that encourage school persistence, improve social skills, discourage the use of drugs and alcohol, and prevent sexual activity and pregnancy, and so on—might qualify as a moral education program.

Broad Character Education refers, then, to a wide range of psychosocial prevention, intervention, and health promotion programs that cover a wide range of purposes, including health education, problem solving, life skills training, and positive youth development, among others. These programs are folded under character education because they bring about desirable outcomes. Moreover, the success of risk reduction interventions and positive youth development are claimed for "what works" in character education because, after all, "they are all school-based endeavors designed to help foster the positive development of youth" (Berkowitz & Bier, 2005, p. 5).

One limitation of Broad Character Education is that it is motivated by literatures that are absent the language of morality, virtue, and character. Developmental science, including developmental psychopathology and the science of prevention, already provide powerful theoretical frameworks for understanding risk, resilience, adaptation, and thriving that has little need for the language of character. The explanation for successful risk reduction interventions never mentions student gains in moral competence or in the acquisition of virtues, but instead refers to constructs and explanatory frameworks of developmental psychopathology. This broad conception of character education does not point to anything distinctive by way of *treatment*; and the only reason to treat them as instances of moral character education is because such interventions reduce or prevent problematic behaviors associated with the "rising tide of youth disorder" so commonly thought to reflect the absence of character education in the schools. But if character education is all of these things, then the singularity of character education as an educational program with a distinctive purpose is lost. Indeed, "there is little reason to appeal to character education, or use the language of moral valuation, to understand the etiology of risk behavior or how best to prevent or ameliorate exposure to risk or promote resilience and adjustment" (Lapsley & Narvaez, 2006, p. 259).

But perhaps this limitation is put too strongly. Broad Character Education has a number of attractive features. For example, it defines character education by its outcome rather than by method or intentions. It might indeed be the case that competent behavior hangs together as a cluster much the way that problem behavior does, and that any good cause in education, whether it be moral character formation or risk reduction, comes down to a common set of instructional practices. In this case it might not matter much if one practice is apportioned to moral character education and another to developmental psychopathology or positive youth development. Moreover, some positive youth development initiatives increasingly make explicit claims about the importance of character (Lerner, Dowling, & Anderson, 2003) or understand its programmatic outcomes as a contribution to moral character education (Elias et al., 2008). Finally, the literature on successful psychosocial interventions has important lessons for moral character education. It must be comprehensive, be guided by explicit theory, involve multiple components, be initiated early in development, and be sustained over time with suitable concern for implementation fidelity. For these reasons we recommend finding a place for Broad Character Education in the preservice teacher education curriculum.

As pointed out above, one characteristic of Broad Character Education is that it tends to define character education in terms of certain desirable outcomes. But what if character education is defined not in terms of outcome but in terms of *treatment*? What if moral character education is seen as the independent rather than the dependent variable?

Intentional Moral Character Education Perspective

The Intentional Moral Character approach addresses moral character education as the independent variable. It includes educational frameworks infused with moral valuation and a transparent theory of action whose objective is to influence the moral formation of children in classrooms and schools. It aims to influence children's moral capacities for the long term. Moral character education purposefully cultivates virtues or orients the dispositional qualities of youngsters toward morally desirable aims for normatively laudable reasons.

Hence, to justify moral character education in the Intentional Moral Character sense would seem to require facility with ethical theory or require some conception of how practice leads to the formation of virtuous dispositions. It affirms that education is not whole or complete without an intentional and sustained focus on the moral and character development of children. This perspective further asserts that "the Best Practice Perspective and the intermittent or occasional focus of the

Broad Character Education Perspective is necessary—but it is not sufficient to equip students with the skills necessary to negotiate the demands of modern life" and that "the task of preparing morally adept individuals requires a more intentional programmatic instructional focus" (Narvaez & Lapsley, 2008, p. 162).

Intentional Moral Character includes schools that endorse core values or have an avowedly religious ethos. Effective schools are those that are infused with a clear moral purpose, and the Character Education Partnership's core values Principle 1 makes this point (see Lickona, Schaps, & Lewis, 2003). Moreover, the most compelling of the CEP principles is Principle 5, which urges schools to give students an opportunity to engage in moral action. This insistence that education include a commitment to moral action makes the CEP principles something more than a mere catalogue of instructional best practice, although it is certainly that as well (Lapsley & Narvaez, 2006).

So this third view considers best practice as necessary but not sufficient for effective moral formation of pupils. Maybe at some point in the halcyon past it was sufficient, but in the present cultural milieu children are reared increasingly in toxic social environments that pose special challenges for their moral and social development (Garbarino, 1999; Garbarino & DeLara, 2004).

The Integrative Ethical Education (IEE; Narvaez, 2006) model is one example of how skill-building character education can be fully integrated into academic instruction and other aspects of school practice. IEE presents an empirically derived set of ethical skills to be taught through a novice-to-expert approach. Educators adapt the research-based framework to local needs (Narvaez, Bock, Endicott, & Lies, 2004). The framework is useful for preparing preservice teachers to become effective character educators, and as classroom- or school-based guidelines to facilitate moral character in their students once they are teachers in their own classrooms (Narvaez, 2006).

The five steps of the IEE model (see Table 8.1) start with the relational focus of caring communities (teacher-student relationships and classroom climate). Teachers design well-structured environments that sustain students by meeting basic needs and fostering flourishing; such positive "moral habitats" facilitate ethical activity and reflection, fostering ethical citizenship (Narvaez, 2010). Step 3 emphasizes skills and subskills in Rest's four components: sensitivity, judgment, focus, and action (Narvaez & Rest, 1995; Rest, 1983). Teacher guidebooks offer ideas for integrating novice-to-expert ethical skill instruction into academic instruction as well as advisory periods (Narvaez, 2006, 2009; Narvaez & Bock, 2009; Narvaez & Endicott, 2009; Narvaez & Lies, 2009). Step 4 emphasizes student self-authorship in moral character building, whereas Step 5 underscores the importance of integrating student flourishing into the fabric of community support.

There are many other curricular approaches to character education that would fit under the Intentional Moral Character Education rubric, with varying levels of conceptual complexity, rigor, and effectiveness (see Lapsley & Yeager, 2013). Our preference for this third approach is conditioned on a pedagogy that is consistent

Table 8.1. Integrative Ethical Education (IEE) Model

Step	Description
1.	Model and establish a close bond and secure attachment with each student
2.	Establish a sustaining classroom climate supportive of meeting student basic needs
3.	Cultivate ethical skills across the curriculum using novice-to-expert pedagogy
4.	Foster student self-regulation and self-authorship
5.	Connect students to and foster skill development with the home and local community

with cognitive-mediational perspectives on learning and constructivist best practice instruction. Moreover, there is recent interest in whether more "stealthy" approaches to moral character education (e.g., encouraging student attributions about the sort of person they are, or altering mind-sets about the malleability of personality) might prove as effective as wholesale curricular and school practice infusion, or else should be a component of such curricular practices (Lapsley & Yeager, 2013).

Summary

We outlined three strategies for preparing preservice teachers for their work as moral educators. The first strategy (Best Practice) focuses on the skills, knowledge, and dispositions to be the best possible teacher. The second strategy (Broad Character Education) is motivated by the language of developmental psychopathology and focuses on the programs, treatments, and interventions suggested by the literatures on risk and resilience, health promotion, and positive youth development. This approach seeks to reduce risk behavior by any treatment that works. The third strategy (Intentional Moral Character Education) is motivated by morality and virtue as treatment or is designed intentionally to effect change in the moral sensibilities of students as outcomes.

Our preference for the third strategy is motivated by the fact that it regards the language of morality (and cognate considerations, such as virtues, character, and values) as the intentional "treatment" fortified by constructivist best practices that also yield outcomes of interest to character education. The novice-to-expert skill-building framework of IEE and the several organizing principles of the Character Education Partnership would be good examples of a commitment to Intentional Best Practice in moral character education.

ALLIANCE FOR CATHOLIC EDUCATION: AN EXAMPLE

Is it possible to organize a teacher certification program that addresses the strategies outlined in this chapter? We teach in an innovative, accredited teacher formation program called the Alliance for Catholic Education (ACE) where these strategies are emphasized. ACE is a 2-year alternative teacher certification program that recruits and prepares approximately 90 classroom teachers each year for service in underresourced Catholic schools in communities across the southern and southwestern United States. Nearly all of ACE enrollees are recent college graduates who earned their baccalaureate degree in a field or discipline other than education. They complete graduate-level coursework and practical internships during a 9-week summer session prior to their first year of teaching, continue their graduate studies throughout the first academic year, and return to campus the following summer to repeat the cycle in their second year of service. ACE graduates earn a master's degree in education and qualify for an Indiana teaching license.

Outlining Course Content

What we would like to highlight here is that even within an alternative and time-constrained academic framework, the ACE program is able to place an intentional curricular focus on moral character education for novice teachers that integrates best practice preparation in classroom teaching. For example, in their second year ACE teachers take a required Development and Moral Education course tailored to the licensure area (i.e., middle school and high school teachers take an adolescence-focused course; elementary education teachers take a child-focused course). The course content is organized around the three pillars of the ACE conceptual framework (community, teacher professional knowledge, and spirituality), but what is emphasized is the seamless weave of teacher instructional strategies that cut across thematic emphases of the conceptual framework.

The 1st week of the course focuses on developmental contextualism whose paradigmatic themes resonate throughout the course and align with the pillar of community. Developmental contextualism highlights the importance of building proper contexts to support learning, development, and behavior, with the implication that character education can never rely simply on "fixing the kids" without also attending to the culture and climate of classrooms and schools. The various contexts of development are addressed (e.g., family, peers, classrooms, and neighborhoods) to undergird the importance of home-school connection and of strong mesosystem connections among the various contexts that contain children and the influence of developmental assets found in communities and neighborhoods. The authoritative leadership qualities of effective parenting and teaching are emphasized, pointing out that these parenting and teaching practices are associated with virtually every outcome of interest to character education, including academic competence and prosocial behavior.

In the 2nd week, taking up the second pillar of the ACE conceptual framework (teacher professional knowledge), students examine the research base supporting instructional best practice, including the literatures on intelligence, intellectual and cognitive development, and how these topics fold into a cognitive-mediational approach to constructivist best practice. ACE teachers learn in the 3rd week that constructivist teacher practices are represented among several of Character Education Partnership's principles of effective character education, with the implication explicitly drawn that good education is indeed effective character education.

The third pillar of the ACE conceptual framework is spirituality. This is a thematic element that is specific to the requirements for teaching in Catholic schools, but it is defined broadly to encompass a concern with values, morality, and character formation. There is explicit instruction in the literatures of moral development and in strategies of sociomoral education from different theoretical perspectives. Several of these strategies have broader applicability across the curriculum. For example, although just-community approaches to moral education evolved out of Kohlberg's specific theoretical paradigm, the key features of the model—such as class meetings, giving students "voice-and-choice," encouraging moral discussion, improving students' sense of connection to teachers and schools, and encouraging a sense of community—are now de rigueur in most accounts of effective schools (Blum, 2005).

Some sections introduce ACE teachers to specific moral character education curricula, such as Integrated Ethical Education designed by Narvaez (2006, 2007, 2008, 2010), or just-community and moral discussion strategies (Power, Higgins, & Kohlberg, 1987). Others introduce teachers to relevant instructional techniques promoted by Lemov's (2010) *Teach Like a Champion* approach, particularly techniques that create a strong classroom culture, set and maintain high behavioral expectations, and build character and trust.

The final week of the course takes up the literatures of risk and resilience and reviews psychosocial intervention and health promotion programs from both a developmental psychopathology and positive youth development perspective. Teachers learn about the elements of effective programs and the role of teachers in educational resilience in pupils.

The capstone event for ACE's Development and Moral Education course is a conference poster session that requires ACE students to prepare a unit in a content area. Students are required to justify pedagogical decisions by reference to relevant scholarly literatures, but also show how it advances moral character education. The poster must also illustrate how the lesson plan accommodates student exceptionalities and how learning objectives will be assessed. This exercise demonstrates how lesson plans have layered instructional objectives that include moral character elements at their very core.

Reflecting on Program Goals

The approach of ACE teacher formation emphasizes instructional goals that are distinctly moral and aim toward explicit character education, including instruction in specific moral character curricula and teaching strategies, while recognizing that these goals are animated and made possible by the pedagogical tools of constructivist best practice. It is Best Practice pedagogy linked with Intentional Moral Character Education content. But note also that our summer ACE class does not neglect Broad Character Education; indeed, it takes up the entire 4th week of instruction.

This intentional focus on moral character formation has particular resonance for ACE teachers insofar as moral and spiritual formation is an explicit charge of the Catholic schools in which they serve. But our recommendation does not hinge on parochial religious concerns but on the necessity of extracting moral language from the hidden curriculum of any school, and hence has wide applicability.

IMPLICATIONS FOR TEACHER EDUCATION

What teachers must know to be effective character educators will depend on what one believes about character education:

- Is it broad or narrow?
- Is it an outcome or treatment?
- Is it a specialized curriculum or a precipitate of best practice?

The three perspectives on how to prepare students for the moral work of teaching take different positions on these questions. The distinctions are not, of course, rigidly drawn, and indeed, teacher preparation would ideally include elements from all three perspectives, insofar as character education might just be all of these things—broad and narrow, treatment and outcome, a specialized curriculum and precipitate of best practice.

Moral education requires pedagogical content knowledge like any other instructional objective. Effective instruction will have good outcomes on a range of behaviors of interest to moral character educators, but such an effect will be catalyzed when best practice is yoked to intentional commitment to the content of morality, virtue, and values. That is, fortify intentional character education as a treatment (Intentional Moral Character) with best practice educational strategies as the intervention (Best Practice). What we gain with this hybrid approach is a framework that starts with best practice as a foundation and builds upon it the "moral cosmopolitanism" required of distinctive moral character education.

But the lessons of Broad Character Education should not be neglected. The frameworks of developmental psychopathology and positive youth development insist that context matters, and so effective moral character education can never be a simple matter of fixing the kids without addressing the instructional press of school culture and climate, and without engaging stakeholders at every level of developmental systems (e.g., family, peers, neighborhood, community). Effective moral character education must also have the features of all effective psychosocial interventions, and this is reason enough for preservice teachers to learn about risk and resilience, prevention, and promotion.

The fundamental challenge for teacher education, then, is to determine how much it wants to take seriously the moral work of teaching, and then to organize a conceptual framework that takes one or more of the three approaches noted here as the way forward. But staging this exercise only makes sense if the immanence and inevitability of moral formation in classrooms is extricated from the hidden curriculum.

One implication for teacher education is that the three approaches should be held in creative tension in coursework that is transparently integrative across the required program. This might require adopting a conceptual framework where the immanence and inevitability of values in education is the core of teacher preparation. In this framework, methods instructors would draw out the implications of best practice for behavioral outcomes of interest to character educators. Content instructors could help preservice teachers see the possibilities for addressing issues of morality and values in lesson planning. But the foundational course for pulling this together would be a "development and moral education" course (much like in ACE) where developmental science meets educational psychology in the service of moral character education.

REFERENCES

Anderman, E. M. (2002). School effects on psychological outcomes during adolescence. *Journal of Educational Psychology*, 94, 795–809.

Battistich, V. (2008). The Child Development Project: Creating caring school communities. In L. Nucci & D. Narvaez (Eds.), *Handbook of moral and character education* (pp. 328–351). New York: Routledge.

Beland, K. (Ed.). (2003). *Eleven principles sourcebook*. Washington, DC: Character Education Partnership.

Berkowitz, M. W., Battistich, V. A., & Bier, M. C. (2008). What works in character education: What is known and what needs to be known. In L. Nucci & D. Narvaez (Eds.), *Handbook of moral and character education* (pp. 414–431). New York: Routledge.

Berkowitz, M., & Bier, M. (2005). *What works in character education: A report for policy makers and opinion leaders*. Washington, DC: Character Education Partnership.

Blum, R. W. (2005). A case for school connectedness. *Educational Leadership, 62*, 16–20.

Bond, L., Butler, H., Thomas, L., Carlin, J., Glover, S., Bowers, G., & Patton, G. (2007). Social and school connectedness in early secondary school as predictors of late teenage substance use, mental health and academic outcomes. *Journal of Adolescent Health, 40*(4), 357.e9–357.e18.

Brooks, D., & Goble, F. (1997). *The case for character education*. Northbridge, CA: Studio 4 Productions.

Carr, D. (1991). *Educating the virtues: An essay on the philosophical psychology of moral development and education*. London: Routledge.

Elias, M. J., Parker, S. J., Kash, M. V., Weissberg, R. P., & O'Brien, M. U. (2008). Social and emotional learning, moral education and character education: A comparative analysis and a view toward convergence. In L. Nucci & D. Narvaez (Eds.), *Handbook of moral and character education* (pp. 248–266). New York: Routledge.

Gabarino, J. (1999). *Raising children in a socially toxic environment.* San Francisco: Jossey–Bass.

Garbarino, J., & DeLara, E. (2004). Coping with the consequences of school violence. In J. C. Conoley & A. P. Goldstein (Eds.), *School violence intervention: A practical handbook* (2nd ed., pp. 400–415). New York: Guilford Press.

Goodman, J., & Lesnick, H. (2001). *The moral stake in education: Contested premises and practices.* New York: Longman.

Hawkins D. J., Guo, J., Hill, K. G., Battin-Pearson, S., & Abbott, R. D. (2001). Long-term effects of the Seattle Social Development intervention on school bonding trajectories. *Applied Developmental Science, 5*(4), 225–236.

Howard, R. W., Berkowitz, M. W., & Schaeffer, E. F. (2004). Politics of character education. *Educational Policy, 18*(1), 188–215.

Kristjansson, K. (2002). In defense of "non-expansive" character education. *Journal of Philosophy of Education, 36*(2), 135–156.

Lapsley, D. K., & Narvaez, D. (2006). Character education. In W. Damon & R. Lerner (Series Eds.), A. Renninger & I. Siegel (Vol. Eds.), *Handbook of child psychology: Vol. 4. Child psychology in practice* (6th ed., pp. 248–296). Hoboken, NJ: Wiley.

Lapsley, D. K., & Yeager, D. (2013). Moral-character education. In I. Weiner (Series Ed.), W. Reynolds & G. Miller, (Vol. Eds.), *Handbook of psychology: Vol. 7. Educational psychology* (2nd ed., pp. 147–178). Hoboken, NJ: Wiley.

Lemov, D. (2010). *Teach like a champion: 49 techniques that put students on the path to college.* San Francisco: Jossey-Bass.

Lerner, R. M., Dowling, E. M., & Anderson, P. M. (2003). Positive youth development: Thriving as a basis of personhood and civil society. *Applied Developmental Science, 7*(3), 172–180.

Lickona, T., Schaps, E., & Lewis, C. (2003). *CEP's eleven principles of effective character education.* Washington, DC: Character Education Partnership.

Loukas, A., Ripperger-Suhler, K. G., & Horton, K. D. (2009). Examining temporal associations between school connectedness and early adolescent adjustment. *Journal of Youth and Adolescence, 38*(6), 804–812.

Loukas, A., Roalson, L. A., & Herrera, D. E. (2010). School connectedness buffers the effects of negative family relations and poor effortful control on early adolescent conduct problems. *Journal of Research on Adolescence, 20,* 13–22.

McClellan, B. W. (1999). *Moral education in America: Schools and the shaping of character from colonial times to the present.* New York: Teachers College Press.

Narvaez, D. (2006). Integrative ethical education. In M. Killen & J. G. Smetana (Eds.), *Handbook of moral education* (pp. 703–733). Mahwah, NJ: Lawrence Erlbaum Associates.

Narvaez, D. (2007). How cognitive and neurobiological sciences inform values education for creatures like us. In D. Aspin & J. Chapman (Eds.), *Values education and lifelong learning: Philosophy, policy, practices* (pp. 127–159). Dordrecht, Netherlands: Springer.

Narvaez, D. (2008). Human flourishing and moral development: Cognitive science and neurobiological perspectives on virtue development. In L. Nucci & D. Narvaez (Eds.), *Handbook of moral and character education* (pp. 310–327). Mahwah, NJ: Lawrence Erlbaum Associates.

Narvaez, D. (2009). *Ethical action.* Nurturing Character in the Classroom, EthEx Series, bk 4. Notre Dame, IN: Alliance for Catholic Education Press (ACE) Press.

Narvaez, D. (2010). Building a sustaining classroom climate for purposeful ethical citizenship. In T. Lovat & R. Toomey (Eds.), *International research handbook of values education and student wellbeing* (pp. 659–674). New York: Springer.

Narvaez, D., & Bock, T. (2009). *Ethical judgment.* Nurturing Character in the Classroom, EthEx Series, bk. 2. Notre Dame, IN: Alliance for Catholic Education Press (ACE) Press.

Narvaez, D., Bock, T., Endicott, L., & Lies, J. (2004). Minnesota's Community Voices and Character Education Project. *Journal of Research in Character Education, 2,* 89–112.

Narvaez, D., & Endicott, L. (2009). *Ethical sensitivity.* Nurturing Character in the Classroom, EthEx Series, bk.1. Notre Dame, IN: Alliance for Catholic Education Press (ACE) Press.

Narvaez, D., & Lapsley, D. K. (2008). Teaching moral character: Two alternatives for teacher education. *The Teacher Educator, 43,* 156–172.

Narvaez, D., & Lies, J. (2009). *Ethical motivation,* Nurturing Character in the Classroom, EthEx Series, bk. 3. Notre Dame, IN: Alliance for Catholic Education Press (ACE) Press.

Narvaez, D., & Rest, J. (1995). The four components of acting morally. In W. Kurtines & J. Gewirtz (Eds.), *Moral behavior and moral development: An introduction* (pp. 385–400). New York: McGraw-Hill.

National Research Council. (2003). *Engaging schools: Fostering high school student's motivation to learn.* Washington, DC: National Academies Press.

Payne, A., Gottfredson, G. D., & Gottfredson, D. C. (2003). Schools as communities: The relationships among communal school organization, student bonding, and school disorder. *Criminology, 41,* 749–778.

Power, C., Higgins, A., & Kohlberg, L. (1989). *Lawrence Kohlberg's approach to moral education.* New York: Columbia University Press.

Rest, J. (1983). Morality. In P. H. Mussen (Series Ed.), J. Flavell & E. Markman (Vol. Eds.), *Handbook of child psychology: Vol. 3. Cognitive development* (4th ed., pp. 556–629). Hoboken, NJ: Wiley.

Schwartz, M. (2008). Teacher preparation for character development. In L. Nucci & D. Narvaez (Eds.), *Handbook of moral and character education* (pp. 583–600). Mahwah, NJ: Lawrence Erlbaum Associates.

Shulman, L. S. (1987). Knowledge and teaching: Foundations of the new reform. *Harvard Educational Review, 57,* 1–22.

Wentzel, K. R. (2002). Are effective teachers like good parents? Teaching styles and student adjustment in early adolescence. *Child Development, 73,* 287–301.

CHAPTER 9

Integrating Social and Ethical Development into the Preservice Curriculum

Building on the Child Development Project

Marilyn Watson, Karen D. Benson, Lana Daly, and Joy Pelton

The Child Development Project (CDP) was an experimental professional development program that successfully helped experienced elementary school teachers in
diverse settings across the United States foster their students' prosocial development. Drawing from research and working with teachers over a 15-year period,
the CDP staff developed a variety of educational practices, supportive curriculum
materials, and video and narrative examples to help teachers integrate students'
social, emotional, and ethical development into their ongoing instructional program.[1] This chapter is about the integration of materials and practices of CDP
into preservice teacher preparation. We begin with an overview of CDP, under
its program director, Marilyn Watson, and follow with how Karen Benson, Lana
Daly, and Joy Pelton adapted core aspects of CDP into two teacher preparation
programs at California State University, Sacramento.

OVERVIEW OF THE CHILD DEVELOPMENT PROJECT

Like teacher preparation programs, elementary schools are mandated to cover several curriculum areas and an expanding number of topics within each area. Knowing these challenges, the CDP staff devised ways to integrate a social and ethical
focus into the academic content and classroom management procedures common
to elementary schools (Watson, Solomon, Battistich, Schaps, & Solomon, 1989).

Thus the CDP presented a promising model for use in the similarly overcrowded preservice teacher education curricula.

The CDP program was initially drawn from the theoretical and empirical literature on the antecedents of caring, cooperative, and responsible behavior available in the early 1980s. From this literature came the project's focus on empathy induction, interpersonal understanding, prosocial action, instruction in social and emotional competencies, and the discussion of prosocial values.

Program Components

Three approaches were at the heart of the original CDP classroom program:

- A literature-based language arts program designed to stimulate children's enjoyment of reading while helping them build empathy for others and a commitment to prosocial values
- A cooperative approach to classroom learning that emphasized learning to work with others in fair, caring, and responsible ways
- Developmental Discipline, an approach to classroom discipline that focused on building caring and trusting relationships with and among students, used induction and a teaching approach to student misbehavior, and involved students in developing and upholding classroom norms and values

With time and experience working in schools, the program developers came to see the creation of a "caring community of learners" as an essential intermediate goal of the project, and the classroom components were seen as both dependent on such a community for their effectiveness as well as vehicles for creating community (Solomon, Watson, Battistich, Schaps, & Delucchi, 1996). The nature and role of the classroom community became a central part of the CDP program. At this point in the project's evolution, CDP's view of children's learning and social development integrated theory and research on attachment and socialization within the family with constructivist pedagogical theory. Additionally, the evidence of the undermining effects of extrinsic rewards and punishment on intrinsic or internal motivation (Lepper & Green, 1978) led the project to develop pedagogical and classroom management strategies that minimize or eliminate the use of extrinsic rewards and punishments.

The nature of the community that emerged as core to the CDP program incorporated ideas that were consistent with several educational theorists and researchers. It was democratic (Dewey, 1916/1980), caring (Noddings, 1984, 1992), just (Power, Higgins, & Kohlberg, 1989), and constructivist (Piaget, 1932/1965; Vygotsky, 1978) and explicitly focused on meeting the psychological needs of students for reasonable autonomy, belonging, and competence (Deci & Ryan, 1985). (For a more thorough description of the CDP program, see Battistich, 2008.)

Supporting Teachers in the Implementation of the CDP Program

For many teachers, the CDP represented profound changes in their beliefs about teaching and learning and substantial changes in their long-standing classroom practice. In particular, the project's curriculum and pedagogical strategies stressed the importance of fostering students' intrinsic motivation. At the time the project was first implemented, and prevailing today, many teachers believed that students are primarily motivated by self-interest and that classroom motivation needs to involve competition, rewards, and punishments.

Similarly, the project's constructivist approach to teaching was different from the direct instruction used by most teachers in the 1980s and 1990s. The CDP's curriculum and pedagogical practices focused on helping students construct their understanding of both academic and social-moral issues, while encouraging teachers to take a scaffolding or guiding, rather than telling, approach to instruction.

To scaffold the teachers' understanding of the project's goals and processes, the staff created curriculum materials to support teachers' performance of its component activities; that is, guidelines for

- Class meetings (Developmental Studies Center [DSC], 1996)
- Collaborative learning (DSC, 1997a)
- Literature (DSC, 1998a, 1998b)
- Cross-grade buddy activities (DSC, 1997b)

Further, the CDP staff created videotapes of the program components as they unfolded in classrooms of experienced teachers.

Evaluation and Outcomes

When a majority of teachers in a school implemented the program, CDP had wide and long-lasting effects. Students showed positive changes in a broad range of areas, for example, greater commitment to democratic values, better conflict resolution skills, more concern for others, trust in and respect for teachers, prosocial motivation, and altruistic and positive interpersonal behavior. Students in these schools also showed increased intrinsic academic motivation, class engagement, enjoyment of class, and liking for school (Solomon, Battistich, Watson, Schaps, & Lewis, 2000).

Positive findings were also found in two middle school follow-up studies. Students from CDP program schools were more engaged in and committed to school, more prosocial, had a higher sense of personal efficacy, and engaged in fewer problem behaviors than comparison students. Program students also had higher academic performance, and they associated with peers who were more prosocial and less antisocial than their matched comparison students (Battistich, Schaps, & Wilson, 2004).

One consistent finding of the CDP that has had a significant effect on approaches to moral education relates to the importance of school and classroom community. In all three studies of the effects of the CDP, students' sense of community was related to a broad range of positive student outcomes (Battistich, Solomon, Watson, & Schaps, 1997).

CDP and Preservice Education

Once it became clear that the CDP program had positive effects on students' social and ethical development, Watson began integrating the materials and practices into a course on social and moral development in the Developmental Teacher Education program at the University of California, Berkeley. The students were generally receptive to the CDP ideas and practices and found the curriculum materials and videos helpful. Still, the preservice students wanted to know, how does one get from the beginning of the year, before a trusting community has been built, to the classrooms of trusting, collaborative students depicted in the videos?

This experience led Watson to decide to videotape a classroom starting with the first day of school and periodically throughout the year. An appropriate classroom would need to satisfy three criteria:

- Anyone would see it as a "difficult" educational setting.
- The teacher would need to be a good implementer of the CDP program.
- The teacher would need to be open to having others see her difficulties and missteps as well as her successes.

Laura Ecken and her full-inclusion, combination 2nd-/3rd-grade class, in a school that shared a chain link fence with the largest housing project in the state of Kentucky, fit all the criteria. Laura agreed, and the taping began on the first day of school and continued periodically across 2 school years. From these tapes and weekly conversations with Laura, Watson crafted the book *Learning to Trust: Transforming Difficult Elementary Classrooms Through Developmental Discipline* that chronicled the instructional, discipline, and management practices that Laura used to mold her struggling class into a caring community of learners (Watson & Ecken, 2003).

Watson then began a series of weeklong summer institutes for teacher education faculty to introduce the developing CDP materials and gain guidance on how to further shape the materials to serve the goals of preservice teacher educators. Because many teacher educators are guided by the same theory and research that shaped the CDP program, she hoped that they would find the materials useful in their own unique teacher preparation programs. Teacher educators from across the country integrated the practices and materials in different ways. What follows is the story told by Benson, Daly, and Pelton of how CDP was integrated into two separate teacher preparation programs at California State University, Sacramento (CSUS).

STRENGTHENING THE CSUS FOCUS ON
EDUCATION FOR DEMOCRACY

In the late 1990s we and other teacher education faculty at CSUS believed that our program needed a stronger focus on education for democracy. The faculty shared Dewey's view of the classroom as a cauldron for building students' understanding of and commitment to the principles of democracy, but realized that this view wasn't receiving enough emphasis in our programs. To make Dewey's view more central would involve intentionally educating teacher candidates about how to build democratic classroom communities and develop in their students the skills, values, and understandings that undergird a democratic way of life.

Given the crowded curriculum, adding a course was out of the question. Yet the current course in classroom management was not equipping our students with the knowledge and competencies they needed to build democratic classrooms. The solution was to reorganize the classroom management course into a comprehensive 2-semester pedagogy course that included classroom management, discipline, community building, and effective teaching strategies. This integration would enable our students to build the kind of moral, democratic communities we envisioned.

At CSUS the teacher preparation programs are fifth-year programs run in semiautonomous "centers" located in different Sacramento area school districts. All centers focus on preparing teachers for urban, multicultural settings. Students are grouped into cohorts of approximately 25 to 30 students, and each center has a coordinator and its own faculty. While the programs at all centers involve the same set of core courses, center programs can differ in emphasis and length (2 semesters or 3 semesters with student teaching, and 2-year internship programs), and the faculty can use different texts and student assignments. This semi-autonomous "center" structure allowed us to incorporate the principles of CDP into the CSUS program in unique ways.

What follows is how the CDP principles were incorporated in a center in the Folsom/Cordova District that involved 2 semesters of coursework and student teaching, and a center in the Sacramento City District that began with summer coursework followed by 2 years of full-time teaching, weekly coaching, and evening seminars.

As our center programs were being reorganized, we were introduced to the CDP program at the institutes for teacher educators described earlier in this chapter. We then worked to reshape the two CSUS centers' programs to better achieve the goals of CDP: a Deweyan, constructivist philosophical focus and an integrated approach to social/ethical teaching and discipline.

LEARNING AND PRACTICING DEVELOPMENTAL DISCIPLINE:
INSTRUCTIONAL STRATEGIES

Many of our students come expecting they will achieve classroom control through the careful use of rewards and "consequences." This is not surprising since most of our students were in elementary school during the heyday of Assertive Discipline (Cantor, 1976). Yet most also arrive quite daunted by the idea of managing a classroom of children from different cultures and socioeconomic backgrounds. They expect they will be given "recipes" for how to manage students so they can "teach." We view both of these attitudes as incompatible with building a democratic community and fostering students' intrinsic desire to learn and to act kindly and responsibly.

In our two centers we teach students a single, well-grounded approach to classroom management and discipline. We chose to use the CDP approach, Developmental Discipline, described earlier in the chapter. Instructing our preservice students in the theory and practices of Developmental Discipline enabled us to focus on building democratic classroom communities, while also providing our students with concrete instructional and management practices that would enable them to create such communities in their own classrooms. For example, to meet children's need for autonomy, our teacher candidates are taught ways to give students voice in the classroom by involving them in class meetings to decide class rules and procedures and providing student choice in academic activities. To meet children's need for belonging, our teacher candidates are taught to build caring relationships with and among students, for example, by engaging them in relationship-building activities, providing opportunities for them to work together, teaching them how to be friends, and refraining from punishment. To meet children's need for competence, teacher candidates are taught to scaffold students' learning, use differentiated instruction, and avoid competition as a means of motivation. We help our candidates understand that their students are in the process of developing their understanding of fairness and their abilities to regulate their emotions and understand others.

Learning and practicing Developmental Discipline is not easy, especially given our students' preconceptions of discipline as a set of techniques for controlling children, and the current atmosphere in many schools where teachers are pressured to use "efficient" reward/punishment-based approaches to classroom management. To help them shift toward Developmental Discipline, we used four instructional strategies—experiential learning/modeling, real-life examples, supportive curriculum guides, and careful course coordination.

Experiential Learning/Modeling

We immerse our teacher candidates in the same kind of social and moral learning community we are teaching them to create.

Creating Community. We place our students in cohorts, engage them in community and relationship building, involve them in determining how our classes will be run, and problem-solve with them when things go awry. By undergoing their own concrete experiences of community in the Educational Foundations and Pedagogy classes, they learn ways to create similar learning experiences with their own students. From the very first day, we engage our students in relationship-, community-, and trust-building activities, reflecting with them on how these activities create a sense of belonging and build a community that supports their learning. As the following comments from students' course reflections indicate, these experiences of community are not lost on them.

> Pedagogy class—gives our cohort the chance to BE the community we're always talking about. I LOVE the way we actually experience [moral education] rather than just hear a lecture. (Student, 2-semester program)

> I've really enjoyed feeling what it is like to be a part of a community. . . . Having this experience [helps] me to effectively institute these practices in my own classroom. (Student, 2-semester program)

Providing Autonomy Experiences. While our program, like all teacher preparation programs, has a long list of required competencies for students to master, we strive to incorporate autonomy experiences for them. We provide students choice in how they carry out course assignments, and we have developed an autonomy experience called Paravision in which individual students voluntarily conduct a conversation and reflect with their cohort around a classroom incident or issue with which they are struggling (Benson et al., 1995). Students describe incidents or issues and invite comments, questions, and suggestions from fellow students. Each student privately decides how to use whatever ideas surface during the Paravision session.

Cooperative Learning Activities. We want our students to learn to conduct cooperative learning lessons that incorporate instruction in social and moral as well as academic competencies and engage their students in reflection on their learning. Therefore, we regularly engage them in and reflect with them about small-group activities in which we emphasize academic, social, and moral learning.

In the Educational Foundations and Pedagogy courses, and through student-teaching supervision, we not only use the pedagogical techniques described above but also periodically ask the students to reflect and identify instances of these approaches that they have experienced in their classes. We constantly convey the message that the experiential process of our classes is a big part of the content of the classes. This consistent modeling and reflection builds our students' deep understanding of these pedagogical techniques and their commitment to using these techniques in their classrooms.

I love that you use some of the techniques you suggest <u>we</u> use with our kids—on us! Seriously, it speaks to the sincerity of your message and the earnestness of your belief in these methods—and that is very important to me. (Student, 2-semester program)

Real-life Concrete Examples

The selection of cooperating teachers in our program is very careful and deliberate; nevertheless, few of our cooperating teachers exemplify all the approaches to instruction and classroom management we are teaching our students. We realized our teacher candidates needed examples of teachers using the most current pedagogical, management, and disciplinary techniques we are intending them to use in their future classrooms. We provided this with three different types of examples: (1) Watson's rich narrative of one teacher's classroom experiences (Watson & Ecken, 2003), (2) guided observations in and conversations with selected local teachers, and (3) CDP videos of lessons and activities from a variety of classrooms across the country.

The Laura Factor. Perhaps our most powerful example is provided by the story of Laura Ecken and her class of 2nd- and 3rd-grade students. In *Learning to Trust* (Watson & Ecken, 2003), Laura offers direct access to the thinking, practices, successes, and failures of a real teacher using Developmental Discipline with a classroom of inner-city kids beginning on the 1st day of school and continuing across 2 years. Our student teachers use this book across all semesters, reflecting on Laura's goals, practices, successes, and failures, as well as her students' behaviors, motivations, and responses. They compare their students to Laura's and their classroom situations to those that Laura faces and report that they frequently ask themselves, "What would Laura do?" when faced with classroom challenges. Because our student teachers are intentionally placed in very diverse classrooms, their experiences are akin to Laura's. This powerful narrative text has been extremely useful in helping our candidates understand their students, especially their more challenging ones, and believe in the possibility of establishing in their own classrooms a caring and democratic learning community, plus understand the intricacies involved in doing so.

Learning to Trust is so relevant and important to what I am doing in my teaching right now. I feel very connected to the situation in Laura's class and have reactions to her class's actions and attitudes as if they were students in my classroom. (Student in 2-semester program reflecting on her student teaching experience)

Laura, in *Learning to Trust,* provides examples of how she orchestrates a powerful learning environment in a diverse context while building a caring community. Her examples also reveal her students' internal motivation to be good learners as well as good people. As our preservice teachers read and learn, they develop a personal connection that helps them translate the theory into their own classroom experiences. They appreciate that Laura makes mistakes, and her reflections on her mistakes provide a comforting model for them as they make their own inevitable mistakes.

> I feel a very strong connection to Laura because she is not perfect and she makes mistakes, but she still genuinely loves her students and cares about their well being. (Student intern reflecting in her dialogic journal)

Guided Observations. A question student teachers often ask us is, "If social, moral, and emotional development of students is this important, how come I don't see more teachers doing it in many of the classrooms we are in?" To respond, we find other exceptional teachers, like Laura Ecken, who emphasize moral and social development, practice Developmental Discipline, and are willing to invite the student teaching cohort into their classrooms to observe. We call this experience *guided observation.* The student teachers prepare questions ahead of time for the "guided observation teacher" about what they would like to "see." The teacher models how he or she incorporates strategies for community building as well as social and ethical learning into the curriculum. After the observation, the teacher debriefs the experience with the student teachers.

> It only took a few hours in Danielle's [guided observation teacher] class to see the bottom line: Developmental Discipline is worth it. The joy that we all bought into, from the songs, from Danielle's infectious enthusiasm, from the classroom atmosphere, from seeing kids making good choices, that is good enough reason to put in the time and effort [to build community]. (Student, 2-semester program)

Classroom Videos. We also show videotapes of aspects of CDP in a variety of classrooms from different communities across the country. For example, a video called *September* depicts beginning-of-the-year class meetings in which a class of 5th- and 6th-grade students determine the norms they want their class to live by. Another called *Teasing* shows that same class reflecting at midyear on how well they have lived up to their norms. *Two Boys/One Chair* shows a Kindergarten teacher scaffolding the problem solving between two boys who struggle to occupy the same chair. *Inside a Learning Community* presents a variety of community building activities in Laura Ecken's 2nd- and 3rd-grade classroom.[2]

Supportive Curriculum Guidelines

We use several theoretically consistent, detailed curriculum guidelines for classroom activities to illustrate how to build caring communities, to help support students as they struggle to accommodate the demands of schooling, and to increase students' social, moral, and academic competencies. Two books published as part of the Responsive Classroom series, *The First Six Weeks of School* (Denton & Kriete, 2000) and *The Morning Meeting Book* (Kriete & Bechtel, 2002), help our students view the start of school through their students' eyes, explain activities that help students make a successful entry into the classroom, and model how to build a caring community. Our students also find the book *Tribes: A New Way of Learning and Being Together* (Gibbs, 2001) useful in designing activities to help their students exchange personal information, build caring relationships, and develop resilience. Marvin Marshall's *Discipline Without Stress, Punishments or Rewards* (2002) emphasizes student self-responsibility for behavior and provides our students additional examples of an approach to classroom discipline focused on intrinsic motivation and social/moral instruction.

Blueprints for a Collaborative Classroom (DSC, 1997a) provides detailed guidance and support as our students struggle to orchestrate small-group learning experiences that are both cooperative and academically productive. The book provides models or blueprints for 25 different types of cooperative lessons. While our preservice teachers might observe students working in groups in their placement classrooms, they seldom see small-group lessons that involve clear social and ethical, as well as academic, instruction and reflection. The book's clear guidelines, lively activities, helpful hints gleaned from experienced teachers, and illustrative vignettes have proven extremely useful in building our students' commitment to cooperative learning strategies and their ability to successfully implement them.

> The purpose of one of the collaborative lessons that I implemented was to build inclusion for the success of the culminating activity of the gold rush unit. . . . Due to the fact that each student felt his or her ideas were respected and considered in the group decision, they transitioned smoothly into the academic task of representing and sharing themselves through the graphic arts strategy with ease and confidence . . . the measure of control over the learning was transferred to the students in a productive way [and] . . . helped me to understand what we as educators mean when we say that we want a student-centered approach to learning. (Student reflecting on her solo student teaching experience)

Course Coordination

We have carefully coordinated student teaching supervision with the content of our Educational Foundations and Pedagogy courses. The student teaching supervisor and the faculty of these courses communicate frequently about issues raised by our students. For example, in Educational Foundations our students read Dewey (1916/1980) on democracy in the schools, Noddings (1984, 1992) on the importance of caring, and Kohn (1991) on the harmful effects of extrinsic motivators in the classroom. At the same time, in Pedagogy our student teachers are being introduced to practical approaches for fostering intrinsic motivation, building caring relationships, and establishing democratic classroom communities. Concurrently, in their student teacher placements, students are practicing how to teach social and emotional skills, develop discipline plans that focus on intrinsic motivation and avoid rewards and punishments, and create and conduct cooperative classroom academic lessons that also focus on teaching social and ethical competencies. Coordination between the educational content of the Pedagogy class and the practical experiences of student teaching is enhanced by the biweekly reflections our student teachers write comparing the educational practices and student learning and behavior in their placement classrooms with Laura's classroom in *Learning to Trust.*

ASSESSING OUR SUCCESS

Based on our students' reflections, projects, and student teaching, we are confident that most students graduate from our programs with the knowledge and commitment they will need to integrate social and ethical learning into the academic curriculum.

One of the culminating program assignments is the creation of a discipline and management plan for leading their own future classroom and managing all the details of classroom life, one that is consistent with their educational goals for and beliefs about children and that focuses on managing the learning environment as well as the children. These plans typically include:

- Class meetings and other community- and relationship-building activities
- Instructional strategies that provide students with choice and involve them in partner or small-group learning experiences
- Strategies for managing student behavior that involve reflection, teaching, and a focus on intrinsic reasons for good behavior

When the student teachers solo teach, they implement their plans as much as possible, keeping in mind the policies of their cooperating teacher. They leave our program with an integrated plan for managing their future classrooms. But, do our students successfully implement their plans and hold on to their beliefs and goals in today's high-pressure, high-stakes classroom and school environments?

To find out how sustainable the principles and practices of our fledgling student teachers were, we sent out surveys to 163 of our graduates from the past 7 years to help us answer the above question. SurveyMonkey® made it possible for the responses to be returned anonymously. Forty-six e-mails bounced, and we received 40 completed surveys, including voluntary comments. These completed surveys represented every grade level from Pre-K through middle school, and the average number of years of teaching experience was 4.8 years, ranging from 1 to 9 years. Our main goal for the survey was to gain information about the degree to which our former students have maintained a focus on (1) reflective practices, (2) the teaching of social and moral competencies, and (3) the integrated approach to classroom management and discipline they developed while in our program. We ended the survey by asking about job satisfaction.

Reflective Practices

Sixty-five percent of respondents indicated that they engage their students in reflection about their behavior every day with the remaining 35% indicating that they did so one to three times a week. The use of reflection on learning was less frequent, with 50% reporting daily reflection and 37% two to three times a week. Four respondents commented that they believed they should reflect more frequently with their students about their learning, but find it difficult to take the time.

> The day goes by so fast, I find it hard to stop and take a moment for reflection. (Years teaching and grade level(s) not indicated)

Teaching Values and Social and Emotional Competencies

Ninety-seven percent of respondents reported that the teaching of values and social and emotional competencies were important to their teaching goals, with 87% indicating that such teaching was very important. Only one respondent checked that the teaching of values and social skills was unimportant, and a second indicated that while the teaching of values is somewhat important, there is "no time in the real world of teaching." The comments that many students added to the survey helped us see just how truly invested these former students are in the moral work of teaching.

> Both of these are at the heart of everything we do each day. (Seven years teaching, 2 in 5th and 5 in 8th grade)

> It's our job not just to teach children about what it means to be a good student, but what it means to be a good person, and to have pride in themselves. (Five years teaching 1st grade.)

> Character education was a large component of my daily classroom activities— my students' social and emotional skills were extremely diverse, from several children identified as emotionally disturbed to children who were heavily involved in all sorts of school clubs and leadership organizations. We, as a class (me included), had to learn how to "read" one another and how to

communicate appropriately with one another. (Three years teaching, 2 in 4th grade and 1 in middle school)

To the degree that these respondents are representative, it seems that the teaching of values and social and emotional competencies have remained important goals for our graduates.

Classroom Management and Discipline

As described earlier, for a culminating assignment in our programs, all our students are required to create an integrated classroom management and discipline plan. To assess how large a role these plans actually play in their teaching, our survey asked, "How important is the management/discipline plan and philosophy that you developed in your Pedagogy class to your teaching goals?"

Ninety-seven percent of students indicated that the plan remained important to their teaching goals, with 75% indicating that their plan remains very important. The individual comments offered by several former students further support the conclusion that the discipline plans they created while in our program are still central to their teaching.

It is the foundation for my classroom practice. (Two years teaching 1st grade)

Using the techniques taught in the program, I was able to easily transition into a classroom management routine that I was able to build on. (Five years teaching 4th grade)

I have been recognized by my principal as a beginning teacher with excellent classroom management. She and my assistant principal often have other teachers ask me about my methods. (New teacher, 1st grade)

We also asked about the individual parts of the discipline plans, for example, the use of relationship- and community-building activities, competition, rewards, and punishments. The responses to these questions were a little more difficult to interpret.

Relationship Building. While 97% of respondents indicated that relationship- and community-building activities are important to their teaching goals, five indicated that pressure on academic performance keeps them from doing these activities as much as they believe they should. Still, several comments indicate that most of the respondents use relationship- and community-building activities regularly and understand the importance of these activities to their ability to "manage" their classrooms.

No matter what special events or schedules are thrown our way, we NEVER miss a morning meeting, even if it has to be an afternoon meeting. The children want it, ask for it, and own it. I wouldn't have the classroom management success that I do without these activities. (Five years teaching 1st grade)

It is critical at any grade level to establish and develop a strong classroom community. Through activities students are able to express themselves, make connections to others, and build trust and a safe place to learn. (Number of years teaching and grade level not indicated)

Competition, Rewards, and Punishment. The most complex survey responses to interpret were related to the use of competition, rewards, and punishments. In our program we argued against the use of all three as means to motivate students. Unfortunately, our survey questions that asked our former students how frequently they used each of these common management and discipline strategies offered only the following response options: "once a month," "1–2 times a week," and "every day." For competition, 17 respondents indicated the minimal response, 10 left the question blank, and 13 reported using competition at least weekly. For rewards, 4 indicated the minimum response, 9 left the question blank, and 27 reported at least weekly use. For punishment, 7 indicated the minimum possible response, 10 left the question blank, and 23 reported using punishment at least weekly. More than half of the respondents who omitted the question or checked the minimal response added explanatory comments indicating that they rarely or never use competition, rewards, or punishments.

Rarely use competition, punishment, or rewards. Limited use based only around schoolwide character trait building system and logical consequences. (Two years teaching 1st grade)

Punishments rarely used; individual conferencing usually solves the problem. (Eight years teaching grade 7 and 8)

If we combine minimal responses with omitted responses that are qualified by comments indicating rare or no use of competition, punishments, or rewards, it appears that 59% of the respondents use little or no competition, 42% use little or no punishment, and 26% rarely use extrinsic rewards. While only 11% of respondents reported daily use of competition, 28% reported using rewards and 24% punishment daily. Some explained that the use of rewards and punishments was part of a schoolwide management system.

Punishment is a mandated behavior method of colors, that is, [there are] 2 verbal warnings, third warning is a timeout to reflect and write down problem and how to solve it, 4th warning is an incident report/call home, 5th warning is parent conference, 6th warning is principal visit. (Two years teaching 3rd grade; 1 year, 1st grade)

Finally, several respondents indicated complex views of rewards and punishments, but it was not easy to discern from their brief comments how well they understand that consequences, no matter how logical, meted out to a child by their more powerful teacher are punishments, or that celebrations or "free time" following individual or class accomplishments are rewards.

I don't "punish" at all, but I do use logical consequences and occasional time-outs or removal to another classroom along with a behavior reflection sheet. . . . Sometimes, if we've accomplished something as a whole class, we might have a class-reward such as playing an educational game or earning a few minutes of free time. (Three years teaching 4th and 7th/8th grades)

Punishments are not used in my class in the traditional way. Consequences are created by my students, both individually and as a class. (Four plus years teaching Kindergarten, 1st, 4th, and 8th grades)

I rarely use competition or punishment in the classroom. I try to reinforce the effects of the choices we make. I am not sure if that constitutes . . . punishment or rewards. (Five years teaching 4th grade)

Job Satisfaction

"How satisfying do you find teaching as a whole?" was the final question in our survey. During these times when teachers are under so much stress, we were heartened to find that all of the respondents indicated that they found teaching satisfying, with 80% reporting that teaching is very satisfying. One respondent's comment captured what we hold as a goal for all our students.

[Teaching]—Nothing like it. There are no 2 days that are exactly the same. To have the opportunity to learn and grow with these students is an invaluable gift. Each day I am provided with numerous opportunities to make a difference and let children know that they impact the world, make unique contribution, and have a choice in the matter of who they get to be . . . it is absolutely extraordinary. (Years teaching and grade level(s) not indicated)

REFLECTING ON OUR SURVEY DATA

Although we cannot rule out response bias, and the data that we have gathered represent only a third of our responding graduates, we believe that our sample is reasonably representative. The respondents were equally distributed across grade levels and years of teaching, and their individual responses varied from question to question and represented all points on the scale.

Overall, we find the results of our survey encouraging. The responses indicate that a number of these former students have maintained a clear focus on teaching social, emotional, and moral competencies and take Dewey's concept of the classroom as a caring, democratic community seriously. Their level of satisfaction with teaching implies that they are being reasonably successful in achieving their teaching goals.

The results related to the use of extrinsic motivation were at first puzzling but eventually enlightening. We were pleased that 97% of respondents reported frequent reflection with students on their behavior, and the continued relevance of the management and discipline plan developed in their pedagogy class, a plan that did not involve extrinsic rewards or punishments. Still, a significant percentage reported at least some use of rewards and punishment, and 30% added comments indicating they are struggling with understanding whether aspects of their motivation and classroom control practices constitute rewards or punishments. It became clear to us that we needed to place additional focus on helping our students better understand the extrinsic versus intrinsic nature of common approaches to classroom management as well as anticipate the obstacles that might hamper their efforts to minimize the use of extrinsic control.

We continue to help our students understand a number of external factors that might make an intrinsically oriented management system difficult to maintain. For example, we explicitly explore with our students the following obstacles:

- The punitive American justice system and the long tradition of classroom management and family socialization practices that stress the importance of meting out unpleasant consequences for misbehavior as well as pleasant consequences for desired behavior
- Our students' own experience with such systems as Assertive Discipline when they were in elementary and secondary school
- The extrinsic programs that many schools require their teachers to use
- The relentless pressure teachers feel to prepare their students to perform well on yearly standardized tests
- The difficulty of managing classrooms with increased numbers of students living transient lives marked by poverty and violence
- In many schools, a prescriptive curriculum that makes it difficult for teachers to teach to the interests of students

In addition to helping our students understand the above factors and plan for ways to overcome, circumvent, or minimize them, we place added focus on helping our students analyze the constructs of reward, recognition, celebration, punishment, reparation, natural and logical consequence, redirection, guidance, and fair rule enforcement. One instructional practice that our students have found helpful is to ask themselves two questions:

- What effect did I intend my action to have?
- How might the student view my action?

For example, when they exercise control, we ask them to figuratively "sit in the student's seat" and ask themselves if they would feel manipulated, punished, or helped by their action.

SUMMARY AND IMPLICATIONS FOR TEACHER EDUCATION

Integrating social and moral development into the crowded curricula of teacher education programs can seem daunting. This chapter reviews materials and practices of the Child Development Project that have proven successful in achieving this integration in schools and describes how three of the authors used these materials and practices to achieve this aim in the teacher education program at California State University, Sacramento.

While there are many ways to integrate the moral work of teaching into teacher preparation programs, our experience leads us to propose the following guidelines:

- Present the moral and social goals of schooling not as an extra or add-on, but as how one builds a well-functioning classroom and teaches effectively.
- Follow Dewey's advice and provide teacher candidates with the same kind of caring learning community you want them to offer their students. When teacher candidates themselves experience the power of a caring learning community and are helped to reflect on those experiences, their ability and commitment to carrying a moral focus into their own classrooms is strengthened.
- Finally, provide teacher candidates with models of real classroom teachers who have deeply integrated social/moral learning into their pedagogy. A guided group visit to observe and reflect with a local teacher who has built a caring classroom community grounds such a goal in reality. Additionally, our students have found Laura Ecken's 2-year effort to build a caring community of learners with her inner-city, 2nd- and 3rd-grade students instructive and inspirational (Watson & Ecken, 2003).

New teachers will face many obstacles as they strive to incorporate the moral goals of schooling in today's educational climate. Fortunately, helpful materials are available to scaffold their efforts, and support for sustaining a commitment to teaching with a moral focus is contained in the teaching itself. It's more fun to teach when one has created a caring classroom community, and teaching is experienced as even more fulfilling when its goal involves preparing children to contribute to a just and caring world.

NOTES

1. The Child Development Project as a research and development project ended in 2000. Many of the materials created by the project are available from the Developmental Studies Center (http://www.devstu.org). The center currently offers a staff development program called Caring School Community that incorporates many aspects of the original CDP program.

2. A complete list of the CDP videos used in the teacher education program at Sacramento State University at Sacramento can be obtained from any of the authors. The videos are also available from the Center for Character and Citizenship at the University of Missouri–St. Louis (http://characterandcitizenship.org/index.php?option=com_content&view=article&id=65).

REFERENCES

Battistich, V. (2008). The Child Development Project: Creating caring school communities. In L. P. Nucci & D. Narvaez (Eds.), *Handbook of moral and character education* (pp. 328–351). New York: Routledge.

Battistich, V., Schaps, E., & Wilson, N. (2004). Effects of an elementary school intervention on students' "connectedness" to school and social adjustment during middle school. *The Journal of Primary Prevention, 24*(3), 243–262.

Battistich, V., Solomon, D., Watson, M., & Schaps, E. (1997). Caring school communities. *Educational Psychologist, 32*(3), 137–151.

Benson, K. D., Higuera, S., Farley, S., Perez, N., Peralta, A., Ruffalo, U., . . . Souza, B. (1995). *From supervision to Paravision: Initiating new teachers through dialogical process.* Paper presented at the annual meeting of the American Educational Research Association, San Francisco, CA.

Cantor, L. (1976). *Assertive discipline: A take charge approach for today's educator.* Los Angeles, CA: Lee Cantor & Associates.

Deci, E. L., & Ryan, R. M. (1985). *Intrinsic motivation and self-determination in human behavior.* New York: Plenum.

Denton, P., & Kriete, R. (2000). *The first six weeks of school.* Greenfield, MA: Northeast Foundation for Children.

Developmental Studies Center (DSC). (1996). *Ways we want our class to be: Class meetings that build commitment to kindness and learning.* Oakland, CA: Author.

Developmental Studies Center (DSC). (1997a). *Blueprints for a collaborative classroom.* Oakland, CA: Author.

Developmental Studies Center (DSC). (1997b). *That's my buddy.* Oakland, CA: Author.

Developmental Studies Center (DSC). (1998a). *Reading for real.* Oakland, CA: Author.

Developmental Studies Center (DSC). (1998b). *Reading, thinking, and caring.* Oakland, CA: Author.

Dewey, J. (1980). *The middle works, Volume 9, 1899–1924: Democracy and education* (J. Boydston, Ed.). Carbondale: Southern Illinois University Press. (Original work published 1916)

Gibbs, J. (2001). *Tribes: A new way of learning and being together.* Windsor, Canada: Center Source Systems.

Kohn, A. (1991). Caring kids: The role of the school. *Phi Delta Kappan, 7*(7), 496–506.

Kriete, R., & Bechtel, L. (2002). *The morning meeting book.* Greenfield, MA: Northeast Foundation for Children.

Lepper, M., & Green, D. (1978). *The hidden costs of rewards.* Hillsdale, NJ: Lawrence Erlbaum Associates.

Marshall, M. L. (2002). *Discipline without stress, punishments or rewards.* Los Alamitos, CA: Piper Press.

Noddings, N. (1984). *Caring: A feminist approach to ethics and moral education.* Berkeley: University of California Press.

Noddings, N. (1992). *The challenge to care in schools.* New York: Teachers College Press.

Piaget, J. (1965). *The moral judgment of the child.* New York: Free Press. (Original work published 1932)

Power, C., Higgins, A., & Kohlberg, L. (1989). *Lawrence Kohlberg's approach to moral education.* New York: Columbia University Press.

Solomon, D., Battistich, V., Watson, M., Schaps, E., & Lewis, C. (2000). A six-district study of educational change: Direct and mediated effects of the Child Development Project. *Social Psychology of Education, 4,* 3–51.

Solomon, D., Watson, M., Battistich, V., Schaps, E., & Delucchi, K. (1996). Creating classrooms that students experience as communities. *American Journal of Community Psychology, 24*(6), 719–748.

Vygotsky, L. S. (1978). *Mind in society: The development of higher psychological processes* (M. Cole, V. John-Steiner, S. Scribner, & E. Souberman, Eds. & Trans.). Cambridge, MA: Harvard University Press.

Watson, M., & Ecken, L. (2003). *Learning to trust: Transforming difficult elementary classrooms through Developmental Discipline.* San Francisco: Jossey-Bass.

Watson, M., Solomon, D., Battistich, V., Schaps, E., & Solomon, J. (1989). The Child Development Project: Combining traditional and developmental approaches to values education. In L. Nucci (Ed.), *Moral development and character education: A dialogue* (pp. 51–92). Berkeley: McCutchan.

CHAPTER 10

Reflections on Preparing Preservice Teachers for Moral Education in Urban Settings

Larry Nucci

In this chapter I will share some thoughts about preparing preservice teachers to integrate moral education within urban elementary school settings. Little published research exists on this topic, and preservice teacher preparation remains the weak link in moral education (Jones, Ryan, & Bohlin, 1999; Milson, 2003; Schwartz, 2008). My reflections will make use of the experience and research findings (Nucci, Drill, Larson, & Browne, 2006) from our efforts to make adjustments in the undergraduate elementary teacher education program at the University of Illinois, Chicago (UIC). The focus of the chapter will be on the factors important to making such program adjustments, and the subsequent impact those changes had for the knowledge and self-efficacy of program graduates to engage in moral education. I will also draw upon my more recent experiences working with the Developmental Teacher Education (DTE) master's degree program in elementary education at the University of California, Berkeley. What both programs share in common is their emphasis upon urban education. UIC prepares more teachers for the Chicago public schools than any other university. The DTE program at UC Berkeley places the majority of its student teachers in the public schools of Oakland, Berkeley, and neighboring urban school districts. Both programs include attention throughout course offerings and field settings to issues of cultural diversity, poverty, and linguistic minority status, as well as the fundamental social justice role of urban teachers. Thus these programs are in many ways steeped in similar moral considerations. In addition, some of the changes made in the UIC program discussed in this chapter were inspired by work conducted at UC Berkeley.

The two programs differ considerably, however, in their history and in their design. The UIC program is more traditional in its overall structure and therefore more similar to most teacher education programs in the United States. It is also double the size of the DTE program. For this reason the bulk of this chapter will focus upon the lessons learned from the UIC effort to integrate moral education within teacher preparation. The UIC undergraduate elementary education program draws students from the general population of the Chicago metropolitan area. The UC Berkeley DTE program offers a master's degree (there is no undergraduate major in education in California) and draws students selectively from within California, with some out-of-state and foreign students. It should be noted that both programs use extensive interviews of prospective applicants as part of admission, and both programs are recognized as offering high-quality teacher education ("Best Education Schools," 2012).

The programs that are the focus of this chapter share an overall conception of learning as a constructive process. This places them on one side of the divide that separates the dominant conceptions of moral development and character formation. The field is roughly split between *traditionalists*, who emphasize the cultivation of virtue through processes of social learning and enculturation, and *constructivists*, who place an emphasis on students' moral and social judgments (Nucci & Narvaez, 2008). These perspectives are associated with different emphases in teacher preparation, with the former group attending more to the use of direct instruction and modeling, and the latter placing greater emphasis on developmental processes, group discourse and moral discussion, and social problem solving. As has been pointed out in analyses of "what works" for character education (Berkowitz, Battistich, & Bier, 2008), all of these practices have a place within comprehensive teaching. Good teaching, however, is not simply a collection of practices. It requires an underlying conceptual framework or theoretical perspective to guide the selection and implementation of practices.

THEORETICAL FRAMEWORK AND GUIDING ASSUMPTIONS

Overarching Constructivist Framework

The broad frameworks that guide both teacher education programs are quite similar. They include attention to the classic developmental theories of Piaget and Vygotsky, and to more contemporary cultural historical activity theories, as well as constructivist cognitive psychology and constructivist theories of motivation such as self-determination theory (Deci & Ryan, 1985; Ryan & Deci, 2000). The DTE program at UC Berkeley is, however, more clearly focused upon development as the overarching structure guiding all of the course design and student field experiences. In this respect the DTE program has a more cohesive conceptual framework than is typical of teacher education in most settings, including UIC, making the integration of an emphasis on moral education much easier to implement.

Social Cognitive Domain Theory and Developmental Discipline

With respect to moral development and education, the paradigm introduced to UIC and employed in the DTE is social cognitive domain theory (Turiel, 1983, 2002). This was not by accident. The program leadership for moral education at UIC and UC Berkeley consisted of myself and Elliot Turiel, two of the primary researchers associated with domain theory. Personal bias notwithstanding, domain theory has emerged as arguably the dominant paradigm for current research on moral development of school-age children and adolescents. I would not contend, however, that it is requisite that all teacher education programs adopt our framework. Rather, I would claim that efforts at preparing preservice teachers to engage in moral education require a research-based framework and faculty expertise in the area of moral development and education.

Domain theory emerged in the mid-1970s in response to research challenging some of the basic assumptions of Kohlberg's (1984) then-dominant paradigm of the psychology of moral development. According to domain theory, concepts of social right and wrong are not all of one type, but are organized within distinct conceptual and developmental frameworks (Turiel, 1983, 2002). Concepts of morality address issues of human welfare, rights, and fairness and are constructed out of the child's early social interactions around events such as unprovoked hitting and hurting that have effects upon another person. Morality can be distinguished from concepts of social conventions, which are the consensually determined standards of conduct particular to a given social group. The domains of morality and convention are further differentiated from conceptions of personal matters of privacy and individual discretion. While morality and convention deal with aspects of interpersonal regulation, concepts of personal issues refer to actions that comprise the private aspects of one's life, such as the contents of a diary, and issues that are matters of preference and choice (e.g., friends, music, hairstyle) rather than right or wrong. The distinctions drawn within domain theory among moral, conventional, and personal concepts have been sustained by findings from more than 80 studies conducted throughout the world over the past 35 years (Turiel, 2002).

The importance of domain theory for educators lies in its ability to provide an account for the following:

- The age-related changes associated with concepts within a given system
- Shifts in behavior associated with growth within particular domains
- The forms of social interaction or educational input likely to stimulate growth within a given conceptual system (Nucci, 2001, 2008)

Moreover, in differentiating among moral and nonmoral issues, educators are provided the analytic tools to address moral values of fairness and beneficent treatment of others, rather than conflating such core issues with matters such as dress codes that schools may approach in different ways as a function of local custom and context. Understanding the ways in which morality and convention interact with one another also permits educators to interpret culturally driven interactions among morality and social convention rather than ascribing them to children's developmental stage. For example, Astor (1994) reported that although inner-city African American male elementary and middle school children universally condemned unprovoked hitting as wrong, they tended to view hitting back in response to verbal insult as a justifiable form of retributive justice. Middle-class teachers operating within an urban setting might well misinterpret this tendency toward physical retaliation as evidence of a "lower" level of moral development rather than as a shared view of a morally appropriate response to disrespect. Finally, understanding how cultures instantiate overlaps among morality, convention, and personal prerogative (e.g., customs or conventions that foster discrimination) allows educators to go beyond the development of "nice children," who are compliant followers of the status quo, toward the development of citizens of a democracy prepared to engage in critical moral evaluation of themselves and the social system they inherit (Nucci, 2008).

Domain theory afforded faculty in both teacher education programs a common language for discussions about morality across disciplinary boundaries. Having this shared theoretical underpinning was critical to the level of success attained at UIC since the program, as is true of most preservice teacher education, was not structured around a particular shared orientation beyond the broad umbrella of urban education and constructivism. The adoption of domain theory as the organizing framework for the efforts at moral education allowed faculty to use a common language with students across courses and provided a tool for picking up common threads running throughout the preservice teacher education experience. These would include such things as attention to the social and emotional development of students, awareness of the particular needs and backgrounds of urban learners, and the integration of moral and social values themes through the general curriculum and processes of instruction and classroom management.

The constructivist developmental assumptions of domain theory along with the overarching constructivist underpinnings of both teacher education programs meant that the selection of the approach to classroom management and student conduct would be similarly linked to considerations of children's development. At UIC we adopted what has been referred to as Developmental Discipline (Watson & Ecken, 2003). This approach emerged from the work of Marilyn Watson (see Chapter 9 of this volume) who integrated the assumptions of Attachment Theory with the Self-Determination Theory (Ryan & Deci, 2000) of student motivation to fashion an approach to classroom management that places a premium on engaging children's basic developmental needs to foster their capacity for self-regulation rather than a reliance on external adult control. Watson was one of the original instructors in the DTE program at UC Berkeley, and Developmental Discipline is a cornerstone of DTE teacher preparation.

Although we employed an overarching theoretical framework, we also provided our students with considerable amounts of information on alternative approaches. However, we emphasized the difference between an eclectic and pragmatic use of techniques as opposed to an eclectic grab bag of frameworks that render teaching incoherent. One cannot be a constructivist when it comes to math and a behaviorist when it comes to reading. However, one can employ the use of phonics as a method within an overall approach to reading instruction that accounts for students' learning in terms of the construction of meaning rather than the systematic building up of stimulus-response connections. In a similar vein a teacher may apply a contingency reward system as part of a constructivist approach to classroom management and student motivation (for an excellent discussion of this point, see Ryan & Deci, 2000), as long as the usage of such contingencies is within an overarching emphasis on student meaning making and autonomous self-management.

Moral and Social Development as Integrated Within Academic Instruction

Central to our entire approach is that moral education should take place within the context of regular academic instruction rather than exist as a separate program. This is a lesson that was learned some time ago in the early efforts to stimulate moral development through classroom uses of standard moral dilemma discussion. Although these focused periods of discussion resulted in some improvements in students' stage of moral reasoning as measured with standard Kohlberg interviews, none of the teachers continued with the practice once the university team concluded their research. As Kohlberg (1978) quipped about this attempt at moral education, "The research operation was a success, but the research patient died" (p. 14). Subsequently, working with Ted Fenton, Kohlberg achieved greater success in sustaining efforts at moral education when the uses of moral discussion were integrated within the regular social studies curriculum (Power, Higgins, & Kohlberg, 1989). More recent efforts to promote moral and character development by setting aside a particular day or period for a focus upon a particular virtue ("If It's Tuesday, This Must Be Honesty") have generated similar criticisms for their irrelevance and lack of connection to the normal flow of school and classroom activity (Kohn, 1997). In contrast, our effort at preparing teachers for moral education is based on the principle that moral education is an aspect of the overall climate and practices of the school and classroom (Hansen, 1996) and on the goal of achieving a 2-for-1 benefit of academic growth and moral development through the integration of social and moral growth within the regular academic curriculum (Nucci, 2008).

PROCESS OF PROGRAM CHANGE AND IMPLEMENTATION

The incorporation of moral education within the UIC teacher education program took place over a 2-year period (2003–2005). UIC was one of three universities included in a national grant program to foster preservice moral education sponsored by the Character Education Partnership (CEP). Prior to the grant project there had been little systematic attention to moral education in the UIC teacher education program beyond the particular interest of individual faculty within their own courses.

Assumptions About Professional Development

One of our operating assumptions was that we were not going to be able to establish a separate strand for moral education carved out of the existing space for course offerings within the teacher education program. This was not desirable from the perspective of the teacher education faculty who understood their role as providing prospective teachers, over a very short time period, with the capacity to teach the basic subject matter of math, science, and literacy. Nor was it something that we viewed as necessary for the provision of the skills needed to engage in moral education. As I outlined above, the basic premise of our approach was and continues to be that moral education should be integrated within the teaching of the regular academic curriculum. Thus our effort was directed at working with colleagues to alter their existing courses to include moral education as an aspect of the teaching of their subject matter.

Another basic assumption was that genuine lasting program change would come only from the active involvement of the faculty stakeholders (Penuel, Fishman, Yamaguchi, & Gallagher, 2007). Thus we set out from the beginning to engage in dialogue with the teacher education faculty to find points of commonality and to locate appropriate opportunities for the integration of moral education throughout courses within the teacher education program.

We addressed the need for a course that would provide the basic information about moral development and moral education to the teacher education majors by fleshing out the social development component of the 1st-year required course Child Development and Elementary Education. I was the primary instructor for this course and was obviously engaged in the goals of integrating moral education within our teacher education program. I worked with the two other instructors who taught this course to generate the changes that are discussed below.

Developing a Core Course for Moral Education

For historical reasons that are unlikely to be unique to the UIC program, issues of social development had been generally left to the courses on human development and educational psychology, while the nitty-gritty of teaching, especially of subject matter instruction, took place in subsequent courses. Rather than bemoan that division of labor, we set out to buttress the social development component of this initial course in child development and use the language and activities of that course to establish the context for the integration of moral education throughout the program.

In order to do this, we expanded the amount of course time spent on social and moral development, and fully integrated those aspects of the course with units on student diversity, student motivation, and classroom management. This expansion of coverage of issues of social, emotional, and moral development was achieved through reductions in the amount of time spent on behaviorist theories of learning and specific attention to content instruction better covered in later courses. Approximately 15% of the total amount of instructional class time was reallocated to moral education. This raised to 40% the amount of instructional time devoted to issues of social and emotional learning, moral and social development, and classroom management.

We also sharpened the content of what was covered within the units pertaining to moral education, and introduced a major new assignment focusing on the integration of moral education with the teaching of academic content. We moved away from reliance on the brief presentation of theories of moral development and research presented in most texts to an in-depth focus upon domain theory as the organizing framework for thinking about classroom practices aimed at social and moral growth. This is not to say that we ignored coverage of other perspectives. Students were assigned to read the chapter on moral development covered in their omnibus textbook. However, in addition to this textbook coverage of the general topic, students read *Education in the Moral Domain* (Nucci, 2001), a book that dealt specifically with research on domain theory and its application to educational practice. Unfortunately, this book was written for a graduate student and faculty audience, and was tough sledding for 2nd-year undergrads. (This experience with the UIC undergraduates inspired a subsequent book, *Nice Is Not Enough: Facilitating Moral Development* [Nucci, 2008], written for classroom teachers and preservice teacher education majors. It now serves as the text for the social development course in the DTE program at UC Berkeley.) To reduce the amount of required reading, and to engage the students in a cooperative learning practice associated with moral education, students worked in teams of five or six to share the reading and teach one another sections of the book. This *jigsaw* reading activity (Aronson & Patnoe, 1996) was supplemented through in-class lecture and discussion, as well as a class project that will be described in detail below. We made a similar decision with respect to classroom management. Rather than limit the treatment of classroom management to an overview of general approaches as covered in the basic textbook, students were organized in jigsaw cooperative learning groups to master and teach one another the content of Parts One and Two of *Learning to Trust* (Watson & Ecken, 2003), a sourcebook on Developmental Discipline. Continuity with domain theory was accomplished through connections drawn between practices of Developmental Discipline and domain concordant responses to classroom transgressions as described in *Education and the Moral Domain* (Nucci, 2001). Lectures and discussions of Developmental Discipline and domain theory were supported by presentations of videos of interviews with children, video recordings of elementary school classroom interactions, and discussions of moral issues drawn from regular school curricula.

We also increased the amount of student time devoted to moral education by adjustments in student assignments done outside of the class. Students worked in groups to construct moral and social values lessons employing regular academic social studies and literacy curricular materials used in the Chicago public schools. Lessons were posted on *Taskstream*, a web-based format that permitted the group members and course instructor to make online comments and suggestions throughout the 3 weeks allotted for the assignment. Examples of the lessons constructed by UIC students in the elementary and secondary education programs may be found in Nucci (2008).

Implementation

Full implementation of the changes made in the undergraduate elementary teacher education program coincided with anticipated shifts in the personnel teaching the professional sequence courses for two of the five cohorts of students. This provided us with a natural experiment in which five cohorts of students would all have participated in the redesigned Child Development and Elementary Education course, but only three of the five cohorts would participate in subsequent courses that included systematic follow-through in the areas of moral development and education. Thus we were able to evaluate the effects of fully integrating moral education throughout the preservice program versus simply increasing the time and quality of instruction on moral education in a single child development course.

The most substantial shifts in these courses took place in the classes on the teaching of reading and in the program field components. Lesson building assignments in the literacy courses were altered to include attention to moral and social values. In some cases this entailed refining and extending the lessons constructed in the earlier Child Development and Elementary Education course. In most cases this entailed constructing entirely new lessons and units. To aid their students in carrying out these assignments, faculty in the literacy courses provided a review of the information on social development that had been presented in the prior year's Child Development and Elementary Education course.

In their fieldwork courses students were given assignments in which they were asked to observe and reflect upon how their cooperating teachers made use of opportunities to infuse moral education in the classroom. In one case the instructor, Eleni Katsarou, dedicated a number of seminar sessions associated with the fieldwork to focused readings on Developmental Discipline (Watson & Ecken,

2003) and showed several video clips on classroom teachers' responses to student transgressions. These videos provided examples of teachers engaged in practices consistent with Developmental Discipline and domain-appropriate responses to transgressions.

There were two major assignments associated with the fieldwork. These were both designed to heighten students' ability to analyze classroom discourse. Readings used to guide students' thinking about these issues included both traditional classroom discourse analysis literature (Green & Harker, 1988), as well as teacher-researcher approaches to classroom discourse (Pappas & Zecker, 2001). These readings served to complement the information students had received about Developmental Discipline, as well as the handouts that faculty had developed to guide students' analyses of domain-concordant responses to student transgressions. The first student assignment entailed recording classroom dialogues in their field settings and then analyzing the extent to which the cooperating teacher's responses to student transgressions employed discourse that was domain concordant. The second assignment was exactly the same type of analysis on a lesson that each student conducted with the public school students.

The second year of the program also included student teaching. Students from field course sections that had implemented the new moral education components were encouraged by their student teaching faculty supervisors to implement the integration of moral education based on Developmental Discipline and domain theory within their subject area teaching. The remaining sections completed their student teaching without any specific encouragement with respect to moral education.

OUTCOMES

The results of the formal program evaluation have been published, and interested readers are welcome to seek out that article (Nucci et al., 2006). What I will share here are some of the highlights that are pertinent to the goals of this volume.

Results from Student Surveys

One set of indices we employed to assess the program were student evaluations of the moral development components of the core Child Development and Elementary Education course and student responses to questionnaires at the time of graduation assessing their knowledge of moral development and educational practices, as well as their sense of efficacy to engage in moral education.

Student course evaluations for the three sections of the Child Development and Elementary Education course were quite high (mean of 4.0 on a 5-point scale) with no significant differences in scores for individual instructors. Analyses of scores for different units of the course revealed that the sections on moral education were rated at or above the overall course rating. Indeed, the section that received the highest overall rating was the unit on Developmental Discipline. Thus students reported enjoying and valuing the information they received about social, emotional, and moral development and associated educational practices such as the construction of lessons integrating issues of moral and social development within the regular curriculum.

Our assessment of student knowledge was a brief multiple-choice exam I constructed that asked about basic knowledge of moral development and educational practices. The questions were similar in content to ones that had appeared on exams in the child development course. The assessment of efficacy was based upon a measure developed by Milson (2003) to assess teachers' beliefs about their own capacity to engage in moral education. This measure was modified to fit the developmental assumptions of the UIC program. These assessments were given to three groups:

1. Recent graduates who had not participated in the revised program
2. Students who had participated in the modified Child Development and Elementary Education course, but whose subsequent coursework was with faculty who were not providing continuing work in moral education
3. Students who participated in the entire sequence of courses associated with the changes in preparation for moral education

What we found was quite interesting. For both students' knowledge and their sense of efficacy, participation solely in the enriched Child Development and Elementary Education course had no impact as measured against the control group of UIC program graduates. However, the students who participated in the full program that integrated attention to moral development and education throughout, including student teaching, provided statistically significant higher scores on both knowledge of moral development and educational practices, and self-reports of efficacy to engage in moral education. This finding indicates that the prevailing practice of limiting preservice teacher education majors' exposure to moral development and education to a single course on child development or educational psychology at the beginning of the students' program has little utility when it comes to their knowledge or sense of capacity to engage in moral education at the time of graduation.

Impact on Courses and Student Products

In addition to the use of student surveys, we also looked at the changes in course syllabi and the products that students produced through their progress in the teacher education program. We found that moral education components had been integrated by collaborating faculty within all of the required courses in the program with the exceptions of Teaching and Learning of Mathematics,

Teaching and Learning of Science, and Characteristics of Exceptional Children. Typical changes entailed the adjustment of assignments to incorporate attention to morality and social convention, thus building from the activities initiated in the course on child development. In the pre-student-teaching seminar taught by participating faculty, the class assignments/fieldwork projects were dramatically and qualitatively different from those in previous years. Most students evidenced an increased sensitivity toward issues of moral education and usage of domain theory constructs to reflect upon classroom interactions. This became even more apparent in their reflections during student teaching. At seminar, most notably, there were frequent references to their earlier coursework in educational psychology as well as the subsequent readings and lectures on Developmental Discipline. In many cases our students employed formal assigned readings to accomplish these objectives. For example, one student teacher employed An Na's *A Step from Heaven* (2003) to engage her 5th-grade class in a lesson on social convention and social structure. This was an embellishment of a lesson she and her group had started in their child development course.

The impact of the moral education initiative was also evidenced in the student accounts of their efforts to implement Developmental Discipline. The following illustrative examples are from unedited excerpts of journal entries of one of the seniors during her student teaching semester. She is describing events from her 2nd-grade classroom.

January 13, 2005: Allison and Khari are on the rug and interrupt my lesson. Allison has kicked Khari for taking her chapstick top. Khari has hit her back. Ms. F. has Allison move from the carpet and stand by the board—she begins to cry. Khari stays on the rug. I decide that I can't continue my lesson b/c it wasn't fair—Khari shouldn't stay either. I have Khari go back to his seat and write about what happened—he doesn't do it. I ask the students what would have been a better way to solve their problem. The lesson continues. Allison eventually goes back to her seat.

January 21, 2005: We came in class, did math and then the last 20 minutes of class time I had them sitting around me and we went over the class rules! It was great! I had them give me examples of how each rule can be broken (they used examples of what they've done throughout the week and to each other) and what can be done to prevent it. It was a great reflection for them and I felt like they were realizing things. It was a nice talk that I feel was beneficial.

Great—two boys were having a hard time sharing a bean bag and I heard Mario (often the cause of my problems) mock me in a good way by telling them "to problem solve!" What was more amazing is that N'ne did that first! I heard him and then Mario followed to tell them the same thing. I was doing something else but overheard this. I loudly said, "very smart boys!" They were surprised to see that I knew what was going on since I was involved in something else.

January 31, 2005: Students were throwing paper balls during library. I returned in the room and asked people to raise their hand if they will admit they threw paper balls—to just be honest. Students immediately began fussing and blaming and pointing fingers—I had them immediately settle down by being calm and telling them that I will let one person at a time speak. I listened to a few students and then said, "Whoever would like to follow the rules of respect and being honest, they can go to the writing center and write down what they did and why—an honesty letter." Khari, R. R., Paris, N'ne, Justus, and Malik voluntarily began writing! It was a great feeling of accomplishment, and they then joined in for a math activity. However, I question, is an honesty note a replacement for consequences—should I have still reprimanded these students in some way for their behavior or was it okay that I just accepted their honesty notes and moved on?

April 7, 2005: I am proud to admit that I was finally able to step back and see a dramatic change in their behavior during my time here. This is not to say that there doesn't need to be more work but together, students and I, run a manageable class, and my hard work and dedication to this goal has shown through!

As can be seen in the above excerpts, provided by the instructor, Eleni Katsarou, the process of managing an urban classroom using Developmental Discipline did not come easily or readily to our students. This is consistent with the reports from even experienced teachers (Watson & Ecken, 2003). The student teacher inherited an unruly classroom accustomed to an authoritarian classroom environment. Over time, the students' persistent engagement in community building, respectful dialogue, and problem solving resulted in a classroom based upon trust rather than raw teacher power. Her classroom became not only better behaved, but also evidenced the beginnings of student-teacher and student-student exchanges in which students engaged in self-monitoring rather than compliance to coercive force. This was not without incident, nor without second thoughts by our novice teacher. On balance, however, the lesson we learned from our experience incorporating Developmental Discipline into the urban teacher education program is that it can be accomplished with benefits to both our novice teachers and the students in their classrooms. Thus our experience was that this approach to classroom climate and student discipline is not something to be limited to the work of veteran classroom teachers with unusual skill levels. In preparation for this chapter I confirmed with Eleni Katsarou that she has continued to include

Developmental Discipline as part of the UIC undergraduate teacher education program to this day.

CONCLUSIONS AND FUTURE DIRECTIONS

In this chapter I have recounted the implementation and short-term outcomes of one attempt to integrate moral education within the preservice preparation of undergraduate elementary teacher education majors. The results of that experience indicate that one can successfully incorporate preparation to teach moral education within an already existing teacher preparation program. We were able to adjust course syllabi and student field experiences in ways that were consistent with the broader goals of the teacher education program. Student course evaluations and outcome measures of student knowledge and efficacy indicated that the changes brought about in the program were well received by the preservice teacher education majors and effective in raising their knowledge of moral development and educational practice, as well as self-perceptions of their preparedness to engage in moral education. The encouraging outcomes from that effort have been replicated at one other large urban public university, the University of Missouri–St. Louis (UMSL) (Navarro, Berkowitz, Battistich, Sheilds, & Suess, 2006; see also Chapter 11 of this volume), and a small private faith-based institution, Whitworth College (Mowry, 2005; Schwartz, 2008).

The UIC findings on student outcomes indicate that measurable program effects require the infusion of moral education across the teacher education program and raise serious questions about the standard reliance upon a single course, such as educational psychology, or an inserted special course on moral education to achieve an impact upon student capacity for moral education. There was no significant difference in either knowledge or perceived efficacy for moral education between a control group of prior graduates and students who had experienced the enriched course on child development. This occurred even though the child development course spent a substantial amount of time on issues of moral and social development and included practical experience in lesson creation and the enactment of Developmental Discipline. Significant effects were found for both student knowledge and efficacy among those students who had completed a program that infused moral education throughout their coursework including field courses and student teaching.

Going beyond a single course poses a dilemma for all preservice teacher education programs already struggling for curricular space to meet demands for skills to teach basic academic subjects. This struggle for curricular space is not limited to the United States. Despite a national policy requiring the teaching of morality and character in British schools, the majority of teachers in Great Britain report feeling unprepared to engage in moral or character education (Revell & Arthur, 2007). The resolution adopted at UIC and the other programs mentioned above was to infuse skills for moral education throughout courses within preservice teacher education. For this to occur, faculty in colleges of education would need to cooperate on the content, scope, and sequence of such moral education components. This in turn requires intellectual leadership, connection between the commitment to moral education and the broader mission and goals of the college or program, a willingness of tenured faculty to collaborate and alter syllabi and course requirements, and a process by which faculty can join together to enact these goals.

The attitude assumed by faculty at UIC was to take up a "reform agenda" rather than simply tweak syllabi or student assignments. Such an activist stance is associated with effective professional growth (Penuel et al., 2007). These activities included providing faculty across areas of the teacher education programs with a shared knowledge base of fundamental elements of moral development and moral education pedagogy. Faculty worked to share syllabi and to locate places in which aspects of moral education could be included. These activities included collaborative efforts to coordinate themes and activities across courses. Lessons developed in methods courses were then implemented during field placements. The field course instructors also supported students in their implementation of Developmental Discipline and included *Learning to Trust* (Watson & Ecken, 2003) as a required reading for seminar discussions. The integration of student experiences followed the principles of the "spiral curriculum" (Bruner, 1996). Faculty advisors from the penultimate field course followed students through student teaching and encouraged student teachers to implement what they had learned about moral education.

Of course, a very large question remains from this apparently successful venture into the alteration of preservice teaching to include moral education: Did this carry over into the teaching engaged in by program graduates? Unfortunately, no such follow-up was part of the funding received to engage in program change, and efforts to obtain funding to conduct a follow-up evaluation were unsuccessful. Nor have there been efforts to follow up with graduates at UMSL or Whitworth College. Thus we have no research evidence to respond to this basic question.

My present work at UC Berkeley may afford such an opportunity in the near future. The DTE program has a generation of experience in preparing teachers to attend to all aspects of their development, including moral growth. A major difference between DTE and traditional teacher preparation is that issues of social and cognitive development are each the subject of an individual course rather than being sandwiched into a single class on educational psychology. I currently teach the course on social development that was originally designed by Marilyn Watson and subsequently taught by Elliot Turiel. In the course I include all of the moral education content and activities that were developed at UIC. This semester-long course structure affords extended time to cover the material on children's early social and emotional development that is foundational for moral education, along with a more extensive period in which to delve into the details of Developmental Discipline and the research on moral development and educational practice. This means, for example, that students read the assigned texts in their entirety rather than as a jigsaw activity as was the case at UIC. Moreover, the DTE program structure insures the continual weaving in of issues of development including morality throughout the entire program continuing into student teaching.

Graduates from DTE tend to stay in classroom teaching for many years beyond graduation, and the program has excellent records on the location of past graduates. Thus this program may afford a unique opportunity to answer the question of carry-over with recent graduates and long-term cohorts. Until we have hard evidence that this attention to preservice teaching has an impact on the subsequent teaching for moral education by program graduates, we will be without a key element needed to sustain support for the preservice preparation of teachers for moral education.

REFERENCES

Aronson, E., & Patnoe, S. (1996). *The jigsaw classroom: Building cooperation in the classroom.* Boston: Allyn & Bacon.

Astor, R. (1994). Children's moral reasoning about family and peer violence: The role of provocation and retribution. *Child Development, 65,* 1054–1067.

Berkowitz, M., Battistich, V., & Bier, M. (2008). What works in character education: What is known and what needs to be known. In L. Nucci & D. Narvaez (Eds.), *Handbook of moral and character education* (pp. 370–390). New York: Routledge.

Best education schools. (2012). *U.S. News & World Report.* Retrieved from http://grad-schools.usnews.rankingsandreviews.com/best-graduate-schools/top-education-schools/edu-rankings

Bruner, J. (1996). *The culture of education.* Cambridge, MA: Harvard University Press.

Deci, E., & Ryan, R. (1985). *Intrinsic motivation and self-determination in behavior.* New York: Plenum Press.

Green, J., & Harker, J. (Eds.). (1988). *Multiple perspective analysis of classroom discourse.* Norwood, NJ: Ablex.

Hansen, D. T. (1996). Teaching and the moral life of classrooms. *Journal for a Just and Caring Education, 2,* 59–74.

Jones, E. N., Ryan, K., & Bohlin, K. (1999). *Teachers as educators of character: Are the nation's schools of education coming up short?* Washington, DC: Character Education Partnership.

Kohlberg, L. (1978). Moral education reappraised. *The Humanist, 38,* 13–15.

Kohlberg, L. (1984). *Essays on moral development: Vol. 2. The psychology of moral development.* San Francisco: Harper & Row.

Kohn, A. (1997). How not to teach values: A critical look at character education. *Phi Delta Kappan, 78*(6), 429–439.

Milson, A. J. (2003). Teacher's sense of efficacy for the formation of students' character. *Journal of Research in Character Education, 1,* 89–106.

Mowry, S. (2005, February). Preparing teachers for character education: Whitworth College experience. In M. Schwartz (Chair), *Integrating character education into teacher education: Three grant sites tell their story.* Symposium conducted at the annual meeting of the American Association of Colleges for Teacher Education, Washington, DC.

Na, A. (2003). *A step from heaven.* New York: Putnam.

Navarro, V., Berkowitz, M., Battistich, V., Shields, D., & Suess, P. (2006). *Mapping character: Beliefs and practices in teacher preparation.* Unpublished manuscript. University of Missouri–St. Louis, MO.

Nucci, L. (2001). *Education in the moral domain.* Cambridge, UK: Cambridge University Press.

Nucci, L. (2008). *Nice is not enough: Facilitating moral development.* Saddle River, NJ: Merrill.

Nucci, L., Drill, K., Larson, C., & Browne, C. (2006). Preparing preservice teachers for character education in urban elementary schools: The UIC initiative. *Journal for Research in Character Education, 3,* 81–96.

Nucci, L., & Narvaez, D. (Eds.). (2008). *Handbook of moral and character education.* New York: Routledge.

Pappas, C., & Zecker, L. (Eds.). (2001). *Transforming literacy curriculum genres: Working with teacher-researchers in urban classrooms.* New York: Routledge.

Penuel, W., Fishman, B., Yamaguchi, R., & Gallagher, L. (2007). What makes professional development effective? Strategies that foster curriculum implementation. *American Educational Research Journal, 44,* 921–958.

Power, C., Higgins, A., & Kohlberg, L. (1989). *Lawrence Kohlberg's approach to moral education.* New York: Columbia University Press.

Revell, L., & Arthur, J. (2007). Character education in schools and the education of teachers. *Journal of Moral Education, 36,* 79–92.

Ryan, R. M., & Deci, E. L. (2000). Intrinsic and extrinsic motivations: Classic definitions and new directions. *Contemporary Educational Psychology, 25,* 54–67.

Schwartz, M. (2008). Teacher education for moral and character education. In L. Nucci & D. Narvaez (Eds.), *Handbook of moral and character education* (pp. 583–600). New York: Routledge.

Turiel, E. (1983). *The development of social knowledge: Morality and convention.* Cambridge, UK: Cambridge University Press.

Turiel, E. (2002). *The culture of morality: Social development, context, and conflict.* Cambridge, UK: Cambridge University Press.

Watson, M., & Ecken, L. (2003). *Learning to trust: Transforming difficult elementary classrooms through Developmental Discipline.* San Francisco: Jossey-Bass.

CHAPTER 11

What Are We Trying to Achieve?

Developing a Framework for
Preparing Character Educators

David Light Shields, Wolfgang Althof, Marvin W. Berkowitz, and Virginia Navarro

Over the past decade the University of Missouri–St. Louis (UMSL) has taken a leadership role in the area of character and citizenship education (CE). This chapter describes UMSL's effort to integrate CE into teacher education. We will focus on a "second wave" of this effort that began in 2008 when the dean of the College of Education appointed faculty member David Shields to lead an ongoing and systematized approach to preparing our graduates to be character educators.

The College of Education was well prepared for such an initiative. In 2005 UMSL officially launched the Center for Character and Citizenship (CCC) with Wolfgang Althof and Marvin W. Berkowitz as codirectors. The CCC seeks to influence and promote the fields of character and citizenship education through research, technical assistance, and capacity building.

Supported by a grant from the Character Education Partnership (CEP), a series of programs and activities were designed to accomplish several preparatory tasks (Navarro, 2005; Navarro, Berkowitz, Battistich, Shields, & Suess, 2006). For instance, we held a variety of seminars with outside experts (Merle Schwartz, Marilyn Watson, and Larry Nucci [see Chapters 9 & 10 of this volume]), to stimulate faculty dialogue about how to intentionally train future teachers with the knowledge, skills, and dispositions needed to become successful educators of character, and we launched a program called Character Adventure Day that integrates experiential team-building pedagogy with guided reflection on the principles of CE.

As leader of the core initiative in 2008, Shields established a Faculty Working Group on Character Education to provide guidance to the effort. This leadership team recognized that there were to be two main thrusts to this initiative. First, we would focus on the development of the program itself (i.e., in its course, syllabi, curricula, and related educational elements). Second, we needed to invest in the professional development of those charged with delivering the curriculum (i.e., the teacher preparation faculty). The successful delivery of the revised program would depend upon the motivation and capacity of this faculty.

In the pages that follow we first describe our teacher education programs to provide the context for our effort. Then we discuss our theoretical framework and goals; the "readiness" of the faculty; the development of a taxonomy of knowledge, skills, and dispositions required of an effective character educator; the course-infusion process; the professional development we offered; and the future directions we envisioned, as well as exploring implications for the field of preservice teacher education.

It is important to note at the outset that from here on we will generally use the more parsimonious term of *character education* or simply CE to represent the broader field, character and citizenship education, that we have tackled in this initiative. This is for two reasons. One is simply brevity of language. The other, however, reflects the fact that we have focused more on civic character than on citizenship education more broadly.

THE CONTEXT: TEACHER EDUCATION PROGRAMS AT UMSL

The University of Missouri–St. Louis graduates the largest number of teacher candidates in the state. The Division of Teaching and Learning within the College of Education offers courses that serve several undergraduate degree programs, partly in collaboration with the College of Arts and Sciences. The curriculum of the teacher preparatory programs is organized into three sequential levels. At Level One students take courses that introduce them to the teaching profession, including its history, philosophy, and practice, and to the child learner. Level Two consists of more advanced foundational courses, including educational psychology, special education, and curriculum development, along with methods courses. Level Three is focused primarily on school internships and student teaching, but it also includes a course in classroom management. Field requirements occur progressively over the three levels.

THEORETICAL FRAMEWORK AND GOALS

Theoretical Framework

The predominant theoretical strands guiding the leadership team are (1) constructivism, (2) attachment theory, (3) democratic pedagogy, and (4) socialization theory. Constructivism (Piaget, 1954) posits that development is largely a collaborative project of the self and the context in which one develops. This interactional way of making meaning of the world one is grappling to understand fosters the construction of new and more adequate ways of reasoning about the physical and the social world—about morality, character, democracy, and citizenship when these concepts are valued and modeled. The key pedagogical message of constructivism is that the role of education is to create educational contexts that are optimal for nurturing this grappling with meaning. Such fertile contexts present problems for students to explore and allow them the space and freedom to try to make meaning of the world, rather than solely "spoon feeding" them facts and answers, what Freire (1970) calls a "banking model" of education.

The application of attachment theory to character and citizenship education (Riley, 2011; Watson & Ecken, 2003) extrapolates from the work of John Bowlby (1982) and Mary Ainsworth (1979) concerning the process of infant bonding to primary caretakers and the extensive research on the impact of such attachment on the lifelong development of the individual. Character (both moral and civic) is largely seen as a product of the nature of the relational history of the individual (Berkowitz & Bier, 2005). Therefore, character education strategies highlight the strategic and intentional fostering of healthy relationships among all stakeholders in the life of the home and the school.

Our focus in efforts to integrate character and citizenship education strategies has also been informed through the lens of a democratic society. The reason the Center's name includes both *character* and *citizenship* is that we see a necessary overlap of the two concepts (Althof & Berkowitz, 2006), particularly in the area of civic character (Berkowitz, Althof, & Jones, 2008). Our understanding of the development of both character and citizenship is largely informed by the work of John Dewey (1916/2008). From this perspective, character and citizenship develop best in contexts that exemplify the best aspects of democracy. This is something we have referred to as a *pedagogy of empowerment* (Berkowitz, 2012).

Finally, we recognize, following the notion of democratic pedagogy above (Dewey, 1916/2008), that educators need to take a sociological perspective on classrooms and schools. This is precisely what Kohlberg was aiming for with his notion of moral atmosphere (Power, Higgins, & Kohlberg, 1989), which was inspired by Emile Durkheim's (1973) sociologically informed educational philosophy. The climate and culture of the school and classroom matter. Educating for character and citizenship requires a strategic focus on nurturing certain prosocial, student-empowering school and classroom cultures.

Goals

We began the initiative with six primary goals:

1. Assess faculty readiness for a CE focus

2. Identify the core competencies (knowledge and skills) and dispositions necessary for a person to be an effective character educator
3. Identify where these spheres of knowledge, skills, and dispositions were currently being addressed in core teacher education courses, and where there were gaps
4. Seek to address gaps through modifications of course content
5. Provide resources and professional development opportunities for faculty
6. Assess the impact of the initiative on student outcomes

It should be noted that these goals reflected an initial decision to adopt an "infusion" approach to preparing students to become character educators. By this we mean that CE preparation was not going to be concentrated in one or two courses; students, for example, would not be required to take a specific class on character or citizenship education. Rather, an emphasis on CE would be integrated into a broad range of courses (see also Chapter 10 of this volume; Nucci, Drill, Larson, & Browne, 2005). This parallels the way we believe CE is best implemented in schools and classrooms (cf. Beland, 2003). Rather than teaching character education as one subject among many, effective character educators infuse an emphasis on character into their teaching across the curriculum, as well as into all facets of school life. In our case, focusing on character development in child and adolescent development classes, on effective methods in educational psychology and methods courses, and emphasizing Developmental Discipline in behavior management courses was the preferred structure. Earlier experiences with integrating technology and multicultural themes across the teacher education curricula made us aware of the challenges of quality control when dealing with multiple instructors (including many adjuncts) and sections of courses, but we still felt this was a more powerful way of shaping the program content and culture.

Despite our desire to have CE infused throughout the teacher education curriculum, it was still necessary to specify what CE content and concerns would be addressed in which courses. Correspondingly, we decided to focus most directly on what we called *core courses*. We identified eight courses that were required in most, and in some cases all, of the teacher education programs. These courses included the introductory courses offered at Level One, methods courses and psychology courses at Level Two, and a course on classroom management at Level Three. While these courses became the focus of our intervention efforts, other faculty were encouraged to include dimensions of CE in their courses as well.

ASSESSING FACULTY READINESS

To assess whether faculty would be open to a new CE initiative, Shields developed a faculty survey to assess attitudes toward CE, including their sense of self-efficacy in the area, their desire for additional professional development, and the extent to which they cover the identified competencies in their courses. In October 2008 the four-page survey was distributed to all faculty members, both full-time and adjunct, who taught in one or more of the teacher education programs. Since one goal was to determine what content was currently being taught in existing courses, the questionnaires were not anonymous. The results of the survey were generally encouraging. The key findings were the following:

- Most faculty believed that it was important to prepare students to be character educators.
- Faculty were skeptical about how well our students were currently prepared as character educators.
- While depth of CE knowledge varied, most faculty did not consider themselves to be experts in the field.
- On average, faculty had a moderate sense of self-efficacy when it came to preparing our students to be character educators.
- Many faculty considered professional development in the area of CE to be a priority.

In summary, the survey indicated that there was sufficient belief in the importance of CE and a perception that this was not being met to justify moving forward with the initiative.

CHARACTER EDUCATOR COMPETENCIES

If we are going to prepare students to become effective character educators, it is imperative that we have a clear understanding of the knowledge, skills, and dispositions that are required. While virtually every book on CE designed to guide teachers in their practice provides some background information, discusses selected relevant pedagogical practices and skills, and at least tacitly acknowledges the importance of certain dispositions, there has been no systematic and exhaustive effort to develop such a taxonomy to date. If we are to develop character educators through preservice teacher education, we need a more comprehensive description of the key competencies and dispositions to be cultivated. Only then are we in a place to plan for the scope and sequence in our curriculum.

Of course, there is a massive literature available on which to draw. Obviously, what competencies are emphasized in a given book or article varies with the theoretical orientation of the author, as well as the unique conceptual focus and audience of a particular work. While one author may emphasize cognitive processes, such as moral reasoning, another may focus on social and emotional competencies; a third may focus on shaping prosocial behavior, and so on. One advantage of engaging in this project in the College of Education at the University of Missouri–St. Louis, is the available concentration of scholars with expertise in character and citizenship education due to the existence of the Center for Character and Citizenship. This provides the knowledge base for a comprehensive perspective on a wide range of approaches to the study and promotion of character.

Our intent in developing a scope document of the knowledge, skills, and dispositions of an effective character educator was not to synthesize the entire CE literature. Our more modest yet still highly ambitious aim was to develop a working heuristic that was broad enough to encompass the main themes in the field and specific enough to be useful on a practical, applied level as we reviewed and revised our curricula.

It is important to acknowledge that we specifically rejected beginning with a formal definition of character or character education. Our task force approached the field with somewhat diverse interests and theoretical proclivities, which we viewed as a strength. The one exception was a proactive decision to include civic character as part of our scope. While we used the term *character education* as our umbrella idiom, it was a shorthand way of referring to both character and citizenship education, to the extent that citizenship education addresses dispositional characteristics (cf. Althof & Berkowitz, 2006; Shields, 2011).

The process began with Shields creating a first-draft taxonomy based on his own background in the field and a review of influential books and recent literature. On that basis, judgments were made about what to include and what to leave out, based on a desire to create a manageable list of the most essential knowledge, skills, and dispositions. It was this preliminary taxonomy that was used in the faculty survey described above. The preliminary scope document then was shared with the leadership team. Over the next several months, drawing from the considerable expertise of the group, numerous additions and other modifications were made. Finally, the taxonomy was also sent to several leading experts in the field and their comments were incorporated.

The list of character educator competencies, as currently formulated, is presented in Figure 11.1. Of course, the taxonomy will always remain open to revision. We share it not as a finished product, but simply as a sample of the kind of guiding scope document that we believe is necessary to provide scaffolding for designing efforts to prepare character educators.

One key problem was deciding on the level of generality for concepts. We do not believe there is a "right" level of specificity for such a document. Favoring utility over consistency, some items on the list were left very broad, while others were delineated further depending on what level of specificity we thought necessary for our own planning purposes. Others may make different choices, depending on their specific needs, goals, and theoretical proclivities; clearly, others may also prefer different terminology and may see a need for further additions. Furthermore, while the taxonomy is not exhaustive, it is nonetheless very extensive. In fact, it may be daunting to many to try to cover all the concepts in the taxonomy, but even a significantly reduced set will still comprise a detailed curriculum concerning character education.

Figure 11.1. Character Educator Competencies and Dispositions

GENERAL KNOWLEDGE

Foundations:

Histories of character and citizenship education
Philosophical considerations:
- What values, virtues, moral principles should guide CE?
- Democracy theory/civil society/social capital

Power and culture/social justice
Role of "character" in education
Moral dimensions of teaching
Civic mission of schools
Civic dimensions of schools
Resource centers (e.g., CEP/CCE)

Multidimensional Nature of Character:

Moral character
Civic character
Performance character
Intellectual character

Developmental Processes:

Moral reasoning
Social conventional reasoning
Social-emotional competencies:
- Intrapersonal awareness and regulation
- Interpersonal awareness and relational skills

Moral emotions (e.g., guilt, pride)
Moral identity

Motivation:

Intrinsic/extrinsic
- Role of autonomy, competence, belonging

Achievement motivation (task/mastery and ego/performance)

Sociocultural Influences on Character / Citizenship:

Family
Peer groups
Identity groups/culture
Media
Economics/Poverty

Politics and civil society
School (see below)

School Influences:

Academic curricula
Co-curricular programs (e.g., sports, clubs)
Teacher behaviors
Classroom behaviors
Classroom and school culture
- Sense of community/"culture of care"
- Belonging/attachment/"ownership"
- Physical and emotional safety
- Management and discipline
- Opportunity structure (e.g., leadership opportunities)
Social interdependence (competition, cooperation)
Institutional integrity

PEDAGOGICAL KNOWLEDGE

(Letters refer to categories of skills, listed below)
1. Empowerment strategies (A–G, N, R)
   - Class meetings
   - Democratic decision making/classroom-school governance
   - Peer mediation/conflict resolution/antibullying
2. Relationship building strategies (C–F, H, K, L, R, V)
   - Unity building activities
   - Self-disclosure
3. Moral dilemma discussion (I, J, R)
4. Discussions of current issues (G, J, N, Q, R)
5. Cross-age strategies (A, F, G, H, K, T, V)
   - Buddying, multiaged advisories, peer tutoring
6. Cooperative learning (F, G, K, N, P, V)
7. Developmental Discipline (G, H, L)
8. Curricular strategies (J, K, M, N, R, T, U)
   - Integrating/highlighting CE content in academic curriculum
9. Co-curricular strategies (O, P, U)
   - Integrating/highlighting CE in sports, clubs, field trips
10. Role plays/simulations (R, M)
11. Self-reflection/critical thinking (C, D, I, J, M, N, Q–V)
12. Service learning/community service (F, G, N, R, S, T, U)
13. Culture of learning/community of learners (A–C, F, H, K, N, R, V)
14. Creating partnerships (H, N, T, U, W, X)
    - Parents, other school personnel, community

15.   Differentiated instruction (B, C, F–H, K, T, U, V, Y)
16.   Inclusion strategies (A–D, F, H, K, L, V, W, Y)

SKILLS

(Numbers refer to categories of pedagogical knowledge, listed above)

A.   Create participatory structures (1, 5, 13)
B.   Collaboratively create class norms (1, 13)
C.   Facilitate class meetings (1, 2, 11, 13)
D.   Facilitate conflict resolution (1, 2, 11)
E.   Motivate student participation in school governance (1, 2)
F.   Build participatory skills (1, 2, 5, 6, 11–13)
G.   Motivate student initiative and leadership (1, 4–7, 12)
H.   Build positive relationships (2, 5, 7, 13, 14)
I.   Facilitate moral discussion (3, 11)
J.   Incorporate discussion of issues, policies, events (3, 8, 11)
K.   Structure cooperative learning (6, 2, 5, 8, 13)
L.   Use Developmental Discipline (7, 2, 13)
M.   Integrate CE into lesson plans (8, 10, 11)
N.   Connect class work to meaningful activity (8, 1, 4, 6, 11–14)
O.   Utilize co-curricular activities (9)
P.   Foster positive competition (9, 6, 13)
Q.   Support media literacy (11, 4)
R.   Promote critical thinking (11, 1–4, 8, 10, 12, 13)
S.   Provide opportunities for moral action (11, 12)
T.   Structure effective service learning opportunities (12, 5, 8, 11, 14)
U.   Advocate for a cause (12, 8, 9, 11, 13, 14)
W.   Work effectively with parents (14)
X.   Network with stakeholders (14)
Y.   Develop cultural competence/responsive (15, 1, 2, 4, 6, 7, 14, 16)

DISPOSITIONS

Moral sensitivity
Habit of self-reflection
Desire to model good character
Commitment to professional ethics
Sense of professional self-efficacy
Sense of political self-efficacy (ability to make a difference)
Love and respect for youth
Appreciation of diversity
Commitment to democratic values
Commitment to social justice
Commitment to civic engagement (interest in social/political)

Sense of social responsibility
Concern for the rights and welfare of others and the "common good"
Commitment to nonviolent conflict resolution
Optimism: potential of all
Acceptance of human frailty/humility

The figure is divided into four broad categories: (1) general knowledge, (2) pedagogical knowledge, (3) skills, and (4) dispositions. *General Knowledge* refers to content about aspects of character (such as how it develops, motivational elements, and school-specific influences) as well as foundational knowledge (such as relevant aspects of history and philosophy of education). *Pedagogical Knowledge* refers to specific strategies or approaches that may be used by classroom teachers to promote character. Of course, it is not enough to simply "know" about a strategy. Typically, it takes one or more *Skills* (the third category) to effectively implement a strategy. These include a broad range of pedagogical methods. The categories of Pedagogical Knowledge and Skills have been cross-referenced to capture the interdependence between knowing what works and knowing how to implement what works. Finally, *Dispositions* refer to the personal characteristics of the educator that support effective character education. It would be difficult to engage in a pedagogy of empowerment (Berkowitz, 2012), for example, if one were authoritarian and unable to engage in true dialogic relations.

In addition to compiling the taxonomy of competencies (knowledge/skills) and dispositions, each term in the scope document is described or defined in a separate (and ongoing) document that provides clear and full explanations for future reference. Many of the terms in the list are clearly abbreviations or shorthand ways of indicating a broader set of ideas. This worked fine for planning purposes since "we all knew what we were talking about," but it was also important to have these truncated concepts or themes spelled out in further depth. To illustrate, here are two of these definitions and descriptions from the category of General Knowledge:

Power and Culture / Social Justice: Students should become critically aware of how people live their lives in situated contexts that reflect dynamics of power and culture. "Character" does not exist apart from how people think and act in real situations. "Character" cannot be reduced to individual characteristics or virtues that can be defined or expressed without reference to their broader social implications and consequences. Students should develop sensitivity to how habitual and patterned behavior can support, even unintentionally, differential access to social power and resources. A concern for social justice should be seen as an essential dimension of character.

Performance Character: Performance character refers to "the dispositions, virtues, or personal qualities that enable an individual to accomplish intentions and goals" (Shields, 2011, p. 52). It includes such qualities as perseverance, diligence, courage, resilience, optimism, initiative, and attention to detail. Such qualities relate to the exercise of will and reflect skills in self-management. Often, the qualities of performance character are referred to as virtues, but they need to be distinguished from moral virtues. While moral virtues (e.g., honesty, trustworthiness) are generally thought of as intrinsically good, performance virtues are good only when they serve good ends.

FILLING THE GAPS RATHER THAN REINVENTING THE WHEEL

A key part of our strategy was to map the terrain we were about to traverse. In other words, we needed to do an inventory of what already existed in our teacher preparation curriculum and then compare that to the taxonomy of what we believed ought to be included for course-infusion of character education. One part of the faculty survey asked respondents to indicate the extent to which they address specific character educator competencies and dispositions in their classes, as listed in the first version of this taxonomy. While the whole Teaching and Learning Department faculty was surveyed, along with relevant faculty in other divisions, we focused our analyses on the responses associated with the core courses mentioned above.

The data from the faculty survey are difficult to summarize concisely, but the following three points seem warranted:

1. *There were no glaring gaps in our coverage.* All the competencies were addressed in at least one class, and often in two or more classes.
2. *Key areas for improvement pertain to consistency and depth.* While it appeared that the competencies were addressed, they were not addressed by all instructors of a given course to the same level of depth.
3. *Systematicity and redundancy.* Not surprisingly, there was no systematic blueprint in place for what and where character education was to be covered in the teacher preparation curriculum, This led to some obvious problems, most notably poor sequencing and, in a few places, the same topics were introduced in different classes.

The faculty survey, as mentioned, was based on a very preliminary scope document. As the taxonomy moved through its many revisions, some faculty members were individually interviewed to refine our understanding of what competencies and dispositions were covered in courses. One frequent problem pertained to the lack of consistency that sometimes existed across sections of a given course. Even when using the same or similar syllabus, two instructors often addressed different content, or similar content with different degrees of depth.

We also noted an issue around using variants of CE vocabulary. Even the term *character* was questioned by some who favored alternative language, such as "developing dispositions toward ethical practices." By and large, however, we were successful at developing a relatively consistent vocabulary. Our working assumption was that the development of a common discourse around CE would enhance the message to preservice teachers across the curriculum.

A Model Course Grid

The leadership team spent some time reflecting on the survey results and how best to move forward. We decided that it would be useful to construct a course grid that indicated where we believed key content could best be introduced, where it might be emphasized and elaborated, and where it might be further utilized and/or reviewed. Through a boot-strapping process that involved both thinking about where we believed CE content could best be covered and talking with relevant faculty about their courses, we eventually developed a grid that identified where content was (or should be) addressed. This model loosely echoes the "spiral curriculum" ideas of Jerome Bruner (1960).

The grid lists all of the items in the taxonomy, which are then cross-referenced with each of the eight core courses. In each case, content was included in a course as Introduced (I), Covered (C), Reviewed (R), or not present at all. Frequently, we identified one course where a specific content (knowledge, skill, or disposition) would be introduced, a second course where it would be covered in a more elaborated form, and a third course where it would be reviewed. For example, the concept of "moral reasoning" was introduced in a Level One course dealing with the psychology of the learner. It was expanded in the Level Two educational psychology course around Kohlberg's and Gilligan's theories, and applied in methods and clinical courses looking at real-world dilemmas and applications.

Resourcing the Courses

With a taxonomy of what ought to be covered in hand and a map of the existing coverage, the next step was to begin to fill the gaps by providing the requisite resources. Two interrelated strategies were developed to provide resources for instructors in the core courses.

First, the lead instructor for each course was invited to meet with Berkowitz and Shields. In the meeting, Berkowitz and Shields reviewed the course syllabus and suggested potential additions and/or modifications to course objectives. They also discussed the place of the course in the overall CE initiative, reviewing the course grid described above. Finally, resources (including suggested readings, videos, websites, curricula, and so on) that fit the objectives were discussed and made available. Fortunately, the Center for Character and Citizenship at UMSL has one of the most extensive libraries of such resources and is able to purchase or otherwise procure suggested resources to expand and update the library.

Second, to facilitate integration of CE across the identified courses and to assist instructors with relevant resources, we decided to publish an edited book of seminal and influential articles in character education (Shields, Funk, & Berkowitz, in press). It became clear that a core set of such readings could be used across the curriculum. The plan is for each student who enters a teacher education program to buy the book and then assignments from it will be given by multiple instructors in a number of courses. In this way the book both symbolically and practically suggests the importance and relevance of CE throughout the teacher education program. Articles for the book were selected with an eye to covering the scope document with relevant and readable publications, with sensitivity to the intended undergraduate audience, and with a desire to introduce a number of key figures in the field.

PROFESSIONAL DEVELOPMENT

Despite the concentration of expertise in character and citizenship education at UMSL, courses in the teacher preparation program are mostly taught by faculty who are not associated with the CCC. To help address this, we established a number of professional development opportunities to broaden the base of committed faculty. In cooperation with Berkowitz, the St. Louis–based organization CHARACTER*plus* regularly offers a 3-day CE certificate program to current educators. We decided to sponsor a special version of that program tailored to teacher education faculty and offered the program annually for 3 years. The content covered theoretical foundations, basic concepts and pedagogical strategies, and extended discussion of infusing CE into various curricular areas as well as entire schools. We managed to attract most of the relevant faculty in the first three years, and we invited others to attend which created a rich mix of education faculty, area educators, and preservice teachers.

A TIME OF TRANSITION

The "second wave" initiative entered a transition phase when the dean of the College of Education retired in 2010 and both Shields and Martille Elias, who had become a key leader of the initiative, left for positions at other institutions. At that time, plans were being developed for an empirical investigation of the initiative's impact on students, as well as a continuation of the provision of resources to teacher education faculty. While we believe, with no more warrant than our own informal observations, that the initiative was having a substantial and positive effect, we are also keenly aware of the need to document those positive outcomes and describe the future directions we envision.

With the hiring of a new dean (Carole Basile) who is highly supportive of the integration of both theory and research into practice in general and character and citizenship education expertise into teacher preparation in particular, the initiative is beginning to morph into a third phase. It is still premature to describe what changes, if any, the initiative will experience. For instance, in an anonymous exit survey, graduate students indicated that they think these concepts are integral to their role as teachers, but that they did not feel well prepared as educators of character. In response, the committee designed a new elective course for a master's program in Elementary Education entitled Building Character and Competence with Diverse Students. Our goal was to integrate CE, special education, and TESOL components under a conceptual umbrella relevant to teacher experiences in the classroom.

Currently, many teacher education faculty continue to integrate the material and knowledge they have acquired in their courses. The work of the Center for Character and Citizenship continues to have a significant impact on CE education and theory building through empirical work (both by faculty and by doctoral students), journal articles, and community outreach. The synergy with CHARACTER*plus* continues, and the St. Louis region continues to be a leader in infusing CE into K–12 schools. These latter elements have helped support the transformation of many local schools and districts into showplaces for character and citizenship education. In fact, over the past 5 years (2008–2012), approximately 33% of all National Schools and Districts of Character, as recognized by the Character Education Partnership (www.character.org), are in the St. Louis region. All are members of CHARACTER*plus,* and nearly all are led by a principal who has graduated from the Leadership Academy in Character Education, a program run by the CCC in collaboration with CHARACTER*plus* (Berkowitz, Pelster, & Johnston, 2012).

We hope the taxonomy of CE competencies, along with the forthcoming book of articles targeting teacher CE development, will continue to impact the UMSL program, as well as other programs also working to integrate CE into teacher preparation in thoughtful and productive ways (cf. Bahm, 2012). Given the extreme focus on testing within NCLB mandates for the past 10 years and the economic downturn at the state level for the past few years, teachers are being asked to do more with fewer resources. School culture in many areas around the country is toxic with peer bullying, disrespect toward teachers, and angry parents. Educational leaders, teachers, and staff are looking for strategies to increase a sense of community, a shared good, and a climate of hope. Understanding and naming needed CE competencies, we believe, will provoke generative dialogue about how to better prepare educators of character for tomorrow's children.

IMPLICATIONS FOR TEACHER PREPARATION

Along this journey to craft and implement a high-impact program for promoting the capacity of preservice education students to be effective character and citizenship educators, we have learned numerous lessons that may be of benefit to those

interested in a similar goal at other colleges and schools of education. So, in closing, we offer the following suggestions:

- *Be collaborative.* This kind of endeavor should not rest on the shoulders
  of one or two faculty or administrators. Having a broad-based leadership
  team with diverse perspectives and areas of expertise is recommended.
  Ideally, the majority, but not necessarily all, should have scholarly
  expertise in character and citizenship education.
- *Build leadership.* As is true throughout education (both in P–12 schools
  and districts and in colleges of education), having strong administrative
  support, ideally at the top, is necessary to legitimize the initiative and to
  garner support.
- *Invest in professional development.* The deeper the expertise, the more
  effective the implementation is likely to be. Mentoring, professional
  development workshops, and the provision of high-quality resources
  (books, articles, videos, curricula, and so on) is necessary.
- *Promote saliency and common language.* Making the initiative and its
  mission and goals explicit helps maintain momentum. Having a clear
  and shared language for identifying the initiative and its components is
  also helpful in both communication, in general, and buy-in, in particular.
- *Be comprehensive.* As noted above, we chose not to focus on creating a
  separate mandatory course or two on these topics. Rather we felt that
  integrating CE across the entire curriculum would take it deeper, make it
  more integral to education, and make it more sustainable. Part of being
  comprehensive is also to be multifaceted. We included syllabi reviews,
  professional development, demonstration guest lectures, certification,
  experiential learning, individual consultations, and provision of
  curricular resources, all to support faculty comfort and capacity.
- *Be accountable.* In this day of a fading Elementary and Secondary
  Education Act (NCLB), accountability in education, for some, has taken
  on a negative hue. However, it is desirable in education to know what
  you are trying to accomplish and to have some way to know if you have
  done so. Our taxonomy was the first step in defining the outcome goals;
  our plans for assessing impact will be the other part of this accountability
  equation.
- *Know your context.* We were well served by first mapping what was
  already in place and generally surveying faculty attitudes and knowledge.
  Building the initiative on the foundation that existed allowed us to make
  it fit the context and not waste time on inappropriate or redundant steps
  or elements.

These tenets taken together represent the distillation of insights from a core
group of faculty with expertise and commitments to integrating character and

citizenship-related knowledge, skills, and dispositions into teacher education. As in all change processes within large complex institutions, leadership, collaboration, and persistence are the yeast to change climate.

REFERENCES

Ainsworth, M. (1979). Infant-mother attachment. *American Psychologist, 34,* 932–937.

Althof, W., & Berkowitz, M. W. (2006). Moral education and character education: Their relationship and their roles in citizenship education. *Journal of Moral Education, 35,* 495–518.

Bahm, K. L. (2012). *The integration of character education and its impact on teachers' professional practice* (Unpublished doctoral dissertation). University of Missouri–St. Louis.

Beland, K. (2003). *Eleven principles sourcebook: How to achieve quality character education in K–12 schools.* Washington, DC: Character Education Partnership.

Berkowitz, M. W. (2012). *You can't teach through a rat: And other epiphanies for educators.* Boone, NC: Character Development Group.

Berkowitz, M. W., Althof, W., & Jones, S. E. (2008). Educating for civic character. In J. Arthur, I. Davies, & C. Hahn (Eds.), *The Sage handbook of education for citizenship and democracy* (pp. 399–499). Los Angeles: Sage.

Berkowitz, M. W., & Bier, M. C. (2005). The interpersonal roots of character education. In D. K. Lapsley & F. C. Power (Eds.), *Character psychology and character education* (pp. 268–285). Notre Dame, IN: University of Notre Dame Press.

Berkowitz, M. W., Pelster, K., & Johnston, A. (2012). Case Study 17B: Leading in the middle: A tale of prosocial education reform in two principals and two middle schools. In P. Brown, M. Corrigan, & A. Higgins-D'Alessandro (Eds.), *The handbook of prosocial education* (pp. 619–626). Lanham, MD: Rowman & Littlefield.

Bowlby, J. (1982). *Attachment.* New York: Basic Books. (Original work published 1969)

Bruner, J. (1960). *The process of education.* Cambridge, MA: Harvard University Press.

Dewey, J. (2008). *The Middle Works, 1899–1924: Vol. 9. 1916: Democracy and education* (J. Boydston, Ed.). Carbondale: Southern Illinois University Press. (Original work published 1916)

Durkheim, E. (1973). *Moral education: A study in the theory and application of the sociology of education.* New York: Free Press.

Freire, P. (1970). *Pedagogy of the oppressed.* New York: Herder and Herder.

Navarro, V. (2005, February). Character education partnership initiatives. In M. Schwartz (Chair), *Integrating character education into teacher education: Three grant sites tell their story.* Symposium conducted at the annual meeting of the American Association of Colleges for Teacher Education, Washington, DC.

Navarro, V., Berkowitz, M. W., Battistich, V., Shields, D. L., & Suess, P. (2006). *Mapping character: Beliefs and practices in teacher preparation.* Grant Report. Washington, DC: Character Education Partnership.

Nucci, L., Drill, K., Larson, C., & Browne, C. (2005). Preparing preservice teachers for character education in urban elementary schools; The UIC initiative. *Journal of Research in Character Education, 3*(2), 81–96.

Piaget, J. (1954). *The construction of reality in the child.* New York: Basic Books.

Power, F. C., Higgins, A., & Kohlberg, L. (1989). *Lawrence Kohlberg's approach to moral education.* New York: Columbia University Press.

Riley, P. (2011). *Attachment theory and the teacher-student relationship: A practical guide for teachers, teacher educators and school leaders.* New York: Routledge.

Shields, D. (2011). Character as the aim of education. *Phi Delta Kappan, 92*(8), 48–53.

Shields, D., Funk, C., & Berkowitz, M. W. (in press). *Becoming character educators.* Charlotte, NC: Information Age.

Watson, M., & Ecken, L. (2003). *Learning to trust: Transforming difficult elementary classrooms through Developmental Discipline.* San Francisco: Jossey-Bass.

COMMENTARY

Part IV concludes the book with a commentary by teacher education scholar Virginia Richardson in Chapter 12. The chapter provides a broad analysis of the implications of the previous chapters for teacher education research and practice. Her commentary takes up issues ranging from the challenges of programmatic change in higher education, to strategies to increase the validity of studies on the moral work of teaching in teacher education.

Teaching Moral Teaching in Teacher Education

Virginia Richardson

I have enjoyed reading the chapters in this book, and thank the editors for asking me to comment on them. For a number of years, a growing body of research has focused on the moral elements of classroom life and teachers' manner and actions that affect them. It is certainly time for the next steps to be taken in introducing and supporting moral teaching in the K–12 classroom: the preparation of teachers for this important endeavor. I use the term *moral teaching* to focus on teachers who explicitly and consciously consider ethics in their own and their students' classroom actions.

The editors have chosen authors who represent a variety of perspectives on moral teaching and approaches to teacher education. The variety is important and helpful for those who are planning a teacher education class or program with an emphasis on moral teaching. As a set, the chapters include descriptions of K–12 and teacher education programs, and teacher education curricula or syllabi that represent different ways of thinking about and approaching moral education. The theoretical and research frames include philosophical theory, learning theory and research, educational research, and the results of the editors' research on their students' beliefs, learning, and development. Each chapter instantiates a particular stance toward moral teaching through a description of the goals, curriculum, and content of a teacher education class or program, such that the chapter writers' approaches and beliefs can be understood more clearly through the portrayals of practice. Thus the chapters are eminently readable and useful, and present teacher education as an intellectually interesting field of study and practice.

In this chapter I focus on a small set of topics and issues related to teacher education that struck me as I read the book. These include ways in which moral teaching is conceptualized; the importance of student beliefs; bringing together theory, research, and practice; the contexts of teacher education that affect the programs; and research/assessment.

CONCEPTS OF MORAL TEACHING AND TEACHER EDUCATION

This section examines the concepts and teaching of moral education within the two dominant disciplines of philosophy and psychology that are represented in the chapters. Before moving into differences, however, it is important to acknowledge the strong agreements across the chapters. First, the authors all agree that ethics is an essential element of teaching whether the teacher recognizes this or not, and that helping teachers understand and find ways of thinking about the ethical import of their actions is an important element of moral education in the classroom and in teacher education classes. Second, there is an agreement that moral teaching, as a specific form of the moral, requires its own analysis, study, development, and implementation into practice. In these chapters, the implementation takes place primarily through teacher education, with some mention of professional development. And third, whether the emphasis in the teacher education program is on teaching morally, teaching morality, or both, it is expected that the results will play out in teachers' classroom actions in ways that affect their students' thinking, learning, and development in positive directions.

The chapters in this book represent different disciplinary stances that help drive the authors' conceptions and instruction of moral teaching as well as teacher education practice. Sanger, Osguthorpe, and Fenstermacher (Chapter 1) differentiate among the chapters in terms of two approaches to the moral work of teaching: teaching morally and teaching morality. Another way of analyzing the chapters is from the disciplines that frame the conceptions, goals, curricula, and teaching of moral education in a given class or program. The two dominant disciplines represented in these chapters are philosophy and psychology. These disciplines are quite distinct in terms of the nature of concept analysis and development, the place of empirical research, measurable outcomes, and eventually program implementation. Within teacher education programs, they have traditionally been placed in two different classes or sets of classes. Philosophy is usually located within the educational foundations classes, and psychology within the educational psychology or learning and development classes. It is exciting to note that faculty members from both disciplines are working hard to bring the moral work of teaching into their teacher education classes and programs such that moral teaching will find its way into our K–12 classrooms. All chapters except Chapter 2 are easily placed within a disciplinary category; there Osguthorpe and Sanger combine the two categories, and their chapter will be discussed in the next section on student beliefs.

Philosophical Chapters

There are five philosophical chapters: Campbell, Chapter 3; Stengel, Chapter 4; Blumenfeld-Jones et al., Chapter 5; Fallona and Canniff, Chapter 6; and Johnson et al., Chapter 7. Each has adopted or adapted a system of ethics which is then developed into a concept of moral teaching that drives the content and processes

of their teacher education classes and programs. For purposes of teacher education, they place the system of ethics within learning and teaching theories such as
constructivism and the democratic classroom. But the major focus is on a conception of moral teaching and the primary goal is to help their students develop an
understanding of moral teaching.

Campbell's classes are grounded in a set of moral virtues that she considers
as a foundation of moral teaching. The virtues are used in her class to help students ethically consider professional practice. Stengel's foundations course is built
around the concepts of moral responsibility (Dewey and Niebuhr) and practical
reasoning. She does this, in part, through democratic education theory as both the
content and process of her classroom.

Blumenfeld-Jones et al. concentrate on different systems of ethics and, with
these, help their students uncover the "hidden curriculum" and consider how
these systems can be used in classrooms. Further, they have developed their own
system of ethics, humility ethics, which they present to the teacher education students and to practicing teachers.

In the teacher education programs described by Fallona and Canniff at the
University of Southern Maine, the mission focuses on preparing teachers fully
committed to equity. The equity mission is grounded in the moral and intellectual
virtues, specifically justice and wisdom, and this stance is carried across the classes
in the program.

Johnson et al.'s teacher education program at Winthrop University looks at
the moral work of teaching as a humanistic and equitable disposition. The program is designed to help teacher education students develop four cognitively based
dispositions: fairness, integrity, commitment, and communication. After working
out the goals of the program, the faculty reconstructed their teacher education
program to meet these goals.

Each of the chapters in this category describes a classroom or program that
takes its curriculum cues from a particular approach to the moral and its instan-
tiation in programs designed to prepare teachers for teaching morally. The next set
of chapters approach the teacher education process in a somewhat different way.

Psychological Chapters

The psychologically oriented chapters focus on preparing teachers to help
their students learn and develop the foundations of teaching morality: Lapsley
et al., Chapter 8; Watson et al., Chapter 9; Nucci, Chapter 10; and Shields et al.,
Chapter 11. Each uses a number of psychology-oriented learning, development,
and educational theories and research, and some philosophical theories (Dewey
and Noddings being mentioned the most). The content of the courses includes
knowledge of psychological theories and research, and skills shown to be effective in teaching morality. The classes are taught using many of the strategies that
the students are expected to eventually use in their own classrooms. In addition,

those who have developed and possibly studied specific character development programs in schools use their knowledge and experience to consider the nature of teacher education that would prepare candidates to teach these programs.

Lapsley et al. build on the considerable research and development work in character education to consider the best approach to prepare teachers to acquire skills in teaching character education. Their approach focuses on explicit best teaching practices, with intentional character education included as a treatment. Watson et al. use the Child Development Project (CDP) program that has been implemented in many schools across the country as the foundation for the teacher education programs described in their chapter. The content and processes in the teacher education classes are designed to prepare teachers in developing CDP classrooms through values and strategies of CDP forms of classroom organization, management and discipline, and reflective practice. Nucci draws on cognitive psychology in his description of two teacher education programs: one at UC Berkeley, and the second at the University of Illinois, Chicago (UIC). From these sources, he and his colleagues developed an overall, coherent theoretical framework for their program that includes constructivist, cognitive, and motivation theories, and social cognitive domain theory. Shields et al. built their program from reviews of good practices and from their taxonomy of knowledge, skills, and dispositions for teachers of character education.

The authors of these psychology-oriented chapters understand the nature of learning and development in classrooms, as well as the dispositions held and strategies used by teachers who teach morality effectively. They center their efforts on preparing teachers to bring explicit moral education into their classrooms. The courses that are described focus on knowledge of moral development in children and on teaching strategies. Teacher education takes place in classrooms that are themselves structured for constructivist, practice-based education.

Comparisons

How different are these two types of teacher education classrooms and programs: the philosophical and the psychological? Obviously, the content is quite different. The philosophical classes focus on moral and ethical systems and how they play out in classrooms. The goals relate to helping teacher education students develop ways of thinking ethically, making judgments, and acting in classrooms situations that are thought to be full of ambiguity and dilemmas. The psychology chapters focus on the knowledge of theories and research concerning student learning and moral development, as well as strategies for teaching moral and character education. With this focus, the strategies in the psychological approach are somewhat more structured for the students than in the philosophical approach.

The teaching processes in the educational psychology and foundations classes have always been quite similar, with a reliance on lectures and discussion sections that focus primarily on readings in theory and research. The teaching processes described in these two sets of chapters still appear to be similar, but have shifted from the traditional lecture to various democratic and constructivist activities that are designed to bring theory/research and teaching practice together in the minds and actions of the teacher education students. With the content of moral teaching represented in these two different forms of teacher education classes, in combination with the modeling of moral teaching in the teacher education classrooms, it may be that explicit attention to the moral becomes a common aspect in K–12 classrooms.

STUDENT BELIEFS

One could suggest that a major goal of the chapters described above is to help students understand and develop their own beliefs about moral teaching and how these might affect their actions as future teachers, and consider alternatives to the beliefs that they now hold. Student beliefs about the moral aspects of classroom life are discussed by Osguthorpe and Sanger in Chapter 2. They report on their studies of the beliefs concerning moral teaching held by candidates entering teacher education programs. While the students hold conceptions of and strong commitments to the moral work of teaching, they present challenges to teacher educators in several ways. A number of the beliefs held by the students appear underdeveloped and in need of extensive new knowledge for implementation. An example is the belief that the way to teach morality is through the teacher's modeling of moral action. In addition, the authors pointed to a tension in the responses between the purposes of teaching and reasons to enter teaching. On the one hand, students' reasons are explicitly moral and relate to the expectations of making a difference for others and being a role model. On the other hand, they viewed the purposes of teaching as academic and preparation for work. As pointed out by Blumenfeld-Jones, these conflicting systems of beliefs also show up in policies and writings about the best ways of arriving at good practice in education.

In Tom Green's (1971) philosophical treatise on the nature of teaching, he proposed that an individual may hold beliefs that are incompatible or inconsistent. This occurs because beliefs are held in clusters, and there is little cross-fertilization among belief systems. Thus incompatible beliefs may be held in different clusters. Green proposed that the incompatibility may remain until the beliefs are set side by side and examined for consistency.

Osguthorpe and Sanger point to the need to take into account the entering candidates' beliefs about moral teaching and to help students understand their own beliefs, examine inconsistencies, and consider alternatives. Such work with students will also help them develop a stance that predisposes them to continue such inquiries into their own beliefs and practices as they move into the teaching profession.

Attention to teacher education students' beliefs about moral teaching will be particularly important over the next several years as the explicit moral education exposure and lack thereof will bring into the teacher education programs students with very different beliefs and ways of holding them. In public schools the sense of the relativity of different systems of ethics still dominates: "In this class, this is how you must treat others; whatever you do at home may be different, and that's not a concern here." On the other hand, more and more students are attending charter, voucher, and parochial schools in which ethical systems are explicit and meant to regulate the students' lives in and out of school. While this is not the case for all charter and voucher schools, it appears to be a growing trend. Some teacher education candidates may have been indoctrinated into one ethical system and arrive in the teacher education classroom with little or no understanding of alternative systems. And others may not be fully conscious of the ethical belief systems that they hold. It will be even more important for teacher educators to bring to the surface for discussion the ethical belief systems of their students. Further, teacher educators should themselves consider the nature of their own beliefs as they develop missions for their programs, and curricula for their classrooms.

THE IMPORTANCE OF BRINGING TOGETHER
THEORY, RESEARCH, AND PRACTICE

In surveys of new teachers concerning their teacher education programs, the major complaint has been that their programs did not prepare them for such practices as classroom management, that is, that the theories and research did not tell them how to teach. I ran into this view in my first experience as a teacher educator. I was an instructor of foundations in the teacher education program at the College at Brockport, SUNY. One of the readings in the standard syllabus suggested that teachers should establish warm and caring classroom environments, and we were discussing this notion in class. A student appeared more and more frustrated as the class went on. He finally became quite agitated and, with a bright red face, raised his hand and said: "And what the **** am I supposed to do about a warm classroom? Turn up the thermostat?" This was my first experience with the phenomenon (often joked or complained about by teacher educators and professional developers) of the intense need for teachers and candidates to know what they should *do* in class on Monday morning. It also relates to the many complaints about the lack of relationship between theory and research, on the one hand, and practice, on the other. Formal knowledge, as represented in research and theory readings and discussions, and practical knowledge, gained from experience with acts of teaching, are different forms of knowing and will remain so. Nonetheless, there are ways of bringing them together such that each informs the other.

There are quite different beliefs on the part of teacher educators about how and particularly when to bring formal knowledge and practical knowledge together. In my own teacher education program at the University of Michigan, several professors felt that the students should begin their internship in the K–12 classroom as soon as the class began; while others wanted to introduce their students to the formal knowledge concerning learning, development, and motivation prior to their entering their internship classrooms. Fenstermacher (1993) and Tom (1995) have made the controversial suggestion that extensive internships in classrooms should precede formal teacher education classes, and, in a book edited by Upitis, Luce-Kapler, and Munby (2000), faculty members at Queens University write about their experiment with this structure.

The differences in the decision of when to introduce students to educational practice in relation to theory are represented in these chapters. Stengel, for example, rejects the notion that knowledge acquisition precedes knowledge use and focuses on guided practice as the appropriate process for knowledge acquisition. On the other hand, Nucci focuses on formal knowledge in his classroom, bringing in examples of classroom practices.

Nonetheless, all of the chapters in this book describe ways in which the authors and their colleagues have worked hard to bring these two forms of knowledge together. Nucci, for example, described the attempts to help students learn to integrate moral teaching within regular academic classes by asking them to construct social and moral lessons within curricular materials used in the Chicago public schools; UIC faculty members also use video clips of teachers around specific forms of action such as responding to transgressions. Campbell uses case study pedagogy. Watson videotaped a teacher from the first day of school and periodically across 2 school years to use in her teacher education classes. From these videotapes, the students can see and discuss how a teacher using CDP principles was able to develop her difficult classroom into an inclusive, democratic, and morally responsive experience for her students. Fallona and Canniff describe their process of immersing candidates into classroom life for two semesters and integrating this immersion with their methods and theory courses. Stengel also integrates her class work with internships by, for example, asking the students to take pictures of their field experience classrooms to capture the physical, social, cultural, and economic realities of their particular school, and share these with other students in the class.

These practices are particularly important in bringing the realities of classroom teaching together with the formal concepts of moral teaching learned in the teacher education program. It is seldom that the cooperating teacher spends time with the student teacher to explain the ethical system behind his or her decisions that affect the classroom, often because they are not always consciously known to him or her. Providing moral concepts and a language to the student teacher and providing ways of seeing, considering, and discussing these concepts in practice is critically important to their learning.

THE CONTEXT OF TEACHER EDUCATION: HIGHER EDUCATION

The moral work of teaching classes and programs described in this book takes place within higher education institutions whose history, structure, culture, and decision-making processes create barriers to program change, particularly if the change is the introduction of a conceptual strand that is unknown and/or unappreciated by many of the members of a faculty as well as the leadership. There is no doubt that the introduction of a new class, or the shift of emphasis within a given class, is easier to accomplish than changing a complete teacher education program. Nonetheless, given the limits on the number of classes/credit hours that are imposed on programs, some faculty members may look askance at even a suggestion for a new class or replacement of an existing class.

Many of the chapters discuss the challenge of bringing the moral work of teaching focus into their teacher education programs, particularly those whose authors believe strongly in the integration of moral education throughout all classes in the program. Nucci, for example, describes the difficulties of doing so at the University of Illinois, Chicago. The program began with a revised course in child development, and they were then able to work with some faculty members to integrate moral education into subsequent courses, particularly student teaching. In a natural experiment, they found that students who went through the integrated program gained more knowledge about moral education and had a higher sense of efficacy about being able to teach the program than those who just took the child development course, the latter group scoring the same as the control group.

Campbell, on the other hand, initially agreed with the views of Nucci, Lapsley et al., and Shields et al. that ethics instruction should be infused across the teacher education curriculum. After her experience with such attempts and her research, she decided that the topic could easily become less clear and eventually disappear with an infusion approach. She now feels that there should be an explicit and required course in the cultivation of ethical practice in teaching, which she has been able to develop in her program.

The difficulties of programmatic change in teacher education programs in higher education haunt teacher educators who want to make changes in their own programs. Usually, it won't work without bringing other faculty members into the process, and making sure that the rest of the faculty members understand and accept the concept and goals that surround the change. There is also a problem when faculty members who have been able to make changes retire or leave to join another institution's faculty. The energy and intellectual interest in a particular topic may then dissipate and the new programmatic emphases disappear. It is important, then, that consideration be given to how a program can be structured to survive the founder's leaving. It is also important to develop a critical mass of programs, which include as a focus the moral work of teaching, that survive over a period of time to ensure that this emphasis becomes part of the tradition of teacher education programs.

Two programs that are described in these chapters appear to have been successful in creating teacher education experiences with foundations in moral teaching: the University of Southern Maine (USM) as described by Fallona and Canniff, and Winthrop University, in the Johnson et al. chapter. Both programs have missions or goals that focus on moral teaching. The USM chapter focuses on developing a stance of equity in its students, which involves the moral and intellectual virtues of justice and wisdom. USM also employs these virtues in the criteria for entrance into the program. The Winthrop program is associated with the National Network for Educational Renewal (Sirotnik, 1994), and also focuses on equity, as well as nurturing pedagogy, and responsible stewardship. The goals center on the development of four dispositions: fairness, integrity, commitment, and communication. In the programs at both universities, these values are expressed in the mission of the program, in the teaching and learning standards and assessments, and in the class curricula across the program. The programs are rooted in the concept of equity, and, to a certain degree, in the standards and assessment movement—both usually found as requirements of accreditation. These two successes suggest that program change is possible, and that there are many lessons to be learned from these two cases about ways of approaching the change. These cases may also suggest that it is helpful to use an external impetus such as accreditation requirements to shape and provide a rationale for the reform.

RESEARCH AND EVALUATION

As suggested by a number of the authors, there is considerable research on the moral aspects of classrooms, moral teaching, and effective strategies for teaching character education. There is considerably less research on teacher education that prepares students for moral teaching and teaching morality.

If we distinguish between *research* (to advance more wide-ranging knowledge or theory) and *evaluation* (to provide timely and constructive information for decision making about particular programs), we find more evaluation than research in the moral teacher education area. This may be because of the accreditation requirements for classroom and program evaluation (National Council for Accreditation of Teacher Education, 2008; Teacher Education Accreditation Council, 2012). Most of the chapters in this book discuss their program evaluations of students as they leave the program or several years after they have been teaching. The methods used to assess stance, dispositions, beliefs, and moral values about teaching involve asking graduates to respond to case studies or dilemmas on paper or in focus groups, or surveys that attempt to determine whether graduates are using practices that instantiate the various moral teaching dispositions or actions that were taught in the teacher education program.

While not discussed very much in the chapters, there is also an emphasis on individual student assessment with what would appear to be observation (e.g., during student teaching) or on student work during the class. This process is helped by clearly stated program learning goals or standards and their assessments of the type found in Fallona and Canniff and Johnson et al. These evaluations have been used for programmatic and class change and for accreditation processes. A concern that was highlighted in the chapter by Johnson et al. is the potential lack of validity of the measures being used for such outcomes as student dispositions because students are able to "regurgitate" the course content rather than reveal a true picture of a candidate's moral dispositions and beliefs. If the measures are used in follow-up studies of former students who are now teachers, they may no longer be viewed by the former students as high stakes, thus improving the validity of the measures.

In moving from evaluation to research, there are some intriguing "researchable" issues that emerge from these chapters. An interesting one involves the program at USM. Fallona and Canniff state that their system of selection into the teacher education program involves an analysis of essays as well as an interview to determine whether the applicants demonstrate a predisposition for the moral and intellectual virtues of justice and wisdom. They state that "in most cases our collective experience has taught us that we cannot take teachers who are not predisposed to be just and wise teachers and make them so." What a fascinating topic for research! Another has to do with the language of moral teaching that is stressed in a number of classes and programs such as Shields et al.'s description of theirs at the University of Missouri–St. Louis. It would be interesting to examine the language that the students use upon leaving the program, and the language, as well as actions, that they use after several years of teaching. A large and long-term study of teacher education programs that are able to include moral teaching within their missions and across the classes would be an important and useful study as well.

While there is considerable work on evaluations that inform a specific program, it would be useful to conduct research that not only informs practice, but also contributes to policy analysis and development. This would require larger scale research programs that go beyond those described in the chapters that are small scale and site specific. However, for a number of reasons, large-scale replicable research is difficult to conduct in teacher education, particularly that which attempts to tie program elements with the eventual moral learning and development of students in the classes of the graduates from the programs. For example, the diverse factors that would have to be controlled in order to conduct a non-random study of the relationship between teacher education programs and the eventual achievement of the K–12 students being taught by the teachers who went through the programs include the nature of the higher education institution and its students, the nature of the teacher education program within the schools of education, the type and demographic profile of the school districts, schools, and classrooms, as well as state requirements, and many more.

In looking at this issue, Gary Fenstermacher and I suggested that mid-level studies in teacher education would prove useful to both policy and the improvement of practice (Richardson & Fenstermacher, 2005). Multiple-site case studies are one example of midlevel studies. Another are studies across several institutions that use the same measures—for example, in follow-ups of graduates. Midlevel studies lead to some warranted and somewhat generalizable findings, while allowing for considerations of local situations. Ken Zeichner (2007) called for a type of midlevel studies that are linked self-studies. The example he used was one that was conducted by Moje, Remillard, Southerland, and Wade (1999) who examined the use of case studies in teacher education classes in four institutions and four content areas in transforming student teacher perspectives. An example from the chapters in this book would be the use of follow-up surveys of graduates of a number of programs using some of the same questions, and placing the findings in the context of the particular programs. For example, it may be that teaching one course in moral teaching in a small preservice master's program, without the concept immersed in other courses, can make as lasting an impression on its students as a program in which the concept is integrated across the curriculum. This would be possible to explore across institutions and types of programs. I feel that such studies will be helpful in contributing to the improvement of practice beyond a local institution and could also contribute important understandings to the development and assessment of policy.

CONCLUSION

This book suggests that the moral aspects of classroom life are important and can be consciously affected by the beliefs and actions of teachers, and that the topic should become a foundational element of teacher education programs. It presents descriptions of teacher education classes and programs that have done so and offers some evidence that they have an effect on teacher education students' thinking and actions. I am impressed with the intellectual strength of the work that is represented in this book. I am sure that it will enlighten those engaged in teacher education, and provide a strong base for those who want to continue to develop programs of practice and research in this field.

REFERENCES

Fenstermacher, G. (1993). *Where are we going? Who will lead us there?* Washington, DC: American Association of Colleges for Teacher Education.

Green, T. (1971). *The activities of teaching.* New York: McGraw-Hill.

Moje, E., Remillard, J., Southerland, S., & Wade, S. (1999). Researching case pedagogies to inform our teaching. In M. Lundeberg, B. Levin, & H. Harrington (Eds.), *Who learns from cases and how?* (pp. 73–94). Mahwah, NJ: Lawrence Erlbaum Associates.

National Council for Accreditation of Teacher Education (NCATE). (2008). *Professional standards for the accreditation of teacher preparation institutions.* Washington, DC: Author.

Richardson, V., & Fenstermacher, G. (2005). Research and the improvement of practice and policy in teacher education. *Didacta Varia, 10*(2), 7–26.

Sirotnik, K. A. (1994). Equal access to quality public schooling: Issues in the assessment of equity and excellence. In J. Goodlad & P. Keating (Eds.), *Access to knowledge: The continuing agenda for our nation's schools* (pp. 159–185). New York: College Entrance Examination Board.

Teacher Education Accreditation Council (TEAC). (2012). *TEAC guide to accreditation, 2012.* Washington, DC: Author.

Tom, A. (1995). Stirring the embers: Reconsidering the structure of teacher education programs. In M. Wideen & P. Grimmett (Eds.), *Changing times in teacher education* (pp. 117–132). London: Falmer.

Upitis, R., Luce-Kepler, R., & Munby, H. (Eds). (2000). *Who will teach? A case study of teacher education reform.* San Francisco: Caddo Gap Press.

Zeichner, K. (2007) Accumulating knowledge across self-studies in teacher education. *Journal of Teacher Education, 58*(1), 36–40.

About the Editors and the Contributors

Matthew N. Sanger is an associate professor in the Department of Educational Foundations in the College of Education at Idaho State University. He received his PhD in Educational Studies, along with an MA in Philosophy, from the University of Michigan. He currently teaches courses in the social foundations of education and in research methodology. His research focuses on the moral work of teaching and teacher education, with recent publications appearing in *Teaching and Teacher Education, Curriculum Inquiry,* and the *Journal of Moral Education.*

Richard D. Osguthorpe is an associate professor and chair of the Department of Curriculum, Instruction, and Foundational Studies in the College of Education at Boise State University. His teaching responsibilities include courses in the foundations of education, and he also serves as a liaison in partner schools where he works closely with teacher candidates in clinical field experience. His research combines his work in schools and responsibilities in teacher education with his deep interest in the moral work of teaching.

Wolfgang Althof is the Teresa M. Fischer Professor of Citizenship Education at the University of Missouri–St. Louis. Prior to joining UMSL in 2005 he was in the Department of Education, University of Fribourg, Switzerland, from 1984 to 2004. His research experience includes studies in professional morality; democracy and education in schools; changes in individual conceptions of personal and societal values and morality in East and West Germany after the liquidation of the German Democratic Republic; intergenerational values transmission; and prevention of right-wing extremism and ethnic violence in schools. For over 2 decades, his focus has been on moral/character development and citizenship/democracy education in schoolwide programs and on their contribution to positive youth development.

Karen D. Benson is professor emerita at California State University, Sacramento. She taught elementary school for several years before joining the faculty at CSUS where she taught Educational Foundations in the Department of Teacher Education.

Marvin W. Berkowitz is McDonnell Professor of Character Education and co-director of the Center for Character and Citizenship at the University of Missouri–St. Louis.

He also directs the Leadership Academy in Character Education. He earned his PhD in Lifespan Developmental Psychology at Wayne State University. His scholarly focus is in character education and development. He is the author of *You Can't Teach Through a Rat: And Other Epiphanies for Educators* (2012), *Parenting for Good* (2005), and more than 100 book chapters, monographs, and journal articles. He is founding coeditor of the *Journal for Research in Character Education*. Dr. Berkowitz has received numerous honors, including the Sanford N. McDonnell Lifetime Achievement Award from the Character Education Partnership (2006), the Good Works Award from the Association for Moral Education (2010), and the University of Missouri System's Thomas Jefferson Professorship (2011).

Donald Blumenfeld-Jones is an associate professor of Curriculum Studies in the Mary Lou Fulton Teachers College of Arizona State University. He founded and directs an elementary education teacher-prep program titled ARTs (Arts-based Reflective Teaching). He holds an EdD in Curriculum Studies from the University of North Carolina at Greensboro, and has received the James B. Macdonald Prize in Curriculum Studies and Outstanding Alumni Award from UNC Greensboro's School of Human Health, Physical Education, and Dance. He has delivered numerous international keynote speeches addressing human rights, ethics, the arts, and education. He is the author of *Curriculum and the Aesthetic Life: Hermeneutics, Body, Democracy and Ethics in Curriculum Theory and Practice* (2012) published by Peter Lang. His work on Levinas has appeared in journals (*Educational Theory, Teacher Education and Practice*) and in an edited book, *Aesthetics, Empathy, and Education* (Eds. Tracie Constantino and Boyd White), also published by Peter Lang.

Elizabeth Campbell is a professor in the Department of Curriculum, Teaching, and Learning at the Ontario Institute for Studies in Education, University of Toronto. Campbell's work focuses on professional ethics in education and the moral and ethical dimensions of teaching. Her book, *The Ethical Teacher*, was published by the Open University Press in 2003. She is an editor of the journal *Curriculum Inquiry*, for which she has written several editorials, and her work has also appeared in the *Journal of Teacher Education; Teachers and Teaching: Theory and Practice; International Journal of Educational Change; Educational Research and Evaluation: An International Journal on Theory and Practice; Journal of Educational Policy; Journal of School Leadership;* and the *Cambridge Journal of Education*. Her current research project, "The Ethical Curriculum," is funded by the Social Sciences and Humanities Research Council of Canada. Dr. Campbell teaches in the Curriculum Studies and Teacher Development graduate program and the Master of Teaching preservice teacher education program.

Julie Canniff is an associate professor and chair of the Department of Teacher Education at the University of Southern Maine, where she is also the ETEP (Extended Teacher Education Program) site coordinator and supervisor. Dr. Canniff earned her EdD at Harvard University. Her scholarly interests relate to the field of cultural ecology. She is currently focused on the dimensions of teacher resilience.

Mary Crawford has been involved in secondary education for 40 years. She began by teaching English (with emphases in American and British literature) in the Stokes County Public Schools in North Carolina. She moved to Arizona in 1982, working first as a teacher and development associate at the Verde Valley School in Sedona, then as a principal at the Oak Creek Ranch School (Sedona) and the Judson School (Scottsdale). She is currently the principal at Foothills Academy, a college preparatory charter school in Scottsdale, AZ. Her chief focus in her present work is in developing a Common Core Standards-based education embedding ethics in the teaching of leadership, entrepreneurship, service, and activism.

Lana Daly taught in K–8 public schools and co-coordinated the Side By Side Service Learning Program. Currently, she teaches and supervises in the Multiple Subject Credential Program at California State University, Sacramento, and supports first- and second-year new teachers.

Rebecca B. Evers is a professor in the Department of Counseling, Leadership, and Educational Studies in the Richard W. Riley College of Education at Winthrop University. Her primary research focus is dispositions for providing equitable access to learning for students with disabilities and other exceptional needs. She teaches courses in teaching methods for inclusive classrooms, classroom management, and assistive technology to meet needs of students with disabilities.

Catherine Fallona is an associate professor and director of the School of Education and Human Development at the University of Southern Maine. Fallona earned a PhD in Teaching and Teacher Education at the University of Arizona. Her scholarly interests relate to teaching as a moral practice, focusing on studying teachers' actions, intentions, and ways of thinking about teaching and learning related to the democratic and moral missions of schooling.

Gary D Fenstermacher is professor emeritus at the University of Michigan. He is a philosopher of education specializing in teacher reasoning and the moral dimensions of teaching. He and Jonas Soltis are the authors of *Approaches to Teaching*, a teacher education text that has appeared through five editions and has been translated into six languages.

Anthony C. Holter is an assistant professional specialist in the Mary Ann Remick Leadership Program, concurrent assistant professor of Psychology, and a fellow in the Institute for Educational Initiatives at the University of Notre Dame. He holds a PhD in Educational Psychology from the University of Wisconsin.

Lisa E. Johnson is an associate professor and senior associate to the dean in the Richard W. Riley College of Education at Winthrop University. As the director of a nine-district school-university network, Johnson facilitates teacher development through collaborative partnerships. Her research involves preservice and practicing teacher dispositional development in the moral domain, curriculum transformation to meet the needs of diverse learners, and new teacher mentoring.

Daniel Lapsley is a professor and chair of the Department of Psychology at the University of Notre Dame, and coordinator of Academic Programs for Notre Dame's Alliance for Catholic Education. Visit his Adolescent Psychology Lab website to learn more about his work: http://www.nd.edu/~dlapsle1/Lab/

Darcia Narvaez is a professor in the Department of Psychology at the University of Notre Dame and editor of the *Journal of Moral Education*. Visit her website to learn more about her work in moral development and education: http://www.nd.edu/~dnarvaez/

Virginia Navarro is an associate professor in the Department of Teaching and Learning at the University of Missouri–St. Louis. She writes about the intersections of language and identity construction from a sociocultural perspective, particularly in urban contexts and through global experiences. Navarro is currently associate editor of the *Journal of Urban Learning, Teaching, and Research*. As a teacher educator, she integrates character and citizenship strategies into teacher development at the undergraduate and graduate levels.

Larry Nucci is professor emeritus at the University of Illinois, Chicago, and an adjunct professor in the Developmental Teacher Education program at the University of California, Berkeley. Nucci has published extensively on research in moral development and education. He is the author of *Nice Is Not Enough: Facilitating Moral Development* (Pearson) and *Education in the Moral Domain* (Cambridge University Press), and the editor of several books including the *Handbook of Moral and Character Education* (with Darcia Narvaez). He is the editor-in-chief of the journal *Human Development* and is on the editorial boards of the *Journal for Research in Character Education, Cognitive Development,* and *Parenting Science and Practice*.

Joy Pelton was an elementary classroom teacher and cocoordinator of the Side By Side Service Learning Program. She currently teaches and supervises preservice teachers at California State University, Sacramento.

Virginia Richardson is professor emeritus of Education at the University of Michigan. While there, she was chair of Educational Studies and professor of Teaching and Teacher Education. She previously served on the faculty at the University of Arizona, and prior to that was an assistant director in the National Institute of Education, Washington, DC. Her research interests include research on teaching, including teacher beliefs and decision making; teacher-student interaction around the moral dimensions of classrooms; research on teacher change, including teacher education and staff development; teaching policy; qualitative methodology; and evaluation and research design. She has written many articles, chapters, and books, and was the editor of the *American Educational Research Journal* and the *Handbook of Research on Teaching* (4th ed.). She was vice president of Division K of the American Educational Research Association, and was awarded the Lifetime Achievement Award from the American Association of Colleges for Teacher Education.

Don Senneville earned his doctorate in Foundations of Education from the University of Arizona. He also holds an MA in Philosophy from Ball State University. He is the founder and director of Foothills Academy College Preparatory, an Arizona "A" grade prep school serving grades 1–12 in Scottsdale. He has been dean of Prescott College's Adult Degree Program, which delivers a highly experiential teacher training program. Before becoming dean, Senneville was associate dean for Teacher Education at Prescott College. He has had a range of social studies teaching assignments, including a stint at Hawaii's Punahou School. He has been educational consultant to the Philosophy for Children program. Senneville currently teaches an Introduction to Western Philosophy class to seniors and a music ensemble class at Foothills Academy.

David Light Shields led the initiative to integrate character and citizenship education into the teacher education programs at the University of Missouri–St. Louis where he was an associate professor. Author of numerous books and articles related to moral and character education, especially in sports and other competitive contexts, he was a founding member of UMSL's Center for Character and Citizenship. Shields now teaches educational psychology at St. Louis Community College, Meramec.

Barbara S. Stengel is professor of the Practice of Education at Peabody College, Vanderbilt University where she is the director of the Secondary Education Program. Her work in teacher education, at Peabody and previously at Millersville University where she is professor emerita, has been grounded in an understanding of teaching and learning as relational, moral practice, and her publications—including *Moral Matters* with Alan Tom (Teachers College Press, 2006) and "Feelings of Worth and the Moral Made Visible" in *Character* and *Moral Education: A Reader* (DeVitis and Yu, Eds., Peter Lang, 2011)—reflect that perspective.

Jonatha W. Vare chairs the Department of Curriculum and Pedagogy in the Richard W. Riley College of Education at Winthrop University. She holds a doctorate in educational psychology from the University of North Carolina, Chapel Hill. Her research interests include developing and measuring dispositions of equity in teacher candidates, evaluating curriculum and policies that influence educational equity for diverse learners in public schools, and analyzing ways in which school-university collaboration transforms partnership culture.

Marilyn Watson is the author or coauthor of several books and articles on the role of schools and teachers in children's moral growth. She is retired from the Developmental Studies Center where she was the program director of the Child Development Project and headed the center's work in preservice education.

Index